Treasury of the WORLD'S COINS

BY

FRED REINFELD

Sterling PUBLISHING CO., INC.

New York

OTHER BOOKS BY THE SAME AUTHOR

COINOMETRY, An Instructive Historical Introduction to Coins and Currency (with Robert V. Masters)

FIRST BOOK OF CHESS (with I. A. Horowitz)

SECOND BOOK OF CHESS: The Nine Bad Moves

BLAZER, THE BEAR (with Robert V. Masters)

Manufactured in the United States of America

ACKNOWLEDGMENTS

In the course of writing *Treasury of the World's Coins,* the author received advice and criticism from a number of people whom he wishes to thank. These include:

Professor Gilbert Highet of Columbia University, for his penetrating criticisms of the section on the ancient world.

Marianne Singer Andersen for her perceptive reading of many sections of the manuscript.

The author's good friend, Granville Whatmough of Preston, England, for supplying numismatic material that is difficult to obtain in the United States.

Dr. Vladimir Clain-Stefanelli, the noted authority on ancient coins, for drawing on his impressive store of scholarly knowledge and providing illustrations of outstandingly magnificent Greek and Roman coins.

Arnold Andersen of the United Nations, and Ross MacDonald of Toronto, for their helpful comments on the Scandinavian and Canadian sections, respectively.

The Chase National Bank Museum of Moneys of the World, the Standard Oil Company of New Jersey, and Robert Friedberg of Gimbel's Coin Department for permission to use illustrations.

Lewis M. Reagan, General Secretary of the American Numismatic Association, who was patient, thorough, and affable in supplying valuable research material. Vernon Brown, Curator of the Chase National Museum of Moneys of the World; Sawyer McA. Mosser of the American Numismatic Society; Sarah Meduri of the White Plains Public Library; Harvey Stack, and Jerome Eisenberg were also most helpful in this respect.

For information relating to coins and material for illustrations, the author found the following standard works invaluable: Peter Seaby: *The Story of the English Coinage*; John S. Davenport: *European Crowns Since 1800*; Charles Seltman: *A Book of Greek Coins*; Wayte Raymond: *Coins of the World;* Milne, Sutherland, and Thompson: *Coin Collecting;* Gilbert Askew: *A Catalogue of Roman Coins;* Stack's listing of *Dollars of the World* (Kaufman Collection); the *International Coin Catalogue*; and all the issues of *The Numismatist* from 1932 to 1953.

Numerous references are made in this book to Masters and Reinfeld: *Coinometry, An Instructive Historical Introduction to Coins and Currency;* the author has refrained from repeating information contained in that book, and suggests that the reader looking for more information, particularly on United States coins, refer to that work.

The author is particularly grateful to Robert Friedberg, who, despite heavy demands on his time, was always glad to check and supply needed information.

Plate 254. Hungary, gold 100 ducats (1629). *Obverse:* Ferdinand III in high ruff collar and armor. The largest gold coin ever struck, and one of the outstanding rarities. Ferdinand was King of Hungary and Bohemia from 1625 to 1657, and Holy Roman Emperor from 1637 to 1657.

Plate 367. Poland, gold 100 ducats (1621). *Obverse:* Sigismund III in damascened armor and wearing the collar of the Golden Fleece. *Reverse:* crowned shield. One of the greatest European rarities.

Table of Contents

Coin Collecting 6
Ancient Egypt 11
Ancient Greece 14
Ancient Rome 30
The Republic 32
The Empire 47
The Holy Land 59
Medieval Times 63
France 64
Great Britain 76
Ireland 98
Germany 100
The Austrian Empire 113
Italy 121
The Iberian Peninsula 131
Switzerland 136
Belgium 140
The Netherlands 142
The Northern Countries 148
The Baltic Countries 156
Russia 159
The Balkans 162
Tiny European Countries 165
United States of America 166
Canada 173
Mexico 179
Central America 184
The West Indies 187
South America 192
Africa 200
Asia 206
Australia 213
Oceania 214
Values of Coins Illustrated 217
Checklist of American Coin Clubs 219
Values of Currently-Used Foreign Coins 221
Index 222

Coin Collecting

Coins are "living history." One of the great appeals of collecting is that coins recreate the past for us with unequaled vividness. What a thrill you get when you hold in your hand a coin picturing the *Golden Hind,* flagship of Sir Francis Drake who crushed the Spanish Armada in 1588! The magnificent amphitheater of ancient Rome, the Circus Maximus, has been in ruins for centuries, but on a coin issued by the Emperor Trajan you can see this stadium as it was when its gladiatorial spectacles enthralled every Roman. Do you want to see a Viking ship? An Estonian coin reproduces one so faithfully that it brings you back in spirit to those long-past days when the Viking "commandos" terrorized the shores of Europe before visiting a part of North America (long before Columbus). And so it goes—with hundreds, even thousands, of beautiful, romantic and historical coins available to all of us. Many of them are pictured in the pages that follow.

Coins have another attraction, too. Since many are minted from precious metals, it matters little whether they are currently being used in any country as money, for they are likely to be worth their face value "intrinsically"—that is, as silver or gold. For this reason, too, coins seldom will decrease below their face value as is possible with postage stamps, or other objects which people collect.

If you are starting a coin collection, you have to decide *what* coins you will collect. Obviously, you cannot collect "everything," for more than 100,000 different coins in different designs have been issued in the past 25 centuries. To collect all types would be too expensive and too long a job for one person's lifetime. So, at the outset, you must specialize.

Specializing in Collecting

You may want to collect the coins of only one country or group, such as Great Britain or the British Empire. You may specialize in ancient coins, or just in the coins of the Roman Republic or the Roman Empire. If you are a United States specialist, you might collect just Indian Head cents and obtain one of each year of issue—1859 to 1909.

Of course, there are many other ways of specializing. You may limit yourself to coins of historical interest which deal with famous events in history. Or you may "collect" famous men—Alexander the Great, Julius Caesar, Charlemagne, and so on.

There is a never-ending pleasure in collecting modern and inexpensive but exceedingly handsome coins. The issues of Canada, Israel, Poland, Danzig and Brazil include many such appealing coins. The beautiful United States commemorative coins are a whole separate artistic field.

Why Condition Is Important

So great is the demand for United States coins that their values have risen steadily year by year. A collector of "Mercury" dimes wants not merely dimes for each year of issue, from each mint which struck them, but he wants them in the best possible condition.

What do we mean by condition? When you are using coins as money, people accept them readily whether they are dull or shiny and new from the mint. In collecting, however, the condition of a coin is all-important. A "Mercury" dime of 1934 in "good" condition is valued at 15¢; one in "fine" condition has a value of 20¢; an "uncirculated" coin is worth $1.

Here is how coin conditions are generally defined:*

Proof: a coin with a mirror-like surface struck with polished dies on a polished blank. Usually sold at a premium by the mints.

Uncirculated: in perfect condition showing no signs of wear or damage but not necessarily brilliant.

Extremely fine: no definite signs of wear but having a less desirable surface than an uncirculated coin.

Very fine: showing inconsequential signs of wear but only slightly less desirable than the "extremely fine."

Fine: perceptible signs of wear but still a desirable piece.

Very good: definite signs of wear but not altogether unattractive.

Good: worn but lettering and design all clear.

Fair: quite badly worn and usually highly undesirable.

Poor: less desirable than "fair" yet the design can be distinguished.

---

* Definitions by Stuart Mosher, Editor of *The Numismatist.*

Plate 1. **Seven thousand years ago the ancient Chaldeans were using clay tablets to keep track of business deals. Here is a typical "document," an example of their cuneiform (wedge-shaped) writing.**

Why Mint Marks Are Important

To look for a coin of each mint, you need to know about mint marks. Foreign mints sometimes placed marks on their issues, but in the United States, which had seven mints, three of which are still in existence, mint marks are extremely important. Here is a useful tabular summary:

Mint		Mint Mark
Philadelphia, Pa.	1792-	none
Dahlonega, Ga.	1838-61	D
Charlotte, N. C.	1838-61	C
Carson City, Nev.	1870-93	CC
New Orleans, La.	1838-1909	O
Denver, Colo.	1906-	D
San Francisco, Cal.	1854-	S

(The chief mint, at Philadelphia, has never used mint marks—with the exception of some Jefferson nickels on which a small "P" appears over the name of Jefferson's

Plate 2. **In the ancient kingdom which later became French Indo-China, the favorite form of money was called "tiger tongue"—a silver bar between four and five inches long.**

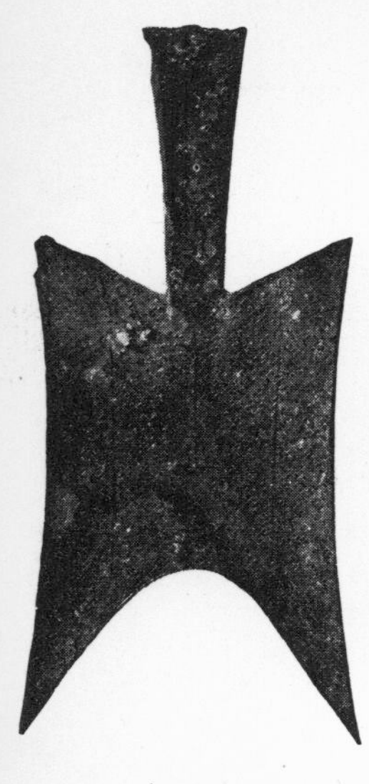

Plate 3. In ancient times the Chinese used spades, hoes, knives and other implements as money. Plate 554 repeats the 4,000-year-old motif on a modern Chinese coin.

Plate 4. On the island of Yap the natives use large chunks of stone for money. "Coins" weighing 50 pounds and more are carried on poles thrust through holes that have been pierced in the stones.

home at Monticello. The New Orleans mint did not operate between 1861 and 1879.)

Values

What do we mean by valuation? All coins in desirable condition have a premium value—a value in excess of their face value. This is determined by a combination of factors: quantity issued; condition of coin; demand for it. In the case of the Mercury dime of 1926, for example, the values in uncirculated condition are:

Philadelphia (no mint mark)	$2.50
Denver (D)	9.00
San Francisco (S)	22.50

Why this wide spread in valuation? The Denver mint issued far fewer dimes than Philadelphia in 1926, and San Francisco issued an even smaller quantity. In a field where demand is strong and growing, relative scarcity raises the valuation.

Valuation refers to the dealer's selling price, the price shown in this and other price lists. When you dispose of a collection or of a smaller quantity of coins, you will realize much less than the catalog value when selling to a dealer. There is nothing unethical about this: if a dealer is to make a profit, he must necessarily purchase at prices lower than his selling prices.

A specialty which has become popular in recent years is collecting proof sets of all the denominations of a given year. In the case of American coins, a proof set would include the penny, nickel, dime, quarter, and half dollar of a given year. Such proof sets are also available from the Union of South Africa, and from Great Britain in coronation years.

Building Your Foreign Collection

Foreign coin collecting is less specialized as to dates of issue. People rarely attempt to collect more than one year of a coin and they pay little attention to mint marks. However, you may want to specialize in one country, or the British Empire, or ancient coins, etc.

Condition is important in the purchase of any coin. In the case of ancient coins, collectors are apt to lower their standards somewhat because, over the centuries, not many coins remained in the finer conditions. A Greek coin in the choicest condition often commands a considerable price. Roman coins were issued in much greater quantities, and therefore their prices are more moderate.

Before starting, you should visit or obtain catalogs from leading dealers. In this way you can get a good idea of the field that interests you, and you can do some "comparison shopping." If you become a member of the American Numismatic Association,* you will receive *The Numismatist* as part of your dues. In this magazine you will find many informative articles about numismatics and detailed advertisements of the leading dealers. Membership in the organization will also make it possible for you to meet other collectors.

Plate 5. **In Malacca, on the Malay Archipelago, the natives assembled tin "coins" on "trees," breaking off "coins" as they were needed for small change. Later on Malaya became one of the world's leading tin-producing regions.**

Cleaning and Storing Coins

Don't try to improve the condition of your coins by cleaning, rubbing or polishing them. If the features of a coin are worn, cleaning will not sharpen them. If a coin is in fine condition, rough polishing or washing may wear down or destroy the features. If you have a coin that is dirty, tarnished or dull, don't try to brighten it up but take it to your coin dealer and let him advise you. Don't let coins rub against each other and always hold a coin by its edges because the oil and sweat from the human hand will tend to remove the shine. Of course, don't drop or plunk coins down to test their soundness if they are in good condition. If you are testing a questionable coin because you suspect it is counterfeit, that is a different matter.

The beginning collector must decide how to store and catalogue his collection. Keeping coins separately in individual small envelopes in a box may be convenient and will prevent rubbing. Dealers usually store their coins this way. However, in order to look at coins readily and exhibit them to your friends, you may find it more impressive to use acetate envelopes or one of several kinds of folders, lucite or cardboard holders, albums or glass cabinets now on the market. It is preferable to show both sides of a coin without taking it out of its holder. Never press a coin into too small a hole or its edges may be marred.

* P. O. Box 577, Wichita, Kansas.

Coining Processes

We are accustomed to taking machine-made coins for granted, but it would be a mistake to think that coining machinery was perfected quickly. Coins probably originated in Asia Minor and Greece and were made by hand for the first 2,000 years of coin history. They were painstakingly hammered out of metal blanks that were not always round, by dies that were engraved by hand. Each coin differed somewhat because the designs wore down quickly, the hammering was not even, and the blanks were also not uniformly thick. It was only in about 1500 that the first coinage machinery came into use in Italy and spread slowly through Europe. How slowly improvements were made can be gauged from the fact that United States mints now turn out more coins in a single day than *the*

Illustration two-thirds size

Plate 6. The disastrous German inflation of the early 1920's resulted in fantastic denominations.

total produced in the United States from 1793 to 1800.

Ingenious new coin machinery is being developed rapidly today. In modern mints, the first step is to prepare the alloy, or combination of metals, in the correct proportion. In silver coins, for instance, the United States uses 900 parts of silver to 100 parts of copper. The metals are weighed separately on a huge balance that is accurate to 1/100 of an ounce. Then the metals are melted and thoroughly blended in an electric furnace. The alloy is poured into molds to form thin bars, and these are checked (assayed) twice again to make sure the proportions are up to par.

After the bars have been put through a series of rollers that soften and stretch them into strips (as much as 8 feet long and 48/1000 of an inch thin), the punch machines hammer out circular blanks from the strips. Since the punching process hardens the metal, it has to go next to an annealing furnace for resoftening. From there, the blanks go through a milling process that thickens their edges to make them last longer. Reeding or corrugating the edges of coins prevents anyone from accumulating precious metals dishonestly by shaving off thin slices from the edges of coins without its being noticed. Therefore, the mint usually reeds the edges of coins of silver and gold.

After the centers of the blanks have been softened with acid, the coins are passed down in a funnel and held, two at a time, by mechanical pincers while an automatic, high-speed press stamps the designs on them. With the coins in position, the upper and lower dies on the press come together with the blanks sandwiched in between them. As much as 160 tons' pressure is needed for striking silver dollars.

Glossary

The *obverse* of a coin is the side known as the "head"—it is almost always the side with the artistic main design. The *reverse* is the "tail" of the coin, usually reserved for technical details, such as the value and date. *Patterns* are trial pieces which may or may not be issued for general use. *Overstrikes* are the striking of new material on an already existing coin, hiding all or some of the original design. An *incuse* coin is one on which the lettering and other details are sunk below the surface of the coin. A coin with a *reeded* edge has lines running across the thickness of the edge from obverse to reverse.

Plate 7. The warning, "Don't take any wooden nickels!" has taken on added meaning since some localities make their "wooden nickels" of cardboard. During the Depression of the 1930's many American communities and business organizations issued wooden nickels, scrip, buckskin bills, and the like.

Ancient Egypt

At first sight it seems very puzzling that this remarkable civilization, which endured for several thousand years, never used coins or currency. Barter was the general form of exchange. Services were paid for in goods, and the same was true of taxes. The Egyptians had developed credit and bookkeeping devices to a high level; they had ample supplies of metal; yet they had no coinage. How are we to explain this puzzle?

Ancient Egypt was a self-contained economy. What foreign commerce there was, was a monopoly of the Pharaoh. All the mines belonged to him. The vast majority of the people were tillers of the soil. Craftsmen worked for the temples or the nobles or the Pharaoh. The government scribes got their pay from the Pharaoh. The priests received huge donations, and much of the best land belonged to the temples.

(In Greece, where coinage appeared early, the situation was quite different. There was not too much good farmland; instead of a single centralized government, there were many small city-states; the Greeks had to trade with each other and with peoples across the Mediterranean. So the Greeks' development of coinage is not at all surprising.)

It is true, however, that the ancient Egyptians, aside from barter, did have more than one medium of exchange. In the early days, they used sacks of corn of standard weight. Linen was another favorite—more valuable than you might think, as the Egyptians were unrivaled in textile weaving.

About 2000 B.C. they began to use metal rings of standard size and weight, also copper utensils, as a medium of exchange. From this time on, they recorded business deals in terms of copper bowls, pitchers, dishes, etc. To get a rough idea of the "money" proportions, you can figure silver as worth 40 times as much as copper, and gold twice as much as silver.

Egypt is the Nile, and the Nile is Egypt. The world's longest river (4,000 miles including its tributaries), the Nile is also the most celebrated. In other lands, an overflowing river brings tumultuous death and

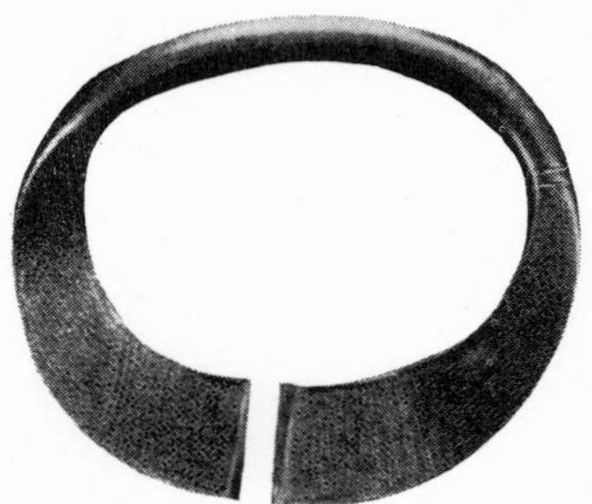

Plate 8. Gold money-ring (about 1680-1350 B.C.). The use of such rings as "money" had become quite customary during this period.

destruction; in ancient Egypt, the overflow of the Nile brought life and prosperity. To the Egyptians of olden times, the river was "All-Father Nile"—a gift of the gods.

During its overflow from June to October, the Nile turns Egypt's parched earth into black, fertile soil. (The ancient name of Egypt was Kemet—"black.") Not too violent, the overflow was readily absorbed by ditches and canals.

The river begins to rise at the summer solstice (June 21). To know the right date was vital to the Egyptians, and they devised their amazingly accurate calendar as early as 4241 B.C. With certain modifications, it is the calendar we use today.

Aside from the blessing of the Nile, Egypt was favored in still another way by geography. Its situation between sea and desert protected it from foreign attack for the most part. Thus, Egyptian civilization had a chance to develop while other empires were wiped out by invasion.

Monumental Builders

The Egyptians were master builders—some say, the greatest the world has ever known. The Sphinx and the monumental Pyramids, built some 5,000 years ago, are still in existence. The colossal Sphinx, half man and half lion, 140 feet long and 34 feet high, continues to look out on the desert with its pitiless and baffling smile. Only a little the worse for wear, it lost its nose when used for target practice by artillerymen at the time of Napoleon's invasion in 1798. The Sphinx is supposed to represent the sun-god.

But the nearby Pyramids, built during the same period, are almost beyond description. One of the most famous is that of Khufu. It was built of 2,500,000 blocks of stone, each weighing anywhere from two to 150 tons! Five hundred feet high, it required the unceasing labors of 100,000 slaves for 20 years. Remember that the Egyptians had no machinery—merely such rudimentary helps as wheels, pulleys, windlasses, drills and saws. They also had the use of donkeys, which had been domesticated by that time.

They moved the massive slabs on long inclines, sending them along on greased timber and rollers. Whatever measuring instruments they had must have been of the crudest—yet the blocks all fit together perfectly. Each Pyramid was the tomb of one of Egypt's kings. In it, the embalmed and mummified body of the Pharaoh rested surrounded by his treasures and the art works he had loved best.

Only second to the Pyramids are the grandiose temples at Karnak and Luxor, staggering in their immensity. At Karnak the buildings cover 60 acres; at one time they contained 86,000 statues.

Plate 9. Copper money-ring (about 1680-1350 B.C.). During the era of the "New Kingdom" the Egyptians had reached the point of putting a "money" value on goods and services.

Plate 11. **Silver tetradrachm:** ***obverse*** **(about 310 B.C.). The first of the Ptolemies issued this impressive coin picturing Alexander the Great with a headdress of an elephant scalp. Compare this with the Lysimachus coin (Plate 34).**

After many centuries, by about 1500 B.C., the civilization of Egypt began to decline. Gradually the provinces in Asia Minor slipped away from Egyptian control. Egypt's domains shrank steadily, foreign tribute decreased, large-scale building slowed down considerably.

In 605 B.C. Nebuchadnezzar, king of the rising Babylonian Empire in the East, defeated the Egyptians in battle. Later, from 525 B.C. on, Egypt was a province of Persia. Then, in 332 B.C. Alexander of Macedon (then northern Greece) conquered Egypt with ease and founded the city of Alexandria at the mouth of the Nile.

With the Greek conquest, coinage came at last to Egypt.

At Alexander's death (323 B.C.), Ptolemy, one of his ablest generals, made himself ruler of Egypt and established a dynasty there. (Actually, it was not until 305 B.C. that he gave himself the formal title of "king.") All the kings who followed had the same name—Ptolemy—and are distinguished only by their numbers and nicknames.

Plate 13. **Gold octodrachm (266 B.C.). The** ***obverse*** **of this rare coin pictures Arsinoe, wife of Ptolemy II.** ***Reverse:*** **double horn of plenty—one of the favorite motifs of ancient coinage.**

Plate 12. **Silver tetradrachm (323-305 B.C.).** ***Obverse:*** **portrait of Ptolemy I—the first coin ever made with the portrait of a living man. The eagle on the** ***reverse*** **reminds us of many an American coin.**

The Ptolemies had a monopoly of commerce, banking, land, and mines. Throughout the life of the dynasty, they continued to issue excellent coinage.

Alexandria, with its far-flung commerce and its importance as a center of Greek culture, was second only to Rome. Unfortunately, after the first five Ptolemies, the dynasty deteriorated more and more. It finally ended when Egypt fell to Julius Caesar; Cleopatra was the last ruler of the Ptolemaic dynasty.

Plate 14. **Silver tetradrachm:** ***obverse*** **(51-30 B.C.). Cleopatra VII, Egypt's last queen, has her place in history as the woman whose beauty captivated Julius Caesar and Mark Antony. Her hair-do, shown on this coin, still is in vogue.**

Ancient Greece

More than 2,000 years have passed since the heyday of Greek civilization. Yet we still consider the Greeks the most gifted people who ever lived. To the Greeks we owe the idea of democratic government; we admire Greek masterpieces of sculpture and architecture; we still look to Plato and Aristotle as the founders of Western philosophy; we still read Homer's *Iliad* and *Odyssey,* both as great poetry and as thrilling stories.

Although the Greeks praised "the golden mean," some Greeks often went to extremes. We see one extreme in the military leader, Alexander the Great, always restless for a new conquest; and the other extreme in the philosopher, Diogenes the Cynic, placidly content to live in rags in a barrel. When the two met and the conqueror asked the philosopher if he needed anything, Diogenes replied that he did indeed: would Alexander stand aside and let the sun through?

To understand Greece, you must understand its geography. Aside from its fertile central plain, Greece is very mountainous. Some of the land is suitable for grazing, very little for farming.

The mountains, too, determined Greek history. Each city, cut off from the others, was a state unto itself—a "city-state." This was good and bad. The comparative isolation and small size of the cities gave democratic government a chance to take hold. On the other hand, the lack of unity was bound to attract formidable foreign invaders. Also, these small but intensely active states constantly quarrelled among themselves. If they could have agreed long enough to found a United States of Greece, they would have changed history even more vitally than they did.

In most of the Greek city-states, it was hard to make a living, and even when the Greeks took to foreign commerce across the seas, population kept growing and this made life very hard. That was one of the reasons why the Greeks were led to found colonies. Of course, some left too because they did not like their government.

Athens, the most famous of the Greek city-states, was dependent on outside sources for its food. The city had a law that no Athenian ship could leave a foreign port without taking grain on board, nor deliver it anywhere but at Athens. In exchange the Athenians exported olive oil, wine and silver from their mines; and made their harbor one of the most important exchange ports between Italy and Asia.

It would be a mistake to think of the Greek mainland as all of ancient Greece.

Plate 15. **Aetna, silver tetradrachm:** ***obverse,*** **slightly enlarged (461 B.C.). The work of an anonymous artist we know only as "the Aetna Master," pictures roly-poly Silenus, companion of "the great god Pan."**

Plate 16. **Rhegium, silver tetradrachm:** ***obverse*** **(about 415 B.C.). A masterpiece in the series of superb coins that appeared in the Greek colonies of Sicily and the Italian mainland. (Lion's scalp.)**

Coin collectors know better, for even a slight familiarity with ancient Greek coins makes it clear that the Greeks lived not only in Greece proper.

Aside from the beautiful islands of the Mediterranean, the Greeks had colonies on the shores of the Black Sea and established flourishing communities on the Mediterranean coast of Asia Minor.

But this was by no means all. To these Greeks, the Mediterranean Sea was "The Sea." They had colonies in Spain; on the north African coast; at Massalia (modern Marseilles); and above all, in Sicily and southern Italy.

To the Greeks, the earth, the sky, the waters were ruled by gods who were far from perfect beings. Though their attitude toward their gods was not always reverent, they invented many myths unequaled in all literature for their charm, their liveliness, and their happy imaginative touches.

The gods were supposed to live on Mount Olympus. Zeus (Jupiter) ruled over gods and men, and the thunderbolt and the eagle were the badges of his power.

Among the other important gods and goddesses were:

Hera (Juno), the wife of Zeus. As a rule, the Greeks pictured her as a majestic matron.

Poseidon (Neptune), god of the sea. His badge of office was the trident (three-pronged spear). He rode the waves in a chariot drawn by foaming white horses.

Athene or Athena (Minerva), daughter of Zeus, goddess of wisdom and the practical arts. She was of course the patron goddess of Athens, and she appears on practically all the coins of the city. Athene's helmeted head and her favorite owl were symbols of Athens just as Uncle Sam and the eagle are symbols of the United States.

Apollo (Phoebus), god of the sun and of poetry and music and the other arts. Greek coins and statues picture him as a very handsome young man. Artemis (Diana), goddess of the moon, was fond of hunting in lonely woodlands.

Hermes (Mercury), messenger of the gods. He was also the patron god of trav-

Plate 17. **Messana, silver tetradrachm (about 460 B.C.).** ***Obverse:*** **nymph driving cart drawn by two mules.** ***Reverse:*** **hare, with small dolphin.**

Plate 18. Macedon, silver tetradrachm (359-336 B.C.), coined by Philip II, father of Alexander the Great. *Obverse:* Zeus: *Reverse:* jockey on horse.

Plate 19. Elis, silver stater (about 460 B.C.). *Obverse:* eagle with hare in its talons: *Reverse:* thunderbolt of Zeus.

Plate 20. Elis, silver stater: *obverse* (about 420 B.C.). Head of Hera.

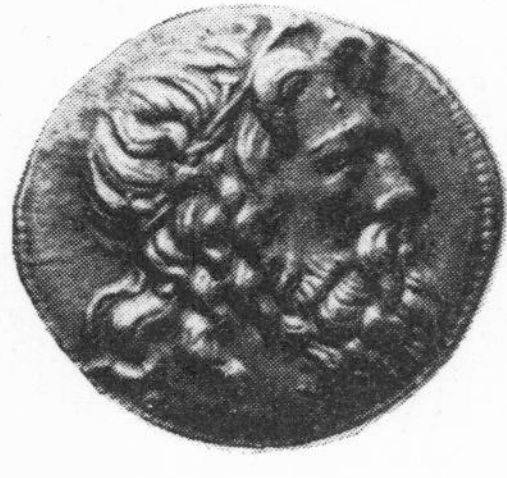

Plate 21. Macedon, silver tetradrachm: *obverse* (253 B.C.). Antigonus Gonatas struck this imposing portrait of Poseidon to commemorate his destruction of the Egyptian fleet.

Plate 22. Athens, silver stater (about 450 B.C.). One of the most famous Greek coins. *Obverse:* helmeted Athene with olive wreath. *Reverse:* Athene's symbol—the owl.

elers and of the marketplace, and had a reputation for being sly and tricky. A familiar figure on coins, he made his way into American coinage on the misnamed "Mercury" dime.

Aphrodite (Venus), goddess of love and beauty. Legend had it that she was born in the white foam of the sea.

Hades (Pluto), god of the dead. His wife was Persephone, who appears on the great coins of Syracuse, because it was near the site of that city that he came up from the underworld to capture her and carry her off.

The Greeks also worshiped many nymphs and local spirits—minor divinities of forests, streams, and the like.

The Greeks enjoyed life fully. Although they were god-fearing their religion was filled with happiness; and therefore some of their greatest religious celebrations centered on athletic sports. The most famous of these was the Olympic Games, held in honor of Zeus. They were founded in 776 B.C. and they were held every four years for about 1200 years continuously. Pilgrims came from as far away as Africa to see the contests. If a war was on, it had to stop during the games!

The contests consisted of foot races, exciting chariot races, and the pentathlon (five events—throwing the discus, running, jumping, wrestling, and throwing the spear). There were also boxing and wrestling matches. The winners received an

Plate 23. Myrina, silver tetradrachm: *obverse* (175-150 B.C.). Beautiful laureated head of Apollo.

olive wreath, prized as one of the greatest honors that could be bestowed on any Greek.

The City-States

So diverse were the Greek city-states that when Aristotle wrote his *Politics,* about 340 B.C., he first had to study 158 existing Greek constitutions!

In the city-states where democracy prevailed, the political ideal was to have every citizen take part in making the laws. The idea of majority rule by vote originated in Greece, an unusual event, to say the least, in an age of despotism.

The city-state that had no use for democracy was Sparta, which favored iron discipline. From childhood on, the Spartan citizen was trained for war.

The Spartan shield was unusually heavy. It was impossible to run away in battle without throwing the shield aside. As you can imagine, a Spartan soldier without his shield was disgraced forever.

Naturally, the Spartans had little use for money. Lycurgus, one of their great kings, did away with gold and silver, allowing the Spartans only a rough kind of iron money. Worth very little and annoyingly bulky, it discouraged the Spartans from any stray thoughts of becoming wealthy. It was impossible to buy any luxuries, and there was no foreign trade to speak of.

Plate 24. Syracuse, silver tetradrachm (about 400 B.C.). *Obverse:* charioteer crowned by flying Victory; below, two dolphins. *Reverse:* nymph Arethusa surrounded by dolphins.

Plate 25. Aenus, silver tetradrachm (470-450 B.C.). *Obverse:* head of Hermes. *Reverse:* goat, and idol on throne.

Plate 26. Athens, silver stater (about 150 B.C.). *Obverse:* head of Athene. *Reverse:* owl standing on amphora. One of the most attractive of all the Athene coins.

Plate 27. Elis, silver stater (about 350 B.C.), issued for the ancient Olympic Games. *Obverse:* head of Zeus. *Reverse:* an eagle, sacred bird of Zeus.

Plate 28. Pergamum, silver stater: *reverse* (about 190 B.C.). Bowcase between two serpents. This coin appeared at a time when Pergamum, a small state in Asia Minor, was an outstanding center of Greek civilization.

The Great Persian Invasions

As long as there was no danger from an outside enemy, the Greek system of separate city-states worked out well enough. But in the sixth century B.C. the Greeks found themselves menaced by the expansion of the Persian Empire. Croesus, the millionaire king of Lydia, lost his throne to the Persians in 547 B.C. From then on, all the rest of Asia Minor was at the mercy of the Persians.

Under modern blitzkrieg conditions, a first-class power like Persia with military superiority would have subdued all of Greece in a very short time. But in those times the conquest took years, and Athens slowed up the process by helping the threatened cities.

Finally, in 490 B.C. it was the turn of the Athenians to submit to the Persians, or to fight against hopeless odds. The men of Athens, greatly outnumbered, decided to fight. Their little army met the Persians on the plain of Marathon, a short distance from Athens.

Although the Persians were considered the ablest fighters of their day, the Athenians outwitted and outfought them. The center of the Athenian army was very thin, but the wings were powerful. After breaking through in the center, the Persians were encircled and crushed by the Athenian wings. (Almost 300 years later, Hannibal was to demolish a Roman army in much the same way at Cannae.)

Fleeing back to their ships, the Persians embarked to attack Athens by sea. However, the Athenian army, losing no time, marched back to their city. The Persians had had enough; crestfallen, they sailed back to Asia Minor.

Marathon was one of the great battles of history. A small city had defeated a mighty empire; a democracy had held its own against a despotic state. Though outnumbered two to one, the Athenians lost only 200 men and slew 6,000 Persians. A messenger reputedly ran the 26 miles from Marathon to Athens to bring the news. From this historic feat, our modern "marathon" race came.

***Plate 29.* Athens, silver dekadrachm: *obverse* (about 480 B.C.). Outstanding Athene-owl coin, issued to commemorate the Greek victory at Marathon. See Plate 45.**

Eager for vengeance, Darius, the Persian King, furiously began his preparations for a "second round." He did not live to see the plans completed, leaving the task to his son Xerxes.

To gain time for holding back the Persians, the Greeks posted 300 men at the narrowest part of a coastal road at Thermopylae. These men were the finest fighters in the whole Spartan army. For two days the Persians charged the pass repeatedly, and each time they were driven back with fearful slaughter.

The Persians were at their wits' end. At this stage, a Greek traitor appeared and showed the Persians how to approach the Spartans by a hidden path. Attacked on an unprotected side, the Spartans fought back for hours against fantastically overwhelming odds, until they were wiped out to the last man.

The pass captured at last, the Persians now had a clear road to Athens. In this grave emergency, the Athenians were saved by Themistocles. A strong believer in sea power, he had persuaded the Athenians to build a large fleet. (Later on, you will see how the Athenians had financed the construction of the vessels by voluntarily returning to the state treasury the great dekadrachms commemorating Marathon.)

Realizing that Athens could not be defended, Themistocles withdrew all the fighting men of the city to his fleet off Salamis. The Persians took Athens, burning much of it and plundering the temples and public buildings. But they still had to fight the Greek fleet, and here they were utterly crushed by Themistocles and his fighters.

Golden Age and Decay

The defeat of the Persians ushered in a Golden Age which lasted almost a century. The victories gave Athens a self-confidence and joyous energy that was manifested in a hundred different ways. The Athenians were lucky in having Pericles as the leader of their democracy. Spending about 30 years (463-431 B.C.) in the service of Athens, Pericles was far from a crude politician. Phidias, the famous sculptor, Sophocles, the great dramatist, and Anaxagoras, a first-rate philosopher, were his close friends and valued advisers.

It was doubtless their influence that stimulated him to make Athens the most beautiful city in the world. The outstanding feature of this program was the construction of the Parthenon, the magnificent temple to Athene. Of course, this ambitious building program had still another purpose —it served too as a project for the unemployed. Pericles understood all too well that Athenian democracy was based on the fact that there were no sharp extremes of poverty and wealth. An aristocrat himself, he widened the democratic powers of the people in many ways.

The Athenian ideal was for every citizen to take an active part in the process of government. The city never had a population of more than 200,000 people, of which perhaps one-sixth, or less, were slaves. Fortunately, the Athenians were never rich enough to have a large number of slaves.

Plate 31. (above). Gela, silver tetradrachm: *reverse* (about 485 B.C.). Man-headed bull (river god).

The city allowed itself the luxury of free speech, which in practice often meant plenty of scurrilous abuse for Pericles.

In time the Athenian democracy became very greedy and materialistic. Power replaced justice as a goal. There were venomous factional disputes. Treachery and intrigue became commonplace. Athens and Sparta shaped up as bitter rivals for the chief power in Greece. The result was the disastrous Peloponnesian War, with most of the Greek cities on Sparta's side against Athens.

The war dragged on from 431 to 404 B.C. At first the two antagonists had trouble coming to grips—Athens was a great sea power, while Sparta's strength was in her army. As the struggle went on, the government of Athens got worse and worse. Eventually the Persians came into the war on Sparta's side. In the end, Athens was crushed and never regained its earlier pre-eminence. Once started, the process of decay continued. The tragic trial and execution of the liberal philosopher, Socrates (399 B.C.) was a sorry admission that Athens was no longer true to its democratic ideals.

The Rise of Macedon

In the hinterlands of northern Greece there was a rough, tough region of burly fighters and hunters. It was called Macedon, and in 359 B.C. Philip II became its king. A man of great ability, he had three ambitions: to create a powerful army, to unite all Greece, and to crush the Persians. Building up a magnificent army of spearmen and cavalry, he created the famous Macedonian phalanx, which was invincible in its day. Philip's program meant the death of the old city-state idea, and he had an easy time brushing aside such feeble resistance as was offered him in Greece.

The city-states had refused to unite when they had the chance; Philip united them by force. However, before he could carry out his ambition to smash the Persians, he was stabbed to death by an assassin in 336 B.C. His young son Alexander succeeded him.

Plate 32 (left). Macedon, silver: *obverse* (about 520 B.C.). Huntsman with horse.

Plate 33 (right). Macedon, silver: *obverse* (about 520 B.C.). Chieftain seated on ox wagon.

Alexander the Great

The people of Greece must have expected a breathing spell when they saw the throne of Macedon occupied by a young man of 20. This raw youth could hardly hope to make an impression in such a turbulent age.

What Alexander accomplished in the thirteen crowded years before his early

Plate 34. Thrace, silver tetradrachm (323-281 B.C.). *Obverse:* head of Alexander the Great. *Reverse:* Athene seated. Struck by Lysimachus, King of Thrace (see page 29).

death, still seems incredible. For four years he had been tutored by the great Aristotle, who instilled in him a deep love for Greek culture and a clear understanding of the problems that confront a ruler. The combination of first-rate education coupled with native genius helps to explain how Alexander was able to conquer Asia Minor, Syria, Egypt, Persia, and even a portion of India during his short life. With an army of less than 40,000, he annexed an area that must have contained close to 2,000,000 men of fighting age.

He minced no words when he set out to conquer Persia. Imagine the feelings of the Persian king when he received this message from Alexander: "I, Alexander, consider the whole of thy treasure, and the whole of thy land to be mine." And he made good his words—it did not take long for him to conquer the Great King and sit on the royal throne under a canopy of gold.

On arriving in Asia Minor, Alexander stopped off in Ilium (the site of the Trojan War), where he offered his armor to the goddess Athene and replaced it with armor that was said to date from the Homeric battles. It was on this expedition that he saw the famous knot at Gordium. According to tradition, the man who untied the knot would rule the world. Alexander tried his hand at the knot and when it did not budge, he impatiently slashed his sword through it.

We often wonder how the soldiers of ancient times were able to trudge thousands of miles and endure untold hardships. One answer is that generals like Alexander shared every privation with their soldiers. In this way Alexander earned a loyalty that fired his men to achieve the impossible. When he invaded India, for example, his men cut steps in steep mountains and crossed parched deserts as well as rainy plains and swollen rivers.

Historians have always ranked Alexander with Caesar and Napoleon among the great conquerors. However, Alexander's conquests had more than a military meaning. He spread Greek civilization far and wide—no wonder his famous tetradrachm was the best-known coin of ancient times.

And yet there was something two-edged about these conquests, for Alexander's armies also received the impact of Oriental traditions, religions, and ways of thinking. He founded 70 new Greek cities (of which Alexandria, in Egypt, is the most famous). He married a Persian princess, and his generals intermarried with the Oriental aristocracies. Displaying a noble tolerance for other religions wherever he went, he treated conquered peoples as equals and not as victims. At the same time his conquests opened up new markets, greatly stimulating commerce between distant regions.

After Alexander

The Macedonian conquests, as we have seen, meant the downfall of the old city-states, and the appearance of great consolidated empires. But it was the Romans, and not Alexander, who were later to carry out the imperial idea in its most lasting form. For Alexander's conquests depended on one man, while the Roman victories were carried out by a government.

Conquest has its shabby side, and Alexander's end was not a happy one. His men, worn out by ups and downs, hardships and easy living, began to grumble. There were murmurs of mutiny. The rough soldiers could not understand a policy that turned old friends into enemies, and old enemies into friends. Alexander became morose, suspicious, subject to hysterical rages. He was only 33 when he died of a fever. As he lay dying, someone asked him which general he wanted to succeed him. His reply: "The strongest."

This answer, worthy of the oracle at Delphi, had just the kind of results that we might expect. Alexander's empire was too young to be stable. His death led to a series of disputes among his generals.

Plate 35. Metapontum, silver stater: *obverse* (about 500 B.C.). Ear of barley overstruck on Corinth "pony."

Yet Alexander's successors played an important role in history. Seleucus, for example, carved out an empire in Asia Minor, and Alexander's successors in Macedon kept in check the roving Gauls, tribesmen from Central Europe, some of whom later occupied what is now France.

You can get a vivid idea of how far the Gauls wandered, from the fact that St. Paul, who lived in the first century A.D., addressed one of his Epistles to the Galatians (Gauls) who lived in Asia Minor. By that time, of course, the Gauls had been thoroughly hellenized ("Greek-ized"). Antigonus Gonatas, one of Alexander's successors in Macedon, put the Gauls in their place by a stinging defeat. This ruler has left us one of the finest coins of ancient times, with a majestic head of Poseidon.

The First Coins

Who made the first coins? To this there is a simple answer: No one knows. Learned men have scoured the museums of the world and pored over faded and torn manuscripts and studied grubby, almost formless bits of metal under the magnifying lens. After a lifetime of research some scholars argue heatedly for China as the source of coinage; others say India, Persia, and Greece. The first *state* was the kingdom of Lydia in Asia Minor.

There is, however, a more sensible, more practical question: Who were the first people to make coins of a standard shape, a standard size, a standard content, and a standard value established by a state?

The Greeks were probably the first to have coins that fit *all* these requirements. They started such coinage in the seventh century B.C. Of course you must take the word "standard" here with a grain of salt. The ancients did not have the kind of powerful and magnificently precise machines we use today for making coins. They made their coins with the simplest of instruments, and their coins were only "approximately standard."

Dr. Charles Seltman, the great authority on ancient coins, has described the Greek coining method as follows:

"An artist or a craftsman would carve an intaglio design on a thick disk of bronze; this was the *obverse* die which fitted into a pit sunk in the top face of an anvil. On the lower end of a square-faced bronze punch the man next carved another intaglio design; this was the *reverse* die.

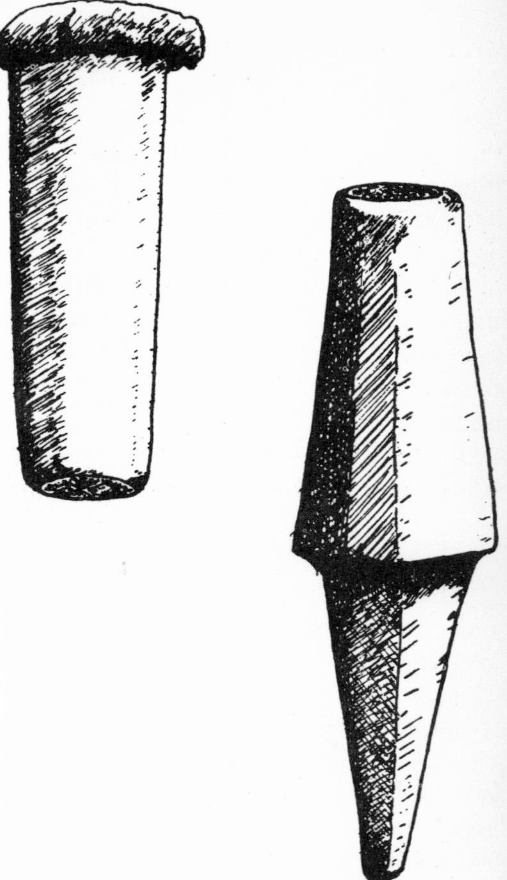

Plate 36. Upper and lower dies for striking ancient Greek coins. (From Peter Seaby: *The Story of the English Coinage*. London, 1952: B. A. Seaby, Ltd.)

"In a little furnace nearby, blank disks of silver, carefully adjusted to the correct weight, were heated to make them adequately malleable, and one by one these silver disks were placed with the aid of a pair of tongs upon the anvil over the sunk obverse die. Down upon each disk came the reverse die on the end of the square-faced punch held in a man's left hand. The hammer in his right hand smote several blows upon the upper end of the punch. The tongs pulled the silver disk away, for it was now a finished coin which required only to refrigerate."

This method of making coins underwent very little change up to about 1500 A.D. And yet, despite these rudimentary methods, the Greeks turned out some of the most beautiful coins ever made. It is interesting that the Greek coins of Sicily surpass even those of the mainland, as far as artistry is concerned.

Above all, the Greek coins had enormous propaganda value in an age which had no newspapers or radio. The "owls" of Athens and the tetradrachm of Alexander the Great and his successors are prime examples of the prestige value of superb coins.

Early Greek Coinage

The earliest Greek coins had a design only on the obverse, usually picturing a patron god or other symbol of the issuing city. Later on, it became customary to have a design on the reverse as well, a fashion that has continued to the present day. The obverse usually pictured a head (Zeus, Athene, Herakles, Apollo, etc.). The reverse was generally more pictorial, showing a bull, an eagle, a winged Victory, a temple, a battle scene, and the like.

Portraits were a very late development, beginning with the Alexander the Great coins issued by his generals after his death in 323 B.C. Ptolemy I of Egypt was the first living man to be represented on a coin (about 300 B.C.).

Incidentally, take a good look at the fierce eagle on the reverse of this coin, standing with wings closed and perched on a thunderbolt. Scholars tell us that this eagle is the ancestor of the American eagle on our 1916-1947 half dollars. On the modern coin the wings are open, to be sure, but the bird is still the eagle of Zeus and is still perched on the thunderbolt.

Having an ample supply of metal from silver mines, the Greeks adopted silver as their standard. For a while they toyed with electrum (a mixture of gold and silver), but this alloy was too untrustworthy. Who could resist the temptation to put more silver and less gold into the alloy?

Plate 37. Macedon, gold stater (about 350 B.C.). *Obverse:* head of Apollo. *Reverse:* charioteer in two-horse chariot.

Gold coins, such as the famous gold stater of Philip of Macedon, were comparatively rare. It was about 550 B.C. that the earliest pure gold coinage appeared. It was issued by King Croesus of Lydia in Asia Minor, the millionaire whose name has become a synonym for wealth. The design on these coins was deplorably crude. In any event, this coinage lasted only a short time for, as we have seen, Croesus soon lost his kingdom to the Persians.

Still another metal, as we learned earlier, was used by the Spartans. Anxious to avoid corruption by luxuries or business dealings, they made a practice of having only iron currency. Heavy, bulky, and of little value, it was ideal for the Spartans' purpose. Six iron pieces were worth a drachm, and the standard coin was a tetradrachm (four drachms). Consequently, the Spartans needed 24 iron pieces as the equivalent of a single tetradrachm. (Perhaps our slang term "iron men" for money comes from these iron pieces!)

The Greeks naturally had other means of exchange before they started using coinage. There was a shortage of cattle, the usual pre-coinage means of exchange; and the experts tell us that the early Greeks used bronze bowls before they had coins. Even after coins came into style, legal fines in Crete were assessed in bowls (*lebetes*). Later on, when the Cretans had silver coins, they stamped the design of a bowl on them. This was by way of telling the people that the coin had the same exchange value as the earlier bowl.

In the Greek colony of Olbia on the Black Sea, a great fishing port, bronze pieces in the shape of fish were used instead of round coins.

Overstriking coins was rather common among the Greeks. The Athenians got their silver from the mines at Laurium, located fairly near Athens. Doubtless the metal was refined at the source, and then minted at Athens. The Athenians used the coins at home for business, and in foreign regions the coins served as bullion as well. In many localities of Asia Minor, the natives restamped the Athenian coins, sometimes so sloppily that the original Athenian design shows through.

The Greek cities of Sicily and southern Italy, which got their silver from Corinth in Greece, did the same thing. Sometimes we can see the Corinthian designs underneath. Athenian and Corinthian coins had a great reputation for quality, so overstriking was quite a time-saver. Instead of melting down the original coins, checking the purity of the metal, and then making new coins, another city could put the original coins to use by simply striking a new design over them.

Sometimes there was another reason for overstriking—a new king or a new government might take the old coins and simply stamp a new legend across the obverse indicating the change of regimes. When Alexander the Great conquered Persia, he decreed that the Persian coins could no longer be used as money. However, these Persian coins stayed in circulation as bullion—plain metal. To indicate this, merchants put marks on the coins with a punch.

Plate 38 **(top). Macedon, silver tetradrachm:** *obverse* **(179-168 B.C.). King Perseus. A masterpiece of portrait coinage.**

Plate 39 **(center). Aegina, silver stater (about 650 B.C.).** *Obverse:* **turtle.** *Reverse:* **punchmark.**

Plate 40 **(below). Aegina, silver stater:** *obverse* **(about 380 B.C.). Tortoise.**

Most scholars believe that Greek coinage started on the small island of Aegina, about ten miles from the Greek mainland in the Aegean Sea. It had a large population that could support itself only by trading. And so its ships plied all over the Mediterranean, to Egypt among other places. As the Egyptians wanted silver, the people of Aegina hit on the idea of getting silver from a nearby island and making coins with it—this being the handiest way of using the metal.

In modern times, explorers have found hoards of these coins in Egypt. On one side, the silver lumps show a turtle (the symbol or "badge" of Aegina). On the other side you can see the mark of the punch that drove the die into the metal. Just as the later Athenian coins were known as "owls," these early coins were called "turtles."

How Greek Coinage Developed

Aegina continued to issue coins for two centuries, until Athens conquered the island. Once Aegina regained its freedom, it issued a new series, but this time with a tortoise, and the letters AI. By 400 B.C. or thereabouts, so many cities were issuing coins that a symbol was no longer enough for identification; the name had to appear as well.

After a while, other Aegean islands began to issue coins with equally simple designs—an ancient coin of Andros, for example, shows an amphora, or wine jar.

Plate 41. Andros, silver stater: *obverse* (about 600 B.C.). Amphora.

These coins, by the way, did not have a denomination—they merely contained a certain amount of metal. The buying power of the coins varied enormously from place to place, depending on supply and demand.

The city of Corinth was among the first to issue coins in denominations, and one of the earliest to have designs on both sides of the coin. This probably happened during the sixth century B.C. The "badge" of Corinth was the winged horse Pegasus, a mythological figure representing flights of poetic inspiration. This image appeared on all Corinthian coins, which is why they were called "ponies."

Plate 42. Corinth, silver stater (about 350 B.C.). *Obverse:* Pegasus. *Reverse:* head of Athene. This is the famous Corinth "pony."

Then Corinth went a step further, with a different design for each denomination—Pegasus always on the obverse, but with varying reverses. These features made the "ponies" among the most popular coins of the Mediterranean region. The favorite denomination was the stater, equal to four drachms.

Another town, Chalcis, made coins not only for its own use—the wheel was its symbol—but also for other towns. One of these was Eretria, with its terrifying symbol of a Gorgon's head.

Plate 43. Eretria, silver stater: *obverse* (about 550 B.C.). According to Greek lore, anyone who looked at the Gorgon's head turned into stone.

About 500 B.C. the coins of Macedon reflect the life of the hunter and farmer. Thebes, the home town of the legendary strong man Herakles (Hercules) issued coins picturing his exploits. One such coin shows him as an infant strangling two serpents.

Plate 44. Thebes, silver stater: *reverse* (about 450 B.C.). Herakles kneeling and drawing his bow. Note the square incuse.

Another set of fascinating coins came from Elis, where Olympia was located. The people there were mostly farmers, and had little occasion for using money. But since pilgrims and tourists came by thousands from all parts of Greece for the Olympic Games, for a short time Elis had a spurt of trade. This explains its issue of several handsome coins commemorating the shrines to Zeus and Hera.

The earliest Athenian coins pictured an amphora because the city did a great export trade in these jars. But after a while Athens switched to an obverse showing the patron goddess Athene, and a reverse picturing Athene's owl. The combination made up what was probably the most famous and most widespread ancient coin up to the time of Alexander the Great. These "owls" turn up very frequently in hoards buried as far distant as central Asia.

Plate 45. Athens, silver dekadrachm (about 480 B.C.). The famous "owl of Marathon" appears on this *reverse* of the coin. See Plate 29.

The finest of all the Athene-owl coins was issued to commemorate the great victory over the Persians at Marathon. If you look closely at the obverse of this coin, you can see that the goddess is crowned with olive leaves, an allusion to the famous victory.

To the Greeks, the connection was even closer, for they believed that Athene, in the guise of an owl, had appeared on the battlefield to assure them of victory. Aristophanes, the famous comic playwright, expressed the idea in his play *The Birds,* in these lines:

How we drove their ranks before us,
Ere the close of eventide;
As we closed an owl flew o'er us,
And the gods were on our side.

Even more remarkable is the further history of this dekadrachm (ten drachms). It seems that every year each citizen of Athens received a bonus of ten drachms from the state. But when Themistocles urged the Athenians to build a great fleet to prepare for the anticipated Persian invasion, his fellow citizens responded patriotically. They turned the beautiful commemorative dekadrachms over to the city treasury as a gift. It was with this money that Themistocles built the fleet which crushed the Persians at Salamis in 480 B.C.

Superb Coins of Western Greeks

The fifth and fourth centuries B.C. were the Golden Age of artistic coinage in Sicily and southern Italy. The Syracusan coins are famous for their device of the quadriga, or four-horse chariot. The Greeks who founded Syracuse hailed from Corinth, noted for its "pony" coins.

At one time during the sixth century B.C. the philosopher Pythagoras was in charge of coinage at Croton, in southern Italy. Pythagoras is remembered for a number of remarkable discoveries and theories. He noted, for example, that the pitch of a musical note depends on the length of the vibrating string. Also he is credited with discovering the (Pythagorean) theorem that the sum of the squares of the arms of a right triangle equals the square of the hypotenuse, or longest side of the triangle. Pythagoras also held, but not for any sound reason, that the earth is a sphere.

As far as coinage is concerned, Pythagoras introduced an interesting incuse style in the coins of southern Italy. The obverse appears in relief (raised above the surface). On the other side of the coin, the design is the same, except that it appears in reverse, sunk below the surface of the coin. The coins of Metapontum, a

Plate 46 (left). **Agrigentum, silver tetradrachm: *reverse* (about 410 B.C.). Eagles attacking hare.**

Plate 47 (right). **Syracuse, silver stater: *obverse* (about 260 B.C.). Charming head of Queen Philistis.**

city near Croton, are famous examples of the incuse method.

Now we come to the coinage of Syracuse. Almost at the same time that the Persians invaded the Greek mainland, the Carthaginians attacked Syracuse. To celebrate the successful repulse of the Carthaginian invasion, the Syracusans issued the first of their commemorative dekadrachms.

After about the middle of the fifth century B.C., political conditions on the Greek mainland became more and more unsettled, and in 430 B.C. a terrible plague raged throughout Athens. Apparently many of the finest artists and craftsmen migrated across the Mediterranean, and it is to them that we owe the later masterpieces of Sicilian coinage.

About 400 B.C. or so, the Carthaginians again invaded Sicily and were again beaten back. The Athenians, seeking to enlarge their empire, also attacked Sicily, and were defeated even more decisively. From these victories came what are perhaps the finest of the Sicilian coins. One of them, indeed, is generally considered the most beautiful coin ever made. Here it is:

Plate 48. **Syracuse, silver dekadrachm (about 400 B.C.). *Obverse*: head of Artemis, Arethusa, or Persephone (the scholars are at odds here!). *Reverse*: Charioteer driving quadriga; flying Victory above, suit of armor below.**

Plate 49. **Syracuse, silver dekadrachm (about 480 B.C.). *Obverse*: head of Arethusa. *Reverse*: charioteer with quadriga, flying Victory above, lion (defeated Carthage) below.**

Plate 50. **Akragas, silver dekadrachm: *obverse* (about 425 B.C.). One of the masterpieces of Western Greek coinage.**

Imperial Coinage

With the coming of Philip and Alexander of Macedon the imperial age began for Greece. The old city-states were in decline, at the mercy of conflicting empires—first the Macedonian, then Alexander's successors, and finally the Roman Empire. Such coinage as was left to the city-states in the third century B.C. and after was, with few exceptions, of poor quality. The best craftsmen were working for the kings, emperors, and satraps.

Meanwhile Greek designs and methods of coining were introduced into the lands of those whom the Greeks called "barbarians." This is a tricky word. We use it to denote people who are wild and savage. In this sense, the hordes of Huns and Goths who overran Western Europe in ancient times were barbarians. But, as far as the Greeks were concerned, anyone who was not lucky enough to be a Greek was a barbarian. To them, "barbarian" simply meant "non-Greek," no matter how cultured or how polished the person might be. Originally, "barbarian" referred to any *language* other than Greek; the word is supposed to have started from the contemptuous use of "bah-bah-bah" to indicate the hideous babble of a foreigner's queer lingo.

We have seen that popular types of Greek coins spread far and wide. When these were scarce in any region, it was quite natural for that locality to make its own coins, which were generally copies of Greek designs. So it is not strange to find imitations of the Athenian "owls" and other popular models in Syria, Arabia, and Mesopotamia. We find them also in ancient Judea, Parthia, Persia, and even further away in Asia.

Going west, we note Greek models in Carthage, Spain, Gaul, and even as far north as Britain. There is little point in reproducing many of these coins, as their workmanship is very poor. Carthage carried on a certain amount of trade with Britain in ancient times, and it is probably to this commerce that we owe the occasional finds of Greek coins in modern-day England. Of course the ancient Britons had not reached the stage of treating the coins as coins. They used the metal for its bullion value. This was still true about the time Julius Caesar invaded Britain toward the middle of the first century B.C.

Plate 51 *(left)*. Mende (Macedonia), silver tetradrachm: *obverse* (about 400 B.C.). Dionysus reclining on donkey.

Plate 52 *(right)*. Leontini, silver tetradrachm: *reverse* (about 440 B.C.). Lion's head.

Philip of Macedon's very popular silver tetradrachm showed Zeus on the obverse and a jockey on horseback on the reverse. Even more popular was his gold stater, naturally much rarer and more likely to be hoarded. It featured a head of Apollo on the obverse and a chariot race on the reverse. (See Plates 18 and 37.)

This gold stater was a great "traveling" coin—it circulated through the Danube valley into northern Europe and finally made its way into Britain. (A Greek named Pytheas made a famous voyage to Britain about 325 B.C. and is known to have left some of the gold staters there. After leaving Britain he went further north and is believed to have stopped off at Iceland.)

Plate 53. Macedon, silver tetradrachm (336-323 B.C.). *Obverse:* head of Herakles. *Reverse:* Zeus holding eagle.

Coins of Alexander the Great

Alexander's silver tetradrachm, with its head of Herakles and the seated figure of Zeus with his eagle and thunderbolt, was certainly the most widespread coin of ancient times. It circulated all through Alexander's empire and continued to be issued by his successors for almost 200 years after his death in 323 B.C.

Some scholars think that in issuing this coin Alexander was claiming descent from Herakles; others believe the head is really a likeness of Alexander. As we have seen, these coins eventually replaced the coins of the individual Greek cities. The tetradrachms have turned up in many hoards. One of the largest was dug up at Demanhur in Egypt in 1905—8,000 tetradrachms, buried about 318 B.C., were unearthed in this find.

Alexander also had a gold double stater which featured a Nike (winged Victory) on the reverse. On the obverse there appeared a head of Athene patterned on a famous bronze statue of the goddess. This statue was one of the outstanding works of the great Phidias. In issuing the coin, Alexander was undoubtedly associating himself with the glorious traditions of Athens.

After Alexander died, several of his generals, as we have noted, pictured him on their coins. Whatever reasons they may have given, their real purpose must have been to get a share of Alexander's fame and prestige, and to point to themselves as his former comrades-in-arms.

Ptolemy I of Egypt issued one of these coins, but the really famous one appeared in Thrace, under Alexander's general Lysimachus. The head of the conqueror is awe-inspiring in the expression of perfection that it conveys. The reverse, a seated figure of Athene, is no less imposing. Several hundred years later two Roman Emperors, Hadrian and Antoninus Pius, copied it for their coins. More than a thousand years later, it turned up as Britannia on a coin of Charles II of England. And 200 years after that, the figure, somewhat modi-

Plate 54. Macedon, gold double stater (336-323 B.C.). *Obverse:* Head of Athene. *Reverse:* Winged Victory. Struck by Alexander the Great.

fied, appeared on the familiar Liberty "seated" type of United States dimes and other coins. (See page 172.)

For an even more striking tribute to the ancient Greek coins, take a look at our Panama-Pacific commemorative piece of 1915 (page 172). The helmeted head of Athene reminds us of the staters of Corinth, and the owl on the reverse harks back to the immortal victory at Marathon. Perhaps the designer is telling us that the completion of the magnificent canal was a feat not unworthy of the men who designed those old coins, so remarkable for their nobility, artistry, and simplicity.

Ancient Rome

Our Debt to Roman Civilization

What remains today of an empire that once stretched from England to the Sahara Desert, and from the Atlantic Coast to the shores of the Black Sea?

Apparently nothing remains—yet Roman civilization plays a great part in our lives, and its language, Latin, is very far from a "dead" language. Half of the words in our own English, and many on coins and currency, are directly derived from Latin.

As a coin collector, you will be interested to know that the words "coin," "numismatics," "obverse," "reverse," "inscription," "design," "commemorative coin," "uncirculated coin," and "proof coin" all have a Latin origin. So do the words "cent," "dime," "quarter," "liberty," and "certificate."

Our characteristically American motto, *E pluribus unum* ("many joined into one") has always been used on our coins and currency in its Latin form.*

All of Europe was greatly influenced by Roman civilization. The Romance languages—French, Italian, Spanish, Portuguese, Rumanian, etc.—are based in large part on Latin. It was the Romans who introduced bullfighting into Spain. The Romans built the finest bridge in Portugal and obtained metal for coins from mines in Dacia (Rumania).

And so it goes—each country showing literally thousands of traces of Roman civilization, Roman ideas, Roman building, Roman law. The institutions begun under Roman law live on in our American law; in fact the legal systems of most of the countries of Western Europe are based on Roman law. After the Empire fell, Roman law became the basis of Church law (or "canon law," as it was called), then medieval law, and finally modern European law.

In zoology and botany, Latin is used for the scientific names of thousands upon thousands of animals and plants. Look at a medical dictionary and you will find pages and pages of Latin terms.

One of the great world religions, Christianity, owes much to Roman civilization. To this day Latin unites Roman Catholics the world over. Churches and public buildings still reflect the Roman influence. Our Capitol in Washington is copied from the Pantheon in Rome.

Latin literature contains many enduring classics, but it is Roman history above all that has fascinated men for two thousand

* For the translation of other Latin phrases that appear on our currency, see *Coinometry,* page 77.

years and inspired great writers like Shakespeare, as well as men of action like the leaders of the French Revolution. This history is a colorful pageant, rich in dramatic and stirring events, with consequences that reach right into our own time.

Our Debt to Roman Coinage

It has been said that coins are materials of history—indeed, they are history come to life. Every day Roman coins are found in sizable quantities in Europe, Asia, and Africa—mute witnesses to the widespread conquests of the Roman Empire. In our own country, of course, we have no physical traces of Roman coinage. But we do have traces—*they are right on our own coins!* Have you ever thought of the vast debt our coinage owes to Roman coinage?

After the fall of Rome in 476 A.D., the victorious barbarian (the Romans used the word now to indicate non-Roman) regimes continued to imitate the Roman coins for centuries. Thus English and Spanish coinage, derived from Roman coinage, has furnished many of the basic ideas and designs of American coins.

The liberty cap, which appears on many early American coins, harks back to the distinctive cap worn by the Roman freedman (freed slave). An even more popular device on our coins, one which is still used today, is the eagle. But this bird was also a favorite figure on coin reverses of the Greeks and the Romans. The eagle was associated with the Roman god Jupiter and hence was a religious symbol. The standards of each legion were topped by an eagle. (Napoleon also copied this idea.) Sometimes the eagles on our coins hold a cluster of arrows or a scroll in their beak. This comes directly from Roman coins.

Aside from this, we have also followed the Romans in showing wreaths and stars on the reverse. Our Goddess of Liberty is

Plate 55. Empire, silver antoninianus (248-249 A.D.). *Obverse:* head of Philip the Arab. *Reverse:* antelope. Philip, Emperor at the time of Rome's thousandth anniversary, struck the coin to commemorate the "Secular Games" held in honor of the occasion.

directly descended from the Roman goddess Libertas and the even older goddess Roma. The diadem wreath is of course also a Roman heirloom. The unusual "radiate" headdress on our Peace Dollar of 1921 is copied from a similar style on Roman coins. In ancient times this coin style reflected the widespread cult of Mithras, the sun-god, whose worship started in Persia and eventually became very popular in Rome.

Our famous "Mercury" dime of 1916 is our most Roman coin. The obverse (head with winged helmet) is an almost exact copy of a device used by the Romans for 600 years on their silver denarius, a coin of about the same size as the dime.

As for the head, we have replaced Roma with Liberty; but the goddesses look like sisters! The reverse of this dime is even more Roman. The fasces (bundle of rods with an ax) was the symbol of authority

Plate 56. Empire. Hadrian, bronze sesterce: *reverse* (117-138 A.D.). This eagle, one of the finest on Roman coins, was the predecessor of the eagle on American coins.

of the Roman Lictors, who protected the Consuls. (Mussolini later copied the symbol for his "fascist" regime.)

The laurel wreath is also copied from the Romans; victorious generals were crowned with a laurel wreath on the occasion of a "triumph." Later the laurel wreath became standard headdress for Emperors depicted on a coin.

Our use of mint marks likewise comes from the Romans. As for lettering, our coins—indeed, all modern coins—follow the Roman custom of curving the inscription to follow the circular edge of the coin. Even the Greeks failed to use this technique as much as they might have.

THE REPUBLIC

The Romans are very distant from us in time. The more or less legendary founding of Rome goes back some 2,700 years. Consequently, we can have a better understanding of their history, and the coins that were part of it, if we have some idea of the daily life of the Romans.

The Roman family of the early days was very close-knit. To the end of his life the father was all-powerful; women had no rights to speak of. Despite this stern atmosphere, there seem to have been very strong bonds of affection and respect between husband and wife, and parent and child.

The Romans had a bewilderingly large number of divinities—30,000, according to one Roman writer. In addition to the gods that most of us have read about, there were numberless guardian spirits of the home, the earth, the temples, many gods of abstract qualities, such as Fortune, Liberty, Abundance, and so on. Even Rome was a goddess—Roma.

The reverse of many Roman coins was given over to those divinities. Janus, the two-headed god of beginnings and endings whose temple was kept open in times of war and closed when peace reigned, appears often on Roman coins. The Lares and Penates, the household gods, are favorites on early coins, and temples are pictured very often. Jupiter, Juno, Minerva, Venus, Apollo, Mars, Mercury, and Hercules (a son of Jupiter) were favorite figures on Roman coins.

Mars (the month of March is named for him) was naturally an important god to the warlike Romans. So was Juno, the goddess of marriage and motherhood. (The Greeks, who regarded women as inferiors, often made fun of Juno. The Romans, who had great respect for women, venerated Juno.) To the Romans, the month of June, named for this goddess, was the luckiest month for marriage. Venus, the goddess of love, also had a sacred month—April.

Plate 57. Republic, silver didrachm: *obverse* (about 220 B.C.). Janus, the god of beginnings and endings, for whom the month of January is named.

Why April? Because that is the month when buds open, and "April" comes from a Latin word meaning "to open." The month of May was named for the goddess Maia.

As for Saturn, the god of agriculture, the Romans thought of him as having presided over a Golden Age that might return some day. They dedicated the Saturnalia, their most important festival, to this god. The Saturnalia, which lasted seven days in December, began with solemn thanksgiving services, went on to a noonday feast, and then erupted in a wild, joyous carnival. The Romans put business aside during this holiday, and even slaves were free during the festivities. In some of the Saturnalia customs, such as exchanging gifts, decorating homes with holly and evergreen, and stressing human brotherhood, we see features that are similar to our modern Christmas—the time of "peace on earth and good will to men."

Over all the divinities, in the Roman view, there reigned mighty Jupiter or Jove. "By Jove" was no trifling oath in ancient Rome.

There were a great many priests; particularly powerful were the augurs, who forecast success or failure in all important undertakings of the state by inspecting the entrails of animals.

An important element of the priesthood was the Vestal Virgins, who guarded the sacred fire dedicated to Vesta, the guiding genius of family piety and happy home life.

The Roman conquests of many lands and the intermingling of many races and faiths brought new religions to Rome, some from the East, some from Egypt. The Stoic philosophy, introduced from Greece, stressed reason, justice, and righteous living. It was the noblest element in Roman life until the spread of Christianity, to which it had a certain kinship.

Plate 58. **Republic, silver didrachm:** ***reverse*** **(about 220 B.C.). Jupiter with Victory in chariot. Note the inscription "ROMA." This is the** ***reverse*** **of Plate 57.**

Romans and the Law

Rome's steady expansion over the years called for a legal system that would hold together her domains with the least amount of friction. Also, there was a continual struggle of the common people (Plebs or Plebeians) to wrest more legal rights from the Patricians (the aristocrats who traced their descent from the founders of Rome). For centuries the law evolved peacefully—through decrees passed by the Senate, decisions handed down by the Praetors (judges), and commentaries prepared by legal experts.

Between the Plebs and the Patricians there stood the Knights or Equestrians. They organized commerce and banking so well that Roman civilization was able to spread far and wide throughout the Western world.

Lowest of all the population were of course the slaves, whose numbers increased phenomenally during the great wars of conquest. Though a slave had no legal rights, he was not treated too badly in the early days of the Republic. Some slaves

Plate 59. **Republic, silver denarius:** ***obverse*** **(70-50 B.C.). Head of the goddess Vesta, whose temple was one of the most attractive in Rome.**

were well educated, some did important work, and quite a few either bought their freedom or were granted it. These "freedmen," or their descendants, often rose far above their originally humble station in life.

The main task of Roman law was to adjust harmoniously the conflicting ambitions and jealousies of all these groups.

In broad outline, this is how the governmental system worked in the heyday of the Republic. Elections took place only in the city of Rome. Voting was limited to men who were Roman citizens and who were present in the city on election day. The voters also had to be fairly substantial owners of property.

Citizens were subject to military service between the ages of 16 and 60. Only those who had served in the army for at least ten years could hold public office.

There were two elective lawmaking bodies, the Tribal and Centurial Assemblies. These in turn elected the government officials. Theoretically the Assemblies had considerable power, but the Aristocrats (Patricians) stripped them of any real role in government.

The two most important elected officials were the Consuls, who more or less fulfilled the functions of an American President or British Prime Minister. Their term in office was limited to one year. When Marius had himself elected Consul for six terms, beginning in 104 B.C., it was a signal that the days of the Roman constitution were numbered.

To keep the Consuls in line, the Romans invented the office of the Tribune. There were ten of these in peacetime, fourteen during a war. Theirs was the veto power—in Latin *veto* means "I forbid."

Other officials were the Quaestors, who ran the "Treasury Department"; the Praetors, who were judges; and the Aediles, who supervised public works. Finally, there were the two Censors, who held office for eighteen months, and watched over morals, took the census, prepared the budget, removed members of the Senate for due cause, and had a variety of other duties. When stern old Cato the Elder became Censor in 184 B.C., he had a Senator expelled for kissing his own wife in public.

Plate 60. Republic, silver denarius: *reverse* (118-104 B.C.). Election scene: one citizen deposits his voting tablet, while another is about to receive his.

Plate 61. Republic, silver denarius: *reverse* (70-50 B.C.). Roman citizen placing a voting tablet in a voting basket. This is the *reverse* of Plate 59.

The Senators ("elders") were the chief governing body of Rome, and met regularly in the Senate-house beside the Forum. It was originally limited to 300 members, but in the late Republic rose to 600 and then to 900. At the height of Rome's power it was composed almost wholly of men who had served as officials.

The SPQR—standing for *Senatus Populusque Romanus,* meaning "the Roman Senate and People"—we occasionally find on remains of Roman structures. At the height of its power, the Senate controlled policy on foreign affairs, war, taxes, public lands, and the conquered provinces.

In cases of grave emergency, the Senate often used its power of declaring martial law and appointed a temporary Dictator for a period of six months or a year. Amazing as it may seem, every Dictator appointed (during the first 400 years of the

Plate 62. Republic, silver didrachm: *obverse* (about 260 B.C.). Mars, the god of war, appears often on early Roman coins. Note the use of a Greek denomination for this and other Roman coins of this early period.

Republic) stripped himself of his powers on the date set. Even Sulla, after a reign of terror unprecedented in Roman history, disbanded his army in 80 B.C. and completely renounced all power.

The Roman Army

A Roman general ("Imperator") commanded an army made up of legions. There were 6,000 soldiers in a legion. Under the Imperator came the Tribunes, each commanding 1,000 men (a "cohort"), and the Centurions, commanding 100 men (in later times, 200).

Roman discipline was unbelievably strict. An army commander had the right to execute any soldier or officer for disobeying a command. There is a famous story of a Consul who had his son beheaded in 340 B.C. for disobedience in battle. For cowardice, the penalty was flogging to death. Each legion had a standard—its "eagle"—which it was considered a disgrace to lose in battle. Roman soldiers gladly gave their lives to prevent this.

In keeping with the austere eating habits of the early days of the Republic, soldiers lived mainly on porridge, vegetables, and sour wine. Pay was small, so that from the start the soldiers had a keen interest in plunder; however, there were severe regulations against stealing. Some commanders, like Caesar in the Gallic Wars, amassed millions; Cato the Elder distributed all spoils among his men, left nothing for himself. One feature that made the harsh discipline acceptable was that generals and great fighting Emperors shared the hardships and dangers of their men.

On returning from a victorious war, a general celebrated a "triumph" in the city of Rome if his army had won a major victory against a dangerous enemy. It was a combination of a victory parade and a religious thanksgiving.

In a triumph, the commander formed his parade immediately outside the city, where his forces laid down their weapons before passing through the gates. Then the procession went along the Sacred Way, with musicians, floats, plunder, exotic animals, the defeated leaders of the enemy; then came the victorious general, clothed in a purple toga, wearing a gold crown, and carrying laurel, the insignia of victory. His relatives followed, and the soldiers brought up the rear.

The parade ended at the Capitol, where the victor formally offered his booty to the gods, sacrificed an animal to them, and had his captive leaders slain. (Claudius, in some ways one of the most intelligent and unconventional of the Emperors, astonished Rome after his conquest of Britain in 51 A.D. by freeing Caractacus, the captive king.) An interesting feature of the triumph was that the soldiers in the ranks had the privilege of ridiculing their chief, if they felt like it—apparently a device to keep him from getting a swelled head!

Plate 63. Antioch, silver stater: *obverse* (about 80 B.C.). Tigranes the Great (94-56 B.C.), King of Armenia, struck this coin after he conquered Syria.

Early Conquests and the Punic Wars

It was the Punic Wars that established Rome as a world power. How these wars came about, what happened in them, and what they led to, make up one of history's most fascinating stories.

Situated on seven hills some miles up the Tiber, the biggest river in the west of Italy, Rome had started out as a monarchy. Much later, the Romans threw out their kings and set up the Republic. Their conquest of Italy was a slow, laborious process. Gradually the Romans wore down the Latins, the Samnites, the Gauls, the mysterious Etruscans and welded together the conquered territories by building magnificent roads and founding fortified cities. They completed the Italian conquest around 250 B.C.

There is a saying that appetite grows with eating, and with complete mastery of Italy in sight, the Romans began to cast longing looks at the large and prosperous island of Sicily off the southern coast of Italy. As yet they had no navy, but control of Sicily would be a stepping stone to control of the Mediterranean. And Sicily was a fertile land, valuable as a granary for whatever country possessed it. But Sicily belonged then to Carthage, the great commercial city-empire founded on the north African coast by the Phoenicians. The Phoenicians were an ancient people of Asia Minor, famous for their phenomenal skill in seafaring and trading, and for their development of an alphabet.

Plate 64. Carthage: *reverse* (about 350 B.C.). Lion in front of date-palm tree. Like the Greeks and Romans, the Carthaginians were fond of picturing animals on their coins.

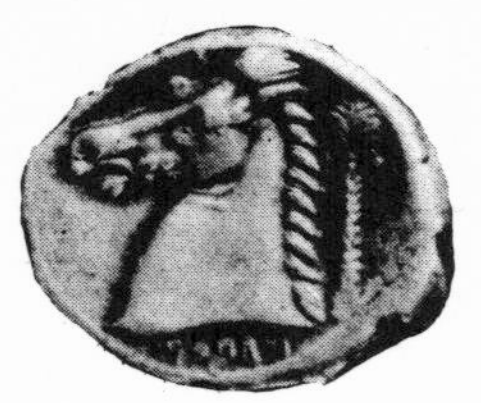

Plate 65. Carthage, silver tetradrachm: *reverse* (330-310 B.C.). Horses were favorites with wealthy Carthaginians who also had cattle, sheep, and goats on their large estates; elephants were used for heavier work.

In those days, north Africa was fertile farmland, with rich fields, gardens, orchards, and vineyards. The Carthaginians sailed through the Pillars of Hercules (Straits of Gibraltar) and then along the Atlantic coasts of Europe and Africa. They also traded inland for elephants, slaves, and precious metals. As they conquered the islands and coasts, they exacted fabulous tributes. The city of Carthage itself, with a population of some 250,000, had 220 magnificent docks. This gives us some idea of its huge commerce. This great city also had impressive temples and stunning public buildings, including a treasury and a mint.

The Carthaginians had coins, based on Greek models, and they also used leather strips with various denominations stamped on them. These were freely accepted throughout their empire—a convincing indication of flourishing business and sound government.

The Romans looked at all this and they didn't like it. Envious, power-hungry, and greedy for the commerce of Carthage, they started hostilities on a pretext. The two antagonists were well matched, and their struggles to the death, which lasted

Plate 66. Carthage, silver stater: ***obverse*** **(about 350 B.C.). Though this handsome goddess wears an African headdress, coin scholars believe this stater is the work of a Greek artist.**

from 264 B.C. to 146 B.C., were known as the three Punic Wars. (The word "Punic" comes from *Poeni,* the Latin word for "Phoenicians.")

The First Punic War lasted more than twenty years. Slowly the Romans assembled a fleet of oared galleys as they laboriously studied the techniques of naval warfare. They studied to good purpose, for their first fleet had over three hundred "quinqueremes" (galleys with five banks of oars). These were a good 150 feet long, with about three hundred slave-rowers and one hundred soldiers. The Romans equipped the vessels with grappling irons and movable gangways for hand-to-hand fighting.

Plate 67. Republic, bronze uncia: ***reverse*** **(250-225 B.C.). Prow of a galley; issued perhaps to commemorate the sea victory over the Carthaginians off Sicily in 256 B.C.**

Despite their inexperience, the Romans trounced the Carthaginians in a great sea battle; but later their fleet was dashed to pieces against a rocky coast. They lost practically all their galleys, and almost 100,000 men were drowned.

There is a famous story from this First Punic War about Regulus, a Roman general who was captured by the Carthaginians and sent back to the Romans carrying the peace terms. The Carthaginians made him promise to return to them if the Romans refused the offer. He brought the terms to the Romans, counseled them to reject the offer, and then, despite the entreaties of his countrymen, insisted on keeping his word. He returned to what he knew was certain death by fiendish torture!

At the end of the war the Romans had Sicily, but both sides knew the fight was only started. The Romans were greatly in need of a breathing spell, for their coinage had depreciated more than 80 per cent. During the "peace" that followed, both sides built up their strength and the Carthaginians planned revenge. By conquering Spain, they obtained a new base of attack against Rome. The Romans in turn began to extend their conquests beyond Italy—now it was Greece they wanted to subdue.

In 221 B.C. the great Hannibal became commander of the armies of Carthage, at the age of 26! Daring and resourceful, Hannibal had a magnificent personality, and his troops idolized him. The writers of the ancient world often compared him with Alexander the Great.

Hannibal formed a brilliant plan to crush the Romans. Setting out from Spain with an army of 60,000 men, he marched through Gaul (France) and then crossed the icy Alps under terrible hardships. He lost half his men in the 17-day passage, and

Plate 68. Carthage, silver stater: ***reverse*** **(about 350 B.C.). Lion and palm tree. This is the** ***reverse*** **of Plate 66.**

the task of getting his elephants carrying supplies through the passes was maddeningly difficult. In forming his plans, Hannibal had relied on the help of Rome's subject peoples in Italy. Failing to get anything like the support he had hoped for, and outnumbered ten to one, he went ahead just the same.

The Romans had a great general, Fabius, who knew that the best way to fight Hannibal was to avoid battle—to wear him out by "masterly inactivity." Hannibal himself realized that this policy held the greatest danger for him, but the Romans chafed under the strategy of Fabius the "hesitater." Plutarch tells how Fabius "always encamped on the highest grounds, where the enemy's horse could have no access to him. Still he kept pace with them; when they marched, he followed them; when they encamped, he did the same, but at such a distance as not to be compelled to an engagement." Far from home, with no prospect of reinforcement or fresh supplies, Hannibal knew that he could not survive this policy.

Bored and irritated by the superhuman patience of Fabius, the Romans replaced him with "men of action." Though greatly outnumbered, Hannibal trounced the Romans several times. Finally he lured a Roman army, twice the size of his own, into battle on the broad plain of Cannae.

Leaving his unreliable allies in the center, Hannibal placed his splendid cavalry on the wings. As he expected, the Gauls

Plate 69. Carthage: *obverse* (about 350 B.C.) of Plate 64. Female head. One of the great rarities among ancient coins.

Plate 70. Carthage, electrum stater: *obverse* (about 270 B.C.). Head of the goddess Tanit. To the Phoenicians, ancestors of the Carthaginians, she was known as Astarte.

in the center quickly caved in, and the Romans heedlessly dashed after them. Then, with a mighty advance of his cavalry on both flanks, Hannibal encircled the Romans and crushed them, winning a victory that has been studied and imitated from that day (216 B.C.) to this. Of the Roman army of almost 100,000 men, half perished and about 10,000 escaped—one of these, Scipio, the man who eventually defeated Hannibal.

Now master of Italy, Hannibal was at a loss to exploit his victory. Said one of his officers: "You know how to win victory, but you do not know how to use it." Hannibal could have taken Rome if he had wanted to, but he could not see how he

Plate 71. Carthage, electrum stater: *reverse* (about 270 B.C.). Horse. This is the *reverse* of Plate 70.

would benefit, still cut off as he was from Carthaginian bases of supply. Hannibal went on for years, content with small-scale battles ravaging the countryside.

Meanwhile another great Roman general, Scipio, gained the mastery of Spain and counterattacked in Sicily, defeating

Plate 72. Republic, silver denarius: *obverse* (about 44 B.C.). Head of Julius Caesar. This was a daring innovation — the first Roman coin to portray a living statesman.

Plate 73. Empire, silver denarius: *obverse* (12 B.C.). Octavian, Caesar's grandnephew and adopted son, who assumed the name of Augustus on becoming Emperor.

IMPORTANT DATES IN ROMAN HISTORY

B.C.	
753	Rome Founded
509	Republic Set Up
443	First Censors
268	First Coinage of Denarius and Sesterce
264-241	First Punic War (Carthaginian War)
241	Naval Victory over Carthage
219-201	Second Punic War
216	Hannibal's Victory at Cannae
202	Scipio's Defeat of Hannibal
150-146	Third Punic War
146	Carthage Destroyed; Conquest of Greece Completed
133-121	Attempted Reforms of the Gracchi
107-87	Marius in Power
83-80	Sulla in Power
60	First Triumvirate: Crassus, Pompey, and Caesar
58-49	Caesar's Campaigns in Gaul
49-44	Caesar in Power
44	Caesar Assassinated
43	Second Triumvirate: Antony, Octavian, and Lepidus
31	Octavian's Defeat of Antony at Actium
27	Augustus (Octavian) Emperor (Reign: 27 B.C.-14 A.D.)
A.D.	
9	Varus Defeated by the Teutonic Tribes
14-37	Tiberius Emperor

A.D.	
30?	Jesus Crucified
37-41	Caligula Emperor
41-54	Claudius Emperor
54-68	Nero Emperor
64	Rome Burned
69-79	Vespasian Emperor
79-81	Titus Emperor
81-96	Domitian Emperor
96-98	Nerva Emperor
98-117	Trajan Emperor
117-138	Hadrian Emperor
138-161	Antoninus Pius Emperor
161-180	Marcus Aurelius Emperor
180-192	Commodus Emperor
284-305	Diocletian Emperor
301	Price-fixing by Diocletian
303-311	Persecution of Christians
305-337	Reign of Constantine
312	Constantine Ends Persecution of Christians
330	Constantinople Founded as Capital of Eastern Roman Empire
403	Ravenna Replaces Milan as Western Roman Capital
410	Alaric Sacks Rome
429	Vandals in North Africa
449	Saxons in Britain
455	Vandals Sack Rome
466	Visigoths in Spain
476	End of Western Roman Empire
1453	End of Eastern Roman Empire

Hannibal's allies there. When Scipio crossed the Mediterranean, menacing Carthage, Hannibal at last returned to defend his homeland. Now 45 years old, he was seeing the city for the first time since he had been taken away as a child of nine to learn the arts of war. In a great battle at Zama (202 B.C.), Scipio crushed Hannibal and the Carthaginians, who were forced to sue for peace. For this sweeping triumph, the Roman Senate gave Scipio the name "Africanus."

But the Romans were not content with their victory and their huge indemnity. Many years later, in 146 B.C., they invaded Africa again in the Third Punic War on a trumped-up pretext. Acting with treachery and cruelty, they broke all resistance and leveled the great city of Carthage to the ground.

The three Punic Wars, the most grueling struggles of the Roman Republic, had made the Romans masters of Sicily, north Africa, and Spain, of fertile farmlands and rich mines, of the teeming commerce of the Mediterranean.

This had not been achieved without great cost. In the Punic Wars, hundreds of thousands of people lost their lives, almost every other farm in southern Italy was put to the torch, and hundreds of towns were wiped out. Swelling the ranks of the city poor, the dispossessed farmers flocked to Rome; the countryside fell into the hands of the rich, who used slaves to till the farms. From then on the populace of Rome was to depend for grain, its staple food, on Sicily and Africa—and was thus left to the mercy of droughts, uprisings, and Mediterranean pirates. Above all, the violence, unrest and physical danger of war got people out of the habit of living together peacefully.

Plate 74. Republic, bronze uncia: *obverse* of Plate 67 (250-225 B.C.). Roma—the spirit of Rome personified as a goddess.

Early Roman Finance and Coinage

Italy is poorly supplied with minerals, but the early Romans had no shortage of metal for coins; mostly farmers, they did very little trading. Up to about 350 B.C., cattle served as a medium of exchange. ("Pecuniary" comes from *pecus,* meaning "cattle.")

As business activity broadened, the problems of financing and the regulation of interest became serious. The Romans had such "modern" contraptions as corporations, mortgages, checking accounts, and interest-bearing savings accounts. As far back as 352 B.C., we find the state helping out creditors, taking over sound mortgages and salvaging investments. During the Punic Wars, businessmen formed many corporations to handle government contracts for war supplies.

The first Roman coins were clumsy lumps of bronze—sometimes cast bars of the metal. (Bronze, by the way, is an alloy made up of 95 parts of copper to 4 parts of tin and one part of zinc.) About 350 B.C. they began to use a cast bronze coin called the "as" (plural: asses), which at first weighed a pound! By the third century B.C., the conquest of Italy had reached a point where the Romans had to compete with beautiful coins from the Greek colonies on Sicily and the mainland.

To meet this situation, the Romans set up a real coinage system in 268 B.C. It provided for coining by a number of mints, basically for military reasons—paying the soldiers stationed in widely separated areas.

The Roman Senate, being in charge of financial matters, naturally controlled the issuing of coins. The Censors contracted to purchase silver bullion. They were assisted by the Quaestors, who paid the government debts. The Senate supervised both of these functions.

Three officials, known as "triumvirs," handled the mechanics of minting. They had the metallic blanks made and were in charge of the slaves who worked on the coins.

The new coins issued in 268 B.C. were silver, well made, and of convenient size and weight. After all, they were intended for trading. The most famous Roman coins were the denarius and the sesterce (or sestertius). Four sesterces equaled one denarius. The as, reissued in a one-ounce weight, was valued at one-tenth of a denarius. Some of these coins continued to be issued until the coinage reform of Constantine the Great in 330 A.D.

During the First Punic War, the Romans suffered such a shortage of money that they "solved" the problem drastically by enormously decreasing the amount of metal in their coins—80 per cent. At the same time, the booty from conquered lands began to bring in vast sums of money. Thus, Scipio Africanus displayed no less than 123,000 pounds of silver after he defeated Hannibal in 202 B.C.

The following figures will give you an even more impressive idea of how profitable the wars of conquest were under the Republic. At the end of the First Punic War in 241 B.C., Carthage had to pay the Romans reparations of 3,200 talents (approximately $18,000,000). After the Second Punic War, which ended in 202 B.C., the Romans fixed the indemnity at 10,000 talents. So profitable were these wars that for some years the Romans were able to get along without taxes!

Plate 75. **Republic, silver denarius: *reverse* (about 40 B.C.). Roman temple for Juno Moneta (goddess Juno, the Guardian or "Monitor") in which Rome's Mint was located. From "moneta" we get our words "mint" and "money."**

Later Republican Coins

The year 146 B.C. was an auspicious one for the Romans; they not only destroyed Carthage that year—they also completed the conquest of the weakened and divided Greek city-states. To assure themselves of a monopoly of Mediterranean commerce, they razed the great Greek trading city of Corinth to the ground.

A host of new influences began to pour in on the city of Rome—many of a kind that sapped the energy and integrity of the once austere and tenacious Romans. Their rule in Spain was notoriously corrupt and bloodthirsty; one of their greatest admirers has said of their policy in Spain: "Never had war been waged with so much perfidy, cruelty, and avarice." It was not at all unusual for proconsuls (provincial governors) to return to Rome with thousands of pounds of silver and every other conceivable kind of booty. Julius Caesar made enough in one year's service in Spain to pay off debts of $10,000,000 to his political "angel," Marcus Crassus.

One man in Rome fought a gallant, sometimes foolish fight against soft living and the quest for easy money. This was Marcus Porcius ("pig") Cato, descended from a family of swine-raising peasants. After he became Censor in 184 B.C., the exasperated Senators made forty-four attempts to get rid of him, but the farmers kept him at his job. We remember Cato for the famous sentence that wound up every speech he made for over 30 years: "Besides this I move that Carthage shall be destroyed." He died three years before his wish came true.

Later Caesar, in his struggle for power, had a special law passed (Lex Julia) giving military commanders the right to issue their own coinage. The effect was to make the troops dependent for their pay on their general rather than on the state.

At the height of the Civil War, in 82 B.C., Sulla brought the Treasury 15,000 pounds of gold and eight times as much silver from his victorious Greek campaigns.

Plate 76. Republic, silver denarius: *obverse* (about 82 B.C.). Venus with Cupid. Issued by Sulla to pay his troops.

More and more we find the generals issuing their own coinage in the first century B.C.—Sulla, Pompey, Caesar, and others. In their jockeying for power, they were giving the Roman coins a personal and private, rather than public, significance. The coinage of Caesar, and later of Mark Antony, clearly reflects the devious groping for power that went on in those troubled times.

As coin collectors we are naturally interested in the designs that appear on these coins. On the obverses we find images of the gods: Mars, Apollo, Hercules, Roma; the reverses feature a horse, or a horse's head, or a figure of Victory. The inscription on the coins is *Roma* or *Romano*. A little later we get more silver coins, with the two-headed Janus (the god of beginnings and endings), and another with Jupiter and Victory in a chariot. Still an-

Plate 77. Republic, silver denarius: *reverse* (about 190-180 B.C.). Castor and Pollux, the Heavenly Twins, were sons of Jupiter and according to legend, helped the Romans defeat the army of the Latin League.

other pictures the legendary heroes, the twin brothers Castor and Pollux riding into battle. Except for gold coins, the issues of the Roman Republic are still plentiful today and you can buy them for reasonable prices.

With new mints open, mint marks began to appear on Roman coins and there were new types, such as Hercules driving two centaurs. There were also exceptionally interesting coins showing the citizens placing their ballots in an urn or jug on election day. From the second century on, we get a large number of interesting commemorative coins illustrating brilliant achievements in war by the early Romans. How this came about is simple—the mint-masters were all of aristocratic lineage, and each one selected the illustrious deed of an ancestor for his coinage. This kind of boasting was quite natural in an age when Rome was still conquering and plundering much of the known world.

Plate 78. Republic, silver denarius: *obverse* (about 60 B.C.). Head of Hercules. Faustus Sulla struck this coin in memory of his father, "Sulla the Happy," whose nickname appears on the left side of the coin.

Decline of the Republic

By about 100 B.C. it had become clear to all that the Republic was splitting at the seams. Aside from the fierce struggle between the Aristocrats and the Popular Party, new dangers loomed up on all sides. There was revolt in southern Italy; a vast horde of 300,000 German barbarians streamed down from the north; uprisings were reported from Africa and Greece. Two great generals, Marius and Sulla, fought bloody battles to crush the enemies of Rome—and then fought each other. When Marius was in power, he wiped out every Patrician he could lay his hands on.

When Sulla finally came to power, he did exactly what Marius had done—murdered as many prominent men of the opposing party as his assassins and informers could track down.

One act of mercy stands out strangely in Sulla's life: he pardoned Marius' wife's nephew. As if ashamed of this lapse, he remarked, "In that young man go many Mariuses." He was right. The young man's name was Julius Caesar.

There is one striking difference between the two greatest conquerors of antiquity. Alexander the Great died at 33, lamenting, as we have seen, that there were no worlds left for him to conquer. Caesar, before he was 40, had done nothing in keeping with the place he has in history.

Born in 100 B.C., he had lived through the upheavals of the age of Marius and Sulla. He seemed unable to get his bearings or focus his ambitions, and up to 60 B.C. he was apparently content with a cynical, ironic attitude toward the world that was crashing about him. Recognized by all as a brilliant man, he limited himself to love affairs and shady political intrigues.

His ambition awoke in 60 B.C. as he realized that the chaotic situation called for a firm guiding hand at the helm of the ship of state.

Plate 79. Republic, gold aureus: *obverse* (about 61 B.C.). Africa personified. Commemorates the victories of Pompey, "the Great." Note the inscription: *Magnus*.

He began by forming a triumvirate with Pompey and Crassus to rule Rome. Doubtless Caesar was the least important member at the start. Pompey was an imposing figure—a general who had amassed a fortune from his victorious campaigns, while Crassus was the richest man in Rome.

It was during Caesar's brilliant campaigns in Gaul that he established himself as one of the greatest generals of all time. His boldness and resourcefulness created victories out of situations that would have destroyed a lesser man. After a hundred narrow escapes from disaster and death, he added to the Roman realm the most prized of all its provinces. By conquering the barbarians of Gaul, he pushed back the inevitable collapse of Rome by several centuries.

Returning to Cisalpine Gaul (on the Italian side of the Alps) in 49 B.C., Caesar found himself at the turning point of his career. Crassus was dead, Pompey was maneuvering to install himself as dictator, and the Senate was on Pompey's side. Soon

Plate 80. Parthia, silver stater: *obverse* (about 40 A.D.). Bust of King Artabanus II. The Romans fought many battles with the Parthians for control of trade routes that went deep into Asia.

an order came from the Senate: Disband your army! If Caesar obeyed, he was a ruined man. If he refused, he was a rebel. He tried compromise, and was turned down.

Coming to the Rubicon, a small stream separating Cisalpine Gaul from Italy, he asked his soldiers whether they were willing to follow him. Assured of their unswerving loyalty, he is said to have exclaimed, "The die is cast!" and advanced on Rome.

He entered the city without a fight after all—Pompey, flabby and timid, fled with his army to Greece. Now Caesar proved himself a great statesman. He exerted himself to win friends, to mollify enemies, and in general to soothe the savage hatreds of civil war.

It was during this period (49-48 B.C.) that he seized the power of issuing coinage within the city limits of Rome. Previously, generals could issue money only under war conditions and away from the city. Caesar obviously took this unconstitutional step in order to keep his soldiers loyal to him. But the coins also had propaganda value, as they commemorated his triumph in Gaul.

One of these famous coins is a denarius showing an elephant crushing a serpent. Another shows Aeneas, the famous Trojan hero, carrying his aged father from burning Troy. Legend had it that Aeneas, son of the goddess Venus, had escaped from

Plate 81. Republic, silver denarius: *obverse* (about 49 B.C.). Elephant trampling serpent. Issued in celebration of past victories. Caesar used this coin for personal propaganda.

Plate 82. Republic, silver denarius: *obverse* (about 44 B.C.). Caesar wearing priestly headdress. The inscription reads *Caesar Dict(ator) Perpetuo*, proclaiming his dictatorship for life.

Troy and come to Italy where he founded Rome. Caesar claimed descent from Aeneas. Such a noble pedigree would prove useful to him as he prepared to seize the supreme power.

After consolidating his position in Rome, Caesar took his army to Greece. At Pharsalus, outnumbered almost three to one, his forces easily crushed Pompey's army.

The defeated general fled to Egypt. When Caesar followed in hot pursuit, he found that Pompey had been assassinated. Now master of the Roman state, Caesar was urgently needed in Rome to restore order. However, he had been so captivated by Cleopatra, the queen of Egypt, that he dawdled in that country for almost a year.

A large-scale revolt in Asia finally roused him from his infatuation. Now fifty-three, he rushed east, put down the revolt with his customary efficiency and sent home the immortal message: "*Veni, vidi, vici*"—I came, I saw, I conquered. Returning to Rome, he established peace there, and the now subservient Senate voted him a ten-year dictatorship.

Generously paying off his soldiers, he gave them lands, tripled the membership of the Senate to make it unwieldy and hence helpless, and set up a great public works program to help the unemployed. In 46 B.C. he issued an aureus to celebrate his victories in Gaul, Pontus, and Egypt. He eased the harsh debt laws, set up a bankruptcy procedure which stands to this day, filled the empty Treasury, consider-

Plate 83. **Republic, silver denarius:** ***reverse*** **(35 B.C.). Head of Cleopatra. Mark Antony braved public opinion in striking this coin, for the Romans thought of Cleopatra as an enemy of the state.**

ably reduced the taxes of the provinces, installed honest governors.

Nothing escaped his attention; he even found time to reform Rome's jumbled calendar. For the last twenty years Caesar had been Pontifex Maximus ("high priest") of Rome. He had discovered that the Egyptian calendar, though four thousand years old, was much more accurate than the Roman system. Caesar introduced the new calendar in 45 or 46 B.C. We use it to this day—with two changes, one made by Augustus, and one by Pope Gregory XIII in 1582.

Now fifty-six, Caesar worked with feverish haste—perhaps with too much haste. He had many far-reaching plans. But he also had many enemies. In 44 B.C. they formed a conspiracy to murder Caesar. On the Ides of March (the 15th) they assassinated him as he entered the Senate.

A few months before his death, Caesar had "encouraged" the Senate to authorize his issuing a coin with his own portrait—Plate 72—the first Roman coin to have the likeness of a living man. By flouting precedent in this way, Caesar was proclaiming to the whole world that he was the real ruler of Rome. It may be that this projected coin was the last straw, as far as Caesar's enemies were concerned.

Caesar had his way, and the coin duly appeared in circulation. A month later, he was murdered!

Gold coins of the Republic are mostly limited to the first century B.C. They are hard to come by and expensive. After the assassination of Caesar, one of these rare gold coins appeared, bearing the portrait of Brutus. It seems that the conspirator Casca—"envious Casca," Shakespeare calls him—issued this coin.

Plate 84. **Republic, silver denarius (about 42 B.C.).** ***Obverse:*** **head of Brutus.** ***Reverse:*** **liberty cap and daggers.** ***Eid Mar*** **is an abbreviation for "Ides of March," when Caesar was assassinated.**

Antony or Octavian?

When Caesar's will was opened, it was found that he had named Octavian, his grand-nephew and adopted son, as his heir. Nineteen at the time, Octavian was sickly, timid, and no fighter. His appearance was deceptive, for he turned out to be cold and crafty with a patience that Caesar had never had.

Plate 85. **Republic, silver denarius:** ***obverse*** **(about 31 B.C.). Octavian as he looked at the time of his final victory over Mark Antony.**

Octavian's chances of ever obtaining his inheritance seemed slim indeed. His rival had been Caesar's most trusted general: Mark Antony. Fourteen years younger than Caesar, Antony had carried out many important military assignments for him. He was powerful, burly, impulsive, affable. It is true that, as Plutarch says, "there was much of simplicity in his nature." It is also true that he was not a man to cross.

Plate 86. Republic, gold aureus: _obverse_ (about 37 B.C.). Mark Antony struck this portrait of himself in Asia Minor while campaigning against the Parthians.

Mark Antony's coins picture him as a dangerous-looking man with a frank expression, and Roman coins are famous for their artistic honesty. The men who designed Roman coins avoided any "softening of the stupid brutality or the peevish ill humor" that we encounter fairly often among the famous Romans.

The struggle between Antony and Octavian is one of the most fascinating in all history. Antony had the power, Octavian had the brains. It took thirteen years to decide the issue between them.

The struggle had its inner logic. Though adversaries from the start, Antony and Octavian had to unite to crush Caesar's assassins—chiefly Cassius and Brutus, who were raising an army in Greece by the inspired method of collecting ten years' taxes in one year. Once Antony and Octavian disposed of their common enemies, the struggle would start in real earnest.

In 43 B.C., the year after Caesar's murder, Antony and Octavian formed the second triumvirate with Lepidus, an aged nonentity, to rule Rome. Their first act was to carry out a gigantic manhunt; they had about two thousand Equestrians and three hundred Senators butchered—partly to avenge Caesar, partly to extort money, partly to pay off old scores and stifle opposition in advance. With this purge completed, they felt much surer of themselves.

The following year, their joint army met the forces of "noble" Brutus and "lean and hungry" Cassius at Philippi, a Macedonian seacoast town. Antony scored an easy victory without much help from Octavian, who, according to some accounts, hid away from the battle. Returning to Rome, the partners squeezed out Lepidus; Antony elected to rule the eastern provinces, leaving Rome and the western provinces to Octavian.

It was in 41 B.C. that Antony met Cleopatra and they fell madly in love. As far as Cleopatra was concerned, there was method in this madness, for she hoped to bring about a partnership between Rome and Egypt to rule the world.

Cleopatra has been described as "a small, dainty creature, radiant rather than beautiful, with an abundance of soft, dark hair, a fascinating mouth, thoughtful wide-set eyes, a prominent though finely chiseled nose." Plutarch, the historian, adds "it was a pleasure merely to hear the sound of her voice." Incidentally, she was Greek, not Egyptian. From the time of the conquest of Egypt by Alexander the Great about two centuries earlier, the rulers of Egypt had been descendants of Ptolemy, one of Alexander's generals.

Plate 87. Republic, silver denarius (about 32-31 B.C.). _Obverse_: Roman war-galley. _Reverse_: eagle and standards of the famous Tenth Legion. Struck by Mark Antony.

For almost ten more years Antony and Octavian jockeyed for power. It is this situation which lends unusual interest to the series of denarii struck by Antony in 32-31 B.C. He issued these to honor the legions commanded by him. There were eighteen coins, one for each legion, and all had the same design: the legionary eagle on the obverse, and a war galley on the reverse. Coin experts consider this issue the outstanding propaganda coinage of all time. Why?

From Asia Minor to Africa there were many "client" states that paid tribute to Rome. The rulers of these countries had a cruel choice: should they support Antony or Octavian?

By issuing his famous coinage, Antony made sure that this money would circulate all over the Roman area and its tributary states, bearing witness to the size and power of Antony's army. Plutarch mentions eleven kings who sent Antony men and supplies.

However, Antony's efforts were doomed in the long-awaited showdown with Octavian. The great battle was fought at Actium off the west coast of Greece in 31 B.C. Antony's lieutenants favored a land battle, but Cleopatra insisted on a sea battle, and a sea battle it was.

At the height of the struggle, with the outcome still in doubt, Cleopatra became frightened and ordered her ships to leave the scene of the battle. At this, Antony lost his head completely and followed her in a galley. Disheartened by their leader's fantastic desertion, Antony's forces collapsed, giving Octavian a great victory and making him the master of the Roman state.

Both Antony and Cleopatra committed suicide. Thus ended the Republic, after almost a century of struggle between Marius and Sulla, Caesar and Pompey, Octavian and Antony.

THE EMPIRE

The Golden Age of Augustus

Octavian was now in the same position as Julius Caesar had been at the height of his power. But there was this difference: the people of Rome were tired of war, and yearned for peace. And peace was what Octavian wanted too; he had removed all his rivals, and wanted a quiet era in which to heal the wounds of conflict and overhaul Rome's outmoded and corrupt governmental machinery.

Octavian had learned a lesson from his famous grand-uncle's career; unlike Caesar, Octavian treated the Senate with a great show of respect, never failing, however, to get from it just what he wanted. For the first time in 200 years, the temple of Janus was at last closed, signifying that peace reigned in Rome. In 27 B.C. Octavian became Emperor—taking the name Caesar Augustus. As Emperor, he was known for his reforms, his mild rule, his patience and unassuming manner.

Augustus soon embarked on an ambitious building program, which he entrusted to his loyal friend Marcus Agrippa, who had won the battle of Actium for him. Agrippa built hundreds of temples, public baths, roads, aqueducts, and harbors. Many of these public works he paid for out of his own pocket. The Pantheon in Rome, the great temple to all the gods, was Agrippa's outstanding architectural achievement. This structure, later rebuilt by Hadrian, became a Christian church in 609 and is still in existence.

The coinage of the Empire begins of course with Augustus. One of his first measures was to set up eighteen mints throughout the Empire. On many of his coins Augustus commemorated the battle

Plate 88. Pergamum, silver tetradrachm (about 27-20 B.C.). *Obverse:* head of Augustus. *Reverse:* sphinx. The most artistic likeness of Augustus.

of Actium. Among the reverses on his denarii we find triumphal arches, wreaths, winged Victories, crocodiles, and a sphinx.

Gradually as his reign extended and became more widely popular, Augustus was revered as a savior of superhuman powers. In many parts of the Empire he was worshiped during his life as a god. Julius Caesar had been proclaimed a god not long after his death, but Augustus was actually deified during his lifetime.

Augustus seemed like a father to his people. During his reign, the memory of his earlier plots and murders was left far behind. In later times the Romans regretfully recalled the age of Augustus as a "Golden Age." In comparison to what followed, it might well be called that.

Plate 89. Republic, silver denarius: *reverse* of Plate 85 (about 31 B.C.). Like the sphinx on the previous plate, the crocodile is a symbol of Egypt and a reminder of Octavian's triumph over Mark Antony there just prior to his becoming Emperor.

Plate 90. Empire, silver denarius: *reverse* of Plate 73 (12 B.C.). A Gaul kneels to the Emperor Augustus; a bit of boasting on the part of the Romans.

The Empire After Augustus

One of the great defects of the Roman Empire was that there was no clear precedent for succession. Sometimes an Emperor's son reigned after him; in a number of cases, the Empire passed to an adopted son; all too often the new ruler was "chosen" by the army, using such methods as bribery and murder. Here, in brief, is the story of the first two centuries of the Empire.

Augustus was followed by Tiberius, his adopted son. For the first nine years of his reign (14 A.D.–37 A.D.), Tiberius was an excellent ruler. In his old age, fearful of plots against his life, he carried on a brutal reign of terror. All Rome breathed a sigh of relief when the lonely and sinister old man finally died at the age of 79. But his successor Caligula (37-41) proved to be a much worse despot, wildly extravagant, immoral, torturing and killing right and left. Finally a Tribune of the Praetorian Guard murdered the 29-year-old madman.

After the assassination of Caligula, the Praetorian Guard forced Claudius to become Emperor. He rewarded the soldiers later—willingly or unwillingly—with the equivalent of $3,500 apiece; an evil precedent. A timid man of bookish tastes, Claudius made an excellent administrator—one of the better Emperors. In 54 he was poisoned by his wife Agrippina, who wanted the throne for her son Nero.

Nero has the reputation of having been the most vicious of all the Emperors, though he has many formidable rivals for that title. He fancied himself as an actor, poet, and musician. Among many weird extravagances, he had a statue 153 feet high made of himself. Some say he caused the great fire that ravaged the city of Rome in 64, that he played his lyre while Rome burned and that he persecuted the

Plate 91. Empire, bronze sesterce (37-41 A.D.). *Obverse:* head of Caligula; the coin has been slashed by somebody who hated him. *Reverse:* inscription includes SPQR.

Plate 92. Empire, bronze as (41-54 A.D.). *Obverse:* head of Claudius. *Reverse:* goddess Liberty promising just rule.

Plate 93. Empire, bronze sesterce (54-68 A.D.). *Obverse:* head of Nero. *Reverse:* the closed temple of Janus. As the doors were closed only in peacetime, Nero is emphasizing that his policies have prevented war.

Plate 94. Empire, bronze sesterce (72 A.D.). *Obverse:* head of Titus. *Reverse:* Roman soldier standing guard over mourning Jewess. The famous *Judaea Capta* coin, struck by Titus during his father's reign, to commemorate the conquest of Judea.

Christians on the false charge of having started the blaze. In 68 he lost the protection of the Praetorian Guard and committed suicide after several tries.

Out of the ensuing free-for-all among the generals, Vespasian emerged as Emperor in 69. A man of humble origin, Vespasian gave himself no airs. He scraped together revenue from every possible source, but his administration was honest and efficient. He died in 79—the first Emperor since Augustus to die a natural death.

His equally popular son Titus lived only two years after becoming Emperor—there is a theory that Titus was poisoned by his brother Domitian (81-96), who succeeded him. A just ruler at first, though exceptionally severe, Domitian finally lapsed into unbearable tyranny. He was murdered by his courtiers.

With the disappearance of Domitian, the Empire entered a new golden age (96-180) under the rule of a series of five Emperors noted for their intelligence and great moral force. Nerva, an old man, reigned for only sixteen months, but he chose Trajan, who was to prove one of the best of all the Emperors, as his successor.

An able general and a man of colossal energy, Trajan had very simple tastes. He treated the Senate with utmost consideration, put the Treasury on a sound basis, constructed great public works and lowered taxes at the same time. A tireless

Plate 95. Empire, bronze as (103-111 A.D.). *Obverse:* head of Trajan. *Reverse:* Trajan's wooden arch bridge over the Danube, built during his Dacian campaigns.

Plate 96. Empire, bronze sesterce: *obverse* (134-138 A.D.). Head of Hadrian. He set the style for Imperial beards; all the earlier Emperors were clean-shaven.

Plate 97. Empire. Hadrian, bronze sesterce: *reverse* (117-138 A.D.). This figure of Pietas (Piety) reminds us strongly of a much older Greek coin of the goddess Athene (Plate 34) and a later Roman coin of Britannia (Plate 98).

builder, he is best remembered for a magnificent bridge across the Danube, the great Triumphal Arch, and the rebuilding of the Forum. He fought many campaigns, the most important being the conquest of distant Dacia (Rumania). We are told that he brought back a million pounds of silver and half a million pounds of gold from Dacia—which, we will see, helped slow down the debasing of Roman coinage.

Before his death in 117, Trajan chose his nephew Hadrian (117-138) to succeed him. One of the three greatest of all the Roman Emperors—the other two are Augustus and Constantine the Great—Hadrian was a man of versatile talents and superlative abilities. He was an even more extensive builder than Trajan; he arranged for the codification of Roman law in its finest form; he renounced the policy of further conquest and consolidated the borders of the Empire.

Plate 98. Empire, bronze as (154-155 A.D.). *Obverse:* head of Antoninus Pius. *Reverse:* Britannia (the spirit of Britain personified) seated on a rock. Apparently this is the first time the name appeared on a Roman coin. Note the similarity of England's first Britannia coins.

Antoninus Pius (138-161), Hadrian's choice for his successor, was a man so amiable, gentle, and tolerant that he has been compared to Abraham Lincoln. Historians have grumbled that his peaceful reign gave them little to write about.

Antoninus selected Marcus Aurelius (161-180) as the next Emperor. A strong believer in the Stoic philosophy, Aurelius worked for "a state in which there is the same law for all, a polity of equal rights and freedom of speech, and the idea of a kingly government that most of all respects the freedom of the governed." Aurelius detested the brutality of the gladiatorial games.

Continuing all the good features of the reign of Antoninus, he was confronted with a grave problem: the numerous northern barbarian tribes were now permanently on the march, menacing Rome. Aurelius

Plate 99. Empire, bronze sesterce (161-180 A.D.). *Obverse:* head of Marcus Aurelius. *Reverse:* spoils from victories over Germanic tribes.

Plate 100. Empire. Trajan, bronze sesterce: *reverse* (98-117 A.D.). Circus Maximus. This beautifully detailed coin shows the huge stadium, which seated 260,000. Note the colonnaded front and the obelisks.

fought them unceasingly for several years, managing to keep them at bay. It was during his campaigns that he wrote his famous *Meditations*.

Roman Spectacles

It has been said that the Roman Emperors kept their people docile with *panem et circenses* ("bread and circuses"). They often gave out grain free or sold it at nominal prices, and they spared no pains to keep the populace amused with spectacles of various kinds.

You can see a picture of the Circus Maximus on a sesterce of Trajan. This magnificent structure was 1,875 feet long and 625 feet wide, with a seating capacity of 260,000. Here the Romans enjoyed chariot races and athletic contests.

The chariot drivers were grouped in teams—the "blues" and the "greens." The Romans followed the chariot races with the same fanatical devotion that we give to baseball and other popular sports. (Caligula was such a passionate "fan" of the "greens" that he gave a charioteer the equivalent of half a million dollars and nominated his horse Incitatus to be Consul.) The spectators had snacks to keep them going through long hours of entertainment.

The races were very exciting. The charioteers had to go around the oval-shaped course seven times. At the curves each driver jockeyed for the favorable inside position, which naturally led to fearful spills. Chariots were overturned, horses ran wild drivers were often seriously injured or even killed. It is said that the crowd's roars of applause could be heard beyond the city limits.

The Colosseum was comparatively "small," seating perhaps 50,000 spectators. The Emperor Vespasian and his son Titus had this stadium built, it is said, by thousands of Jewish slaves, and it was opened in 80 A.D. Here the Roman Emperors offered Christians to the fury of wild animals that had been starved for days in preparation for this "sport." The Colosseum, still in existence, appears on the coins of Titus and several later Emperors.

Boxing was a sport the Romans enjoyed watching. The fighters used a boxing glove called the *caestus*. It was made of "pieces of hard leather having projecting and cutting edges like our knuckle dusters. Often covered with knots and nails, it must frequently have caused death."

Mere displays of athletic skill, which fascinated the Greeks, bored the Romans. More to their taste were the gory animal battles of the huge amphitheaters. There was a battle of 400 tigers against bulls and elephants. The opening performance at the Colosseum featured the fighting death of

Plate 101. Empire. Titus, bronze sesterce: *reverse* (79-81 A.D.). The Colosseum. Titus restaged a spectacular sea-fight here after flooding the arena to produce the proper setting.

Plate 102. **Umbria, bronze triens:** ***obverse*** **(about 250 B.C.). The** ***Caestus,*** **or Roman boxing glove, was used by gladiators not to soften blows but to make them more dangerous. The boxers were very likely to be killed or seriously maimed.**

some 5,000 beasts. Before these struggles there was often a display of unusual creatures—ostriches, giraffes, apes, and other animals that the ordinary Roman was not likely to see elsewhere. Skillful trainers often taught the animals to perform amusing tricks. Elephant ballets were a popular specialty.

Combats between a man and a bull, or another ferocious beast, always delighted the Romans. (Bullfights, by the way, have a long history, dating back before Roman times.) "Best" of all, from the Roman point of view, were the brutal and brutalizing mass combats of the gladiators—most of them condemned criminals and slaves, others trained in professional gladiatorial schools. Nero, Domitian, and Commodus were among the Emperors who took a direct part in killing the arena animals, and we are told that high-born ladies, Senators, and dignified businessmen sometimes tried their hand at it. Nero followed Caligula's example by forcing Senators to perform in gladiatorial combats and chariot races. Even the enlightened Augustus staged eight spectacles involving 10,000 fighters.

Another favorite sport with the Romans was sham naval battles. Claudius staged a mock duel between two "fleets" of 19,000 condemned criminals on a dammed lake in 45 A.D. Many were drowned in the fight.

Roman Coin Values

The aureus, a gold coin equivalent to twenty-five denarii, was issued regularly only under the Empire. There was also the talent, equal to six thousand denarii. The talent, taken over from the East, where it had been known from Babylonian times, was a measure—not a coin. In terms of our present-day money, we might figure the sesterce as worth a quarter, the denarius a dollar, and the talent as $6,000.

The Empire and Its Coinage

The Roman Empire was at its most flourishing about 100 A.D. Taxes were not unreasonable, the coinage was sound, the legal system the most enlightened of its time.

The era of stability that Augustus ushered in is suggested in the soundness of his gold, silver, and copper coinage. With Nero (54-68) the depreciation of the coinage started—not too bad at first, for the Romans still had confidence in their government and prices were fairly level. As time went on, the gold coinage slowly lost its original purity, while the silver was debased at a faster rate.

By 200, the serious military defeats, the rising cost of war, and the steady increase in the cost of living were having their effect on the coinage. The silver coins of Augustus had been 100 per cent pure; under Nero they were 90 per cent pure, under Trajan, the figure dropped to 85 per cent. Caracalla introduced a coin called the antoninianus, with a 50 per cent silver content. By 260, the silver content was 5 per cent, by 284 it was 2 per cent!

During the third century A.D. the famous silver mines of Spain were no longer as productive as they had been. When Aurelian gave up Dacia in 271 because Rome could not guard this distant province any more, the Empire lost its valuable silver mines there. This alone made further currency depreciation inevitable.

There were disastrous inflations in many parts of the Empire. Even the gold coinage had lost 40 per cent of its gold content. The bronze as, originally weighing one pound, had declined to a quarter-ounce in Nero's time. What made conditions even more unbearable for the people of the Empire was that while the government made its payments in the disastrously depreciated silver coin, it insisted on collecting taxes in gold—or even in goods.

The depreciation of the coinage was also reflected in the slow but steady rise in interest rates, from 4 per cent in the time of Augustus to 12 per cent (the maximum permitted) under Constantine the Great. Diocletian introduced a large bronze coin which had a thin overlay of silver. But this coin, the follis, depreciated so rapidly that people had to carry around heaps of the coins in a bag.

It was Constantine the Great (305-337), Diocletian's successor, who finally reformed

Plate 103. Empire, bronze follis: *obverse* (305-306 A.D.). Head of Diocletian. This Emperor is remembered today mainly for his persecution of Christians throughout the Roman Empire.

Plate 104. Empire, bronze follis (about 307-308 A.D.). *Obverse:* head of Constantine the Great. *Reverse:* Sun-god. Eastern religious cults were tremendously popular in the Empire at the time.

the coinage system. At his new capital, Byzantium (Constantinople), he issued a gold coin, the solidus. It lasted for 700 years and the later coinages of England, France, Spain, Italy, Denmark, and Sweden were derived from it. This coin (also known as the besant, bezant, and byzant) weighed 72 to the pound.

Collecting Roman Coins

Because Roman coins are so old, it is easy to assume that they are rare and expensive. This is not necessarily true. The Roman state existed for hundreds of years, with very extensive coinage in the days of the Empire. Because there were so many Emperors, there are numerous types of coins—thousands of them—issued by mints in various parts of the Empire. During unsettled times, people often hoarded coins. Seldom does a day pass without some of these buried coins being dug up in Europe, Africa, and Asia. Thus we have a steady, substantial addition to our stock of Roman coins.

The bronze coins are particularly plentiful and therefore reasonably priced. This is all to the good as far as the collector is concerned—these bronzes were large and therefore gave the designer scope for large, detailed images. Those of the first century A.D. were generally the size of a silver dollar; later on, they became somewhat smaller. You can obtain these coins, and many others like them, at prices ranging from $1 to $5 for specimens in excellent condition.

The denarii (silver) are also available at reasonable prices; but the denarius, about the size of our dime, left much less room for interesting detail. If you want some Roman coins just for the thrill of having them, you can buy them for prices well under a dollar; though of course their condition will leave something to be desired. As for the gold coins, they are comparatively rare and expensive.

Coin Portraits

In the coin portraits of the Empire, the Romans reached the heights of artistic excellence, second only to their remarkable statuary heads. Assigning their finest craftsmen to the Emperor's portrait, they often produced coins on which the portrait is first rate, while the lettering is jagged and the reverses merely passable.

Interesting is the fact that the coins of the early Empire are the best; as conditions became more unsettled—then chaotic—the portrait work deteriorated, finally becoming mediocre. So faithful are the early portraits that many of them are unflattering. The Nero and Vespasian coins are particularly striking in this respect. When we consider what tyrants some of these Emperors were, this refusal on the part of the mint officials to curry favor by flattering strikes us as amazing.

Plate 105. Empire, bronze sesterce: *obverse* (117-138 A.D.). Hadrian struck several coin portraits of his beautiful wife Sabina, paying tribute to her character by depicting Pietas on the *reverse* (see Plate 97).

Plate 106. Empire, bronze as (71 A.D.). *Obverse:* head of Vespasian. *Reverse:* Aequitas (personification of Imperial justice) holding scales signifying equal treatment for all.

Sometimes the coins of the Emperors lead us into fascinating if sinister byways of history. Thus there are coins of one Emperor, Maximinus (235-238), issued with the portrait of his predecessor, Alexander Severus, after he had him murdered.

Scholars conjecture that these coins were made before the mintmasters knew what the new Emperor looked like. In one case, that of Marius (268), we have coins of an Emperor who is said to have reigned no more than three days! (He was murdered.) The explanation of the mystery is probably that Marius planned his coup long in advance—time enough to have his coins made.

Reverses on Imperial Coinage

The purpose of featuring the portrait of the current Emperor on the obverse of a coin was to inspire personal loyalty to the *Emperor*. As for the images on the reverse, they served the purpose of inspiring loyalty to the *Empire*.

There was at all times a strong commemorative trend—to honor famous men and notable anniversaries, to celebrate victories and great feats of war, to express pride of ownership in the case of some provinces. Then, too, the coins of the Empire had great propaganda value. The Roman Empire took in many diverse peoples—Italians, Gauls, Spaniards, Britons, Germans, Egyptians, Jews, Greeks, Syrians, and others. There was an equally bewildering variety of races in the city of Rome itself. But the coinage, uniform through the length and breadth of the Roman Empire, proclaimed the unity and universality of Roman law.

Some coins of Augustus, as we have mentioned, commemorated his great victory over Antony at Actium. Other coins call attention to his recovery of the standards lost by the legions of Crassus to the Parthians (see page 57).

Nero's coins (54-68) celebrate his escape from conspiracy—real or imaginary—while other coins, with an image of Victory, express his determination to have his way despite fierce opposition.

Vespasian (69-79), the "common-sense" Emperor, gave us Peace, Plenty, and Equity on his coins, as well as a famous reverse celebrating the conquest of Judea. His son Domitian (81-96), a gloomy tyrant, issued a reverse featuring Moneta, the goddess of money and minting. We see her with scales and the horn of plenty—by way of telling the people of Rome that they are living in a time of great prosperity.

Trajan (98-117), outstanding builder and great general, has a coin showing a Dacian (Rumanian) captive—an allusion to Trajan's conquest of Dacia. The great food markets of Nero and Trajan appear on the reverses of their coins—an obvious propaganda device hinting at plentiful food supplies.

Hadrian (117-138), Trajan's able successor, features *salus publica* ("the well-being of the state"). On another coin he displays a corn-measure, a hint to the populace that he means to keep them well fed. He also has coins honoring Spain, Mauretania (north Africa), and Dacia—probably in connection with his visits to those countries.

Antoninus Pius (138-161), perhaps the most admirable of the Emperors, selects for his reverses such figures as *Clementia* ("leniency"); *Felicitas* ("happiness"); *Indulgentia* ("mercy"); and *Liberalitas* ("liberality"). With devices like these, he keynotes for us the spirit of his reign.

Many of these coins, which take us almost to the end of the second century A.D., have the letters "S C"—standing for *Senatus Consulto* ("by authority of the Senate"). In this way the Emperor politely pays his respects to the Senate.

The Decline of the Empire

One of the main reasons why the Empire debased coins more and more was the tremendous amount spent by the Romans on luxuries from the East. So great was the desire for the gems, spices, and fabrics of India that even in the time of Augustus (27 B.C.–14 A.D.) 120 ships sailed from Rome every year for these Eastern luxuries. Economists have computed that in Imperial Rome the purchase (per capita) of such luxuries was greater than in Napoleonic Europe! Consider that a large proportion of the Roman population were slaves and poor people, and you get some

Plate 107. **Empire. Hadrian, bronze sesterce: *reverse* of Plate 96 (134-138 A.D.). The Emperor raises Africa (personified) to prosperity—represented by the three ears of corn.**

idea of the sharp demand for luxuries among the classes that could afford them.

The more unfavorable Rome's balance of trade became, the more its currency depreciated, and the more urgently it was in need of bullion. Historians tell us that one of the main reasons for Trajan's conquests in Dacia (Rumania) was to tap its rich reserve of minerals.

Mining conditions were so bad that they were practically a form of torture. Miners were recruited from slaves or criminals. Precisely because mining was considered as punishment, mining technique remained on a very low level for centuries.

The third century A.D. saw a steady worsening of conditions in the Empire. Some of the Emperors were shockingly incompetent; the able ones found it was too late to make really lasting improvements. Between 193 and 284 there were 23 Emperors; no less than 20 died violent deaths.

Caracalla (211-217) was notorious for his cruelty and mass killings. Extravagant beyond belief, he is said to have spent his whole inheritance in one day. After he was assassinated at the age of 30, it was found that he had stored away enough poison to kill a great many people.

His one great constructive achievement was to declare all the males of the provinces Roman citizens. One of the results of this policy was to subject them to inheritance taxes, which could be levied only on Roman citizens.

Elagabalus (or Heliogabalus), probably the most depraved monster of all the Emperors, assumed the throne in 218 at the age of 14, and was assassinated at the age of 18. Some of his banquets cost $400,000 apiece, none less than $12,500 or so. Gibbon says that his "inexpressible infamy surpasses that of any other age or country."

Among the later Emperors, the good

Plate 108. Empire, silver antoninianus. *Obverse:* Caracalla. *Reverse:* Sun-god. (215 A.D.). The first coin of this new denomination. Its silver content soon decreased.

ones as well as the bad ones, we notice that the old Roman stock is no longer prominent. Septimius Severus (193-211), an African, said toward the close of his reign: "I have been everything, and it is nothing." Alexander Severus (222-235), like his predecessor Elagabalus, was a Syrian. Philip (244-249) was an Arab, Theodosius (379-395) a Spaniard.

The vigorous Emperors toward the end of the third and the beginning of the fourth centuries, Aurelian (270-275), Probus (276-282), Diocletian, and Constantine, were all of Balkan origin. They were all of humble birth, Diocletian being the son of a freedman (former slave).

These men did what they could to check the steady depreciation of currency and rise of prices. Diocletian went so far as to issue a famous decree freezing prices and wages in 301. It didn't work. There was an epidemic of tax evasion, faked figures, hiding of assets.

In those troubled times rich men began to transform their elegant villas into forti-

Plate 109. Empire, bronze dupondius: *obverse* (220-222 A.D.). Elagabalus, a native of Syria, became Emperor when his mother bribed Roman troops to depose Emperor Macrinus.

fied castles guarded by their peasants, who gave them free labor and military service in return for the use of the land. Diocletian and Constantine went a step further —they bound the peasant to the soil. If the estate was sold, he was sold with it. This arrangement gradually hardened into the feudal system of the Dark Ages. Large-scale trade came almost to a standstill.

But high prices were really inevitable, for the Empire was constantly in a state of war.

Before the end of the third century, the barbarians were attacking simultaneously in different parts of the Empire. Thus they forced the Emperors to fight a war on two or more fronts, as part of the impossible job of defending 10,000 miles of border.

Diocletian saw that the Empire could be held together only by some radical changes. He therefore divided the State into two regions in 286, the Western Empire and the Eastern Empire. In the West, he shifted the capital from Rome to Milan. From this city, north of Rome, it was easier to campaign against the German tribesmen in Gaul and Germany.

Constantine, Diocletian's successor, went a step further by actually moving the eastern capital to Byzantium. Situated right on the Bosporus, it was surrounded by water on three sides, and therefore fairly safe from attack. He began building the new capital in 324, renaming it Nova Roma ("New Rome") and making it the most beautiful city in the world. The city later was called Constantinople and is now known as Istanbul.

Constantine—he figures in the history books as Constantine the Great—reigned from 305 to 337. Actually he was full Emperor only from 323 on. One of the outstanding statesmen and generals in all Roman history, Constantine is famous above all for his edict ending the persecu-

Plate 110. Empire, bronze (348 A.D.). *Obverse:* head of Constantius II. *Reverse:* Christian standard on galley steered by Victory. Issued to commemorate Rome's eleven-hundredth year (see Plate 55).

tion of Christians in 312. Legend has it that before one of his most important battles he saw a flaming cross in the sky, with the inscription, "By this sign thou shalt conquer." In gratitude for his victory, he not only repealed the cruel decrees against the Christians, but favored the once persecuted sect until it became Rome's religion.

We talk of the fall of the Roman Empire as if it were something extremely violent. Actually it was like the gentle death of a very, very old man. In fact, when the "fall" took place in 476, it was completely unnoticed by contemporary chroniclers. Odoacer, a Gothic chieftain, took over the rule of Rome in 476 without violence, and was accepted by Rome's apathetic and greatly reduced population as a matter of course. Sometimes Odoacer's successors described themselves as reigning under the Eastern Empire; but whether they said so or not, they were their own masters.

Plate 111. Empire, bronze (350-353 A.D.). *Obverse:* head of Magnentius: *Reverse:* Chrismon. This is an early Christian symbol intertwining the letters X and P (CH and R in Greek, the beginning letters of Christ's name).

The Byzantine Empire

After the fall of the Western Empire in 476, the Eastern Empire continued to exist for almost another thousand years. We call it the Byzantine Empire, because its capital was Byzantium.

Almost from the start, the Byzantine Empire was more Oriental than Western, more Greek than Roman. Throughout its long history it was an absolute despotism, with corrupt and intriguing courtiers and a large and cumbersome bureaucracy. The people were passionately interested in chariot races, which served as an outlet for political feeling. Each charioteer belonged to a faction similar to one of our political parties.

Justinian, Byzantine Emperor (527-565), was famous for two widely different reasons: he began the building of the beautiful church of St. Sophia, which later was turned by the Turks into an equally handsome mosque; and he had the most thorough compilation made of Roman law, which has been known since his time as the Justinian Code.

The Empire had gold, silver, and copper coinage. The most famous Byzantine coin was the (gold) solidus. Since the coin was used to pay army wages, our word "soldier" was derived from the coin's name.

Plate 113. Bronze. These bits of metal, attributed to the fifth and sixth centuries A.D., give us a vivid idea of the decline of coins and the arts after the fall of the western Roman Empire.

Relations between the Byzantine Empire and the countries of western Europe were always strained. In 1054 there occurred the Great Schism—the final separation of the Roman Catholic Church of the West and the Greek Orthodox Church of the East. When the Ottoman Turks laid siege to Constantinople in 1453, the West looked on without lending a helping hand. The city fell to the Turks, and the last part of the Roman Empire came to an end.

With all its drawbacks, the Byzantine Empire performed two great services. It fought the Arabs and the Turks, giving all of Europe a breathing spell against invasion. Perhaps equally important, Byzantine scholars preserved the texts of the Greek classics. If it had not been for them, these masterpieces would have been lost forever, because they were not preserved by western Europe during the centuries after the fall of Rome.

Plate 114. Byzantine Empire, gold solidus (527-565). *Obverse:* head of Emperor Justinian. *Reverse:* Victory holding long cross. As in most Byzantine art, there is an unnatural air of stiffness about these figures.

Plate 115. Byzantine Empire, gold solidus: *reverse (869-879)*. Christ seated on throne; the right hand is raised in benediction, the left holds a book of the Gospels. The full-face pose, rare in most coinage, is characteristic of Byzantine coins. The religious subject is also typical of coins of this era.

The Holy Land

The tiny Holy Land has had a long history unequaled for turbulence. Stationed at the crossroads of ancient history—between Egypt and Asia, between the Mediterranean and the Arab countries—it has been conquered and plundered again and again.

The Assyrians, the Babylonians (or Chaldeans) under Nebuchadnezzar, the Persians under Cyrus the Great, the Greeks under Alexander the Great, the Romans under Pompey, all made history here. After the fall of Rome in the fifth and sixth centuries, the land fell into the hands of the Arabs, then the Turks, then the Crusaders, then it was reconquered by the Turks, who finally lost it in 1917. The League of Nations established a British mandate over Palestine, which became an independent country under the ancient name of Israel in 1948.

But there is something even more remarkable about this invasion-torn country. It gave rise to two great world religions (Christianity and Judaism) and, of course, to the Bible.

The Old Testament mentions shekels and talents, which were metal bar weights at that time, and later became coin denominations.

During the middle of the second century B.C., a number of empires were locked in mortal combat. At this time the Jews managed to free themselves by a heroic revolt under Judas Maccabaeus. They were able to hold on to their freedom until 63 B.C., when Pompey, at the head of a Roman army, took Jerusalem and extorted a fine of 10,000 talents (about $60,000,000).

It is said that when Pompey entered the Temple in Jerusalem, he was so filled with awe that he could not bring himself to loot it. The Temple was one of the most admired structures of ancient times. Its famous features included bronze doors, 75 feet high and 24 feet wide, at the entrance to the inner temple. Several years later, another Roman general, Crassus,* passed through Jerusalem, and he stripped the Temple of all its treasures.

The Romans gave the country the name of Judea, and installed a "client king" who was a caretaker for Rome. Under Roman rule the country always seethed with unrest; there were constant revolts, which the Romans put down with systematic brutality. In 6 A.D. Augustus made Judea a Roman province. Conditions became even worse; the Roman governors, aside from many other bad qualities, never lost a chance for graft. Because of the Jews' commandment against graven images, they refused to allow any statue of the Emperor

* See page 43.

Plate 116. **First Revolt, silver shekel (67-70 A.D.). *Obverse:* golden cup which held manna. *Reverse:* branch with three pomegranates.**

in the Temple. The hateful sight of the eagles on the Roman Legionary banners was enough to infuriate the hotheads.

The first great revolt broke out in 67 A.D. The occasion for it was a highhanded action by Florus, the Roman governor, who seized 17 talents of the Temple treasure. To retaliate, some youngsters mocked him by going about with baskets and begging alms for him. The Romans hit back by killing several thousand people, beginning a gory fight with no quarter given on either side.

It took the Romans several years to crush the rebels; and they needed another few years for "mopping up" even after they celebrated their triumph in Rome. Jerusalem fell to the Romans only after a long and bitter siege, with the Romans making steady progress with their battering rams and ballistas—huge slingshots that hurled stones weighing more than 100 pounds. Close to a million Jews perished during the siege and the sack of the city.

It is said that Titus, the Roman commander, was anxious to spare the Temple.

Plate 117. **Maccabean Revolt, bronze shekel (about 143-137 B.C.). *Obverse:* two *lulavs* (bundles of twigs). *Reverse:* *esrog* (citron). The *lulav* and *esrog* are associated with the Feast of Tabernacles.**

Plate 118. **Second Revolt, silver shekel (132-135 A.D.). *Obverse:* temple with the Ark of the Covenant and two scrolls of the law. The inscription *(Shimon)* is presumably a reference to the first name of Bar Kochba, heroic leader of the Revolt. *Reverse:* *lulav* and *esrog*.**

During the last desperate fight after the Romans broke through, they set the Temple ablaze, and it was burned to the ground. But before that, Titus was able to seize some of the most desirable treasures, such as the great golden seven-branched candlestick on the altar before the blue, purple, and scarlet veil of the Holy of Holies.

The Romans crucified so many captives that there was a shortage of crosses. Thousands more were sold into slavery, or shipped to the arenas and mines, or reserved for Titus' triumphal return to Rome. There Titus had a beautiful arch built to celebrate his victory. About 400 years later, when the Vandals sacked Rome, they carried off the magnificent candlestick and most of the other Temple loot. But the arch is still in existence, as is the Wailing Wall in Jerusalem, the only standing remnant of the Temple.

In 131 the Emperor Hadrian took severe

Plate 119. **Israel, aluminum 1 prutah (1949). *Obverse:* anchor (replica of a coin of the Maccabean Revolt). *Reverse:* value in wreath.**

Plate 120. **Israel, bronze 10 prutahs (1949). *Obverse:* amphora (replica of a coin of the Second Revolt). *Reverse:* value in wreath.**

measures against the remaining Jews of Judea. There was another gallant, futile revolt, led by Bar Kochba. The uprising was crushed mercilessly by 135, but, as it turned out, the Romans did not have the last word.

All three revolts—the Maccabean, and the two later ones against the Romans—resulted in coin issues which have fascinated scholars for centuries. In 1949, after Israel had established its independence, the new government brought out a set of coins using the designs which had appeared almost 2,000 years earlier. The modern coins are therefore of the greatest historical interest since the originals are rare.

On all the coins, the word "Israel" is inscribed in Hebrew on top, in Arabic below.

Coinage in the New Testament

Scholars have devoted a great deal of study to the interesting references to coins in the New Testament. The use of such terms as "penny" and "farthing" is confusing, as there were of course no such coins in Judea. If we realize that these English names for the coins were inserted

Plate 121 (left). **Israel, silver 250 prutahs: *obverse* (1949). Three ears of wheat (replica of a coin of the First Revolt).**

Plate 122 (right). **Israel, silver 500 prutahs: *obverse* (1949). Branch with three pomegranates (replica of a coin of the First Revolt).**

Plate 123. **Roman Empire. Vespasian, silver denarius: *reverse* (about 72 A.D.). Captured arms and a mourning Jewess. Another "Judaea Capta" coin (see Plate 94).**

by the translators who prepared the King James Version of the Bible at the beginning of the seventeenth century, we are free to speculate about some of the coins mentioned. For example, the scholars ask, what coin did Joseph use when he went with Mary to Bethlehem to pay the Roman head tax? The most likely coin was the silver denarius of Augustus, which was the favorite coin for paying the tax.

In one of Christ's parables there is this famous passage: "What woman having ten pieces of silver, if she lose one piece, doth not light a candle, and sweep the house, and seek diligently till she find it?"

The silver coin referred to is thought to be a denarius of Tiberius, the Roman Emperor who reigned from 14 to 37 A.D. The denarius was probably the "tribute penny" shown to Jesus which led him to reply, "Render unto Caesar the things that are Caesar's and unto God the things that are God's." The obverse of this denarius portrays Tiberius, the reverse his mother Livia. And this coin is apparently also the same one mentioned in the parable of the miracle of feeding 5,000 people, and the parable of the Good Samaritan.

Plate 124. **Roman Empire, silver denarius (14-37 A.D.). *Obverse:* head of Tiberius. *Reverse:* his mother Livia, seated, holding scepter and flower.**

Plate 125. **Bronze coin attributed to Pontius Pilate (about 30 A.D.); the so-called "widow's mite." *Obverse:* wine ladle. *Reverse:* three ears of grain.**

Another New Testament coin that has fascinated coin students is the "widow's mite." Here is the passage that mentions the coin: "And he looked up, and saw the rich men casting their gifts into the treasury. And he saw also a certain poor widow casting in thither two mites. And he said, Of a truth I say unto you, that this poor widow hath cast in more than they all: For all these have of their abundance cast in unto the offerings of God: but she of her penury hath cast in all the living that she had."

Mites were small copper coins (leptons) of trifling value. One school of Biblical research holds that the coin mentioned here was struck by Pontius Pilate. The obverse of this coin shows a *simpulum,* a ladle used at Roman sacrifices to pour wine into a cup.

The thirty pieces of silver paid to Judas for betraying Christ are thought to have been in the form of the large four-drachm piece of the Phoenician city of Tyre, known as the Tetradrachm of Tyre. The obverse of the coin shows a head of the Phoenician god Melkarth in the Hellenized (Greek) form of Herakles, or Hercules. While this theory necessarily involves guesswork, coin experts believe that this coin was circulated very widely in Judea during the first century A.D.

Plate 126. **Tyre, silver tetradrachm (about 125 B.C.-100 A.D.). *Obverse:* head of Melkarth. *Reverse:* eagle. Most scholars favor this coin as the one used to pay Judas his "thirty pieces of silver."**

Plate 127. **Antioch, silver tetradrachm (about 30 A.D.). *Obverse:* head of Augustus. *Reverse:* female figure representing the city of Antioch. This coin is an alternative choice of the scholars for the Judas coin.**

Medieval Times

The collapse of Roman rule in Western Europe led to a free-for-all among the Germanic tribes. Each tribe wanted to be free of any higher control and was just as eager to rule over other groups. Disputes were settled not by appeal to law but by the use of force.

Disorder lasted about five centuries—from about 500 to 1000. Wars, famines and plagues ruined or partly emptied the cities. City dwellers returned to the countryside; trade dwindled; robbers menaced the roads. Some people sought safety in monasteries, others bound themselves as serfs to powerful feudal lords in return for protection.

Many monarchs were Kings in name only. The laws differed from one district of a kingdom to another. The King was the ruler only as far as his army's power extended, and sometimes that was not very far at all. Men were loyal to a local count or duke or bishop; loyalty to a far-off King was a notion not yet developed. Patriotism, as we know it today, hardly existed.

As trade increased over the centuries, bonds grew between one European region and another. Merchants needed uniform laws extending over a large area. So they supported the idea of kingdom, which made possible one set of rules in place of many. Gradually the countries that we know came into existence—and with them came coinage issued for a whole country and not merely for this or that locality.

When times were chaotic and there was little trade, there was correspondingly little coinage. The solidus (or bezant) of the Byzantine Empire enjoyed great prestige. As for Western European coinage, it was crudely designed, and crudely struck.

Not until the thirteenth century do we find artistically admirable coins—the *Gros Tournois* in France, the florin of Florence, and the augustales of Frederick II, the most fascinating of all the Holy Roman Emperors. Increased trade made it desirable to have attractive coins and a vast improvement in metal-working techniques made it possible to have them.

The German cities, which were noted for the excellence of their armor, and the Italian cities, which turned out the finest swords, also became expert in coin designing and production. Later on, the Renaissance exerted a strong artistic effect on coinage. You will find in this book many coins from the fifteenth, sixteenth, and seventeenth centuries that are truly works of art.

The coins are grouped geographically under the names of the current governments and are generally in chronological order under these headings.

France

France, one of the great powers for many centuries, has strongly influenced the rest of the world in art, in music, in literature, in philosophy, in fashion, and in other ways. It is a nation which has had a stormy history. The French themselves often joke about their many political parties and frequent cabinet changes. This tradition of instability goes far back in France's history and sometimes seems at odds with the extremely centralized governmental system which France has had since 1789.

The historical task of welding France together into a single country has been a very slow and laborious one. Back in the fourth and fifth centuries A.D., when the Roman Empire was tottering and decaying, Gaul remained its most flourishing and civilized province. The Franks were the most gifted of the Germanic tribes that were infiltrating into Gaul. Partly by warlike means, partly by clever statesmanship, they eventually took over much of the territory that was to become modern France. The centuries of the Dark Ages that followed were times of general brutality, looting, and treachery.

Yet, when the Moors threatened to overrun Western Europe, the Franks drove them back in 732 near Tours in what scholars now consider one of the greatest decisive battles of all history. The Frankish chieftain who succeeded in rallying his divided people and who led them to this victory was Charles Martel ("Charles the Hammer"), whose son Pepin and grandson Charlemagne were to go on by conquest and diplomacy (including the help of the Popes) to establish a new Empire.

Charlemagne

Reigning from 768 to 814, Charlemagne was the greatest ruler of the Middle Ages. To the Germans, who claim him as one of their own, he is Karl der Grosse; to the French he is their own Charlemagne (from Carolus Magnus, "Charles the Great"). His achievements and his prestige were enormous (and later generations magnified them in legend to even greater heights).

This rough German tribesman led an incredibly strenuous life—he fought over fifty campaigns. He conquered Saxony and northern Italy, he subdued the barbarians who invaded the Danube valley, he fought the Moors in Spain.

Unlike many Kings of the Middle Ages, Charlemagne possessed genuine power and knew how to use it for good ends. He was deeply concerned with the welfare of the poor, and made sincere efforts to wipe out abuses. He organized a remarkable system of supervising his far-flung empire, leaving conquered peoples their own laws and governing with the help of an annual council.

Charlemagne's rule was the wisest and most capable that Europe enjoyed for centuries, but he worked under handicaps and his overseas trade was stifled. The Norsemen made marauding raids on the northern coast of France, and the Arabs controlled the Mediterranean on the south.

Under such handicaps, Charlemagne found it difficult to maintain a reliable coinage system. France had little gold, and the solidus, introduced by Constantine the Great (p. 53), disappeared because of the lack of commerce. The denier (from denarius)—valued at one-twelfth of the solidus—was the most prevalent coin in Charlemagne's empire, and he had 240 deniers struck from one pound of fine silver.

Illiterate most of his life, Charlemagne made a gallant attempt in his old age to learn to write. He spoke a Teutonic dialect, but eventually learned Latin and could understand spoken Greek. His capital was not at Paris, but at Aachen (Aix-la-Chapelle), a German town. (His palace there lasted into modern times, but was destroyed in an air raid during World War II.)

Charlemagne was keenly interested in raising the educational level of his people. He founded a great many cathedral and monastery schools and established the first free schools; later some of them developed into famous universities. Many classical manuscripts were preserved by his efforts. He converted many heathen to Christianity, though his methods sometimes reflected the times he lived in. For example, he had 4,500 Saxons beheaded in one day because they refused to adopt Christianity.

Plate 128. **Charlemagne, silver denier (768-814). These bracteates (see page 101) were struck for use in Italy.**

Charlemagne's most statesmanlike achievement was to have himself crowned Roman Emperor by the Pope on Christmas Day, 800. His motives were not wholly unselfish. Nevertheless, he hoped in this way to unite the different parts of his empire and bring peace and order to western and central Europe.

Unfortunately, Charlemagne's successors were not men of his caliber; they quarreled among themselves and eventually divided up his empire. In time, the modern states of France, Germany, Austria, Italy, Switzerland, Belgium, and Holland arose from Charlemagne's Roman Empire.

France's existence as a separate kingdom is usually reckoned from 843, when the empire was again divided at the Treaty of Verdun. The power of the French kings rapidly declined as authority was increasingly taken over by feudal lords, and the Kings had so hard a time securing power that they were reluctant to share it

Plate 129. **Aachen, silver taler (1568). *Obverse:* Charlemagne enthroned. *Reverse:* Crowned double eagle. This handsome coin, struck more than 700 years after Charlemagne's death, shows how much the art of coinage had advanced since his day.**

with anyone. These were centuries of constant warfare and struggle.

One important consequence was that France never developed a sound system of taxation—one of the prime causes of the French Revolution.

"The Sun-King"

Louis XIV (1643-1715) was the first French King who could truly consider himself an absolute monarch. He raised the Kingship to new heights and made France Europe's leading power. The nobles no longer presented any danger to the Crown. The King acted as his own Prime Minister, and did not dream of convening the States-General. Since he distrusted the aristocracy, he chose all his ministers from the middle class.

The "Sun-King" regarded France as his private property. Work never wearied him. He gave all his attention to his job, which he described as "grand, noble, delicious." Everything Louis XIV did was in the grand manner—from politely lifting his hat to a chambermaid to paying Charles II a huge annual bribe to maintain British neutrality.

The period of Louis XIV's reign is remembered as *Le Grand Siècle*—"the great century." France was the leading country on the Continent and was just beginning to exploit its huge holdings in the New World. Germany and Italy were chopped up into small parts; Spain and Austria had started a long tailspin of decline; Russia had not emerged as a European power.

Plate 130. Louis IX, silver gros tournois (1226-1270). *Obverse:* cross in circle. One of the best-made coins of its time.

The population of France, with over 20,000,000 people, exceeded the combined population of England, Germany, and Italy. No other country could boast of such writers, artists, and composers. Paris was already regarded as the most enchanting city in Europe.

The Sun-King spent most of his life at his palace at Versailles, a few miles from Paris. This vast residence, constructed in 1685 by 30,000 workmen, is famous for its luxurious decorations, rich tapestries, costly marbles, crystal lamps and chandeliers, large mirrors, and delicate furniture inlaid with mother-of-pearl. However, the heating system was inadequate, and there were no plumbing facilities!

Plate 131. Silver louis (1643). *Obverse:* Louis XIII. This is the King of France who appears in Dumas' *The Three Musketeers.*

Plate 132. Silver ecu (1653). *Obverse:* Louis XIV as a child of ten. *Reverse:* crowned shield featuring the lilies of France. Louis XIV reigned for 67 years.

Plate 133. Silver one-twelfth ecu (1675). *Obverse:* Louis XIV. *Reverse:* Crowned cross with lilies.

The court of Versailles had almost 5,000 servants! The cost of the fabulous entertainments—fireworks, parades, fancy dress balls, theatrical spectacles, boating parties, and the like—ran into many millions.

The extravagance of Versailles, costly as it was, was a trifle compared to the losses in men and money that France suffered from 40 years of foreign wars. Louis XIV had a mania for enlarging the territory of France, and was even more obsessed with the glory and glamour of military campaigns.

The lack of a sound system of taxation was aggravated by the fact that lands of the Church and nobles paid only trifling taxes. The burden fell on the rest of the population, and it was made even heavier by the royal custom of borrowing and letting wealthy bankers collect the taxes in repayment. The bankers collected a fat commission—at the expense of the taxpayers, of course.

Another way Louis XIV raised revenue was by selling government jobs—mostly superfluous ones. Louis XIV's minister Colbert calculated that 40,000 of the 45,000 posts in the Justice and Finance departments served no purpose.

In view of these unsound practices, it is not surprising that at the death of the Sun-King in 1715 the French Crown was perilously near bankruptcy.

Louis XV (1715-1774), the great-grandson of Louis XIV, kept aloof from the problem. He was lazy, cynical, and pleasure-loving, and even became involved in a scandalous attempt to corner the market in grain while bread riots were raging.

His grandson, Louis XVI (1774-1792) meant well, but unfortunately he was sluggish and stupid. He loved hunting and had a passion for playing with locks; problems of statesmanship were beyond his grasp. His glamorous Austrian-born queen, Marie Antoinette, was frivolous, erratic, and wholly without understanding of the people.

National bankruptcy was not the only danger that confronted the monarchy. Outmoded privileges and abuses were the targets for attacks by brilliant writers. These writers created a mood of contempt for the high-born, and at the same time they dazzled Frenchmen with prospects of a brave new world guaranteeing Liberty, Equality and Fraternity. Only a short time before, the American Revolution had set a pattern for throwing off the yoke of a monarchy that was taxing unfairly. France, in its historic opposition to England, had aided the American colonists, and while French liberals applauded this, the aid increased the government debt.

Plate 134. Silver ecu (1767). *Obverse:* Louis XV. It was during the reign of this King that France lost two empires (one in Canada, one in India) to the British.

Revolution

In 1788 France was bankrupt. Louis XVI had taken the unprecedented step of calling an Assembly of Notables. It was limited to 144 members of the nobility, who had power to discuss—nothing more.

One year later, the States-General was convened for the first time since 1614. After two months of wrangling by the upper classes, the representatives of the Third Estate (the middle class) left the meeting hall and swore the famous Tennis Court Oath: "Never will we separate until a Constitution for this Kingdom shall be established." Notice that they were talking about a "kingdom," not a republic.

Paris was alive with alarming rumors and seething with unrest. On July 14, 1789, a large crowd gathered, marched on the famous old Paris fortress and prison known as the Bastille, overpowered the guards, released the prisoners, and destroyed the building. (July 14, called "Bastille Day," is now France's Independence Day.)

When Louis XVI heard the news, he remarked dully, "This is a great revolt."

"No, Sire," was the pitying reply, "it is a great revolution!"

Nobles began to flee the country, taking with them whatever money and valuables they could. Now the discontent of centuries gathered into a mighty flood, and events moved with furious rapidity. Less than a month after the fall of the Bastille, the nobles surrendered their right not to be taxed, relinquished their titles of nobility and the collection of feudal rents from their peasants. The National Assembly drew up a constitution; it was signed by the King, and France changed from an absolute to a constitutional monarchy. Every ruler in Europe watched French events fearfully and trembled for his own throne.

Plate 135. Brass 12 deniers (1791). *Obverse:* Louis XVI. *Reverse:* fasces in wreath surmounted by Liberty Cap. These coins were cast from bell metal.

Reign of Terror

By 1791 thousands of aristocrats had fled to Prussia and Austria, where they tried to stir up war against the new French government and later succeeded. The mood of Paris was meanwhile becoming more ugly every day. The people began to wear red liberty caps—a custom taken from the caps worn by freed slaves in ancient Phrygia in Asia Minor. (The Romans had taken this custom over from the Greeks, and in turn American coinage has frequently featured the liberty cap.) The French moderates were losing their grip on the situation. Terrified, the King and Queen decided to flee in the dead of night with their children. The next morning, when their coach was quite near the border, an innkeeper caught a glimpse of the King. He had never seen Louis XVI, but he recognized him from a coin! The royal family was stopped and brought back to Paris.

When Prussia and Austria declared war and invaded France, the King and Queen were arrested and a fearsome reign of terror resulted in the guillotining of over a thousand aristocrats in a few days. It was in these wild times that the stirring *Marseillaise* was composed and became popular throughout France. France became a republic, and began a new calendar dating from September 22, 1792 (the first day of Year One). This step foreshadowed the execution of Louis XVI, which followed

Plate 136. **Copper 2 sols (1794).** ***Obverse:*** **tablet reading: "All men are equal before the law."** ***Reverse:*** **Liberty Cap, wreath, and scales to denote justice.**

ASSIGNAT

de mille francs.

créé le 18 Nivôse l'an 3me de la République.

Hypothéqué sur les domaines nationaux.

Numéro 273.

Série 1106

Plate 137. **Assignat for 1,000 francs (1795). Worth about 8 francs at the height of the inflation.**

in January, 1793. (Marie Antoinette was executed in the following October.)

Ten days after the King was brought to the guillotine, France declared war on the monarchies of Great Britain, Holland, and Spain; she was still at war with Prussia and Austria.

While the reign of terror was going on, French armies were fighting foreign enemies. The new republic had trouble finding capable officers, for military leadership had been one of the prerogatives of the aristocrats. One serious problem had to be taken care of at once: Toulon, the great naval base and arsenal on the Mediterranean, had fallen into the hands of the English. The city had to be retaken—but who could do it? The assignment was given to an obscure 24-year-old captain named Bonaparte, who was said to be a genius in handling artillery. He succeeded brilliantly, and was promoted to the rank of brigadier-general.

Inflation

The French Revolution caused the most disastrous inflation known up to that time. Gold coins immediately went into hiding. The émigrés took large sums as they escaped from France. Tax collections dwindled.

In August, 1789, the government tried to raise a loan of 30,000,000 livres. Only 2,500,000 livres were subscribed. Other expedients, like overstamping existing coins with ten times their value, also failed. And so, inevitably, the government turned to paper money.

In November, 1789, the States-General confiscated all Church property in France. A few months later, the first issue of assignats appeared in the amount of 400,000,000 livres. The assignats were paper money, bearing interest and secured with confiscated property. From the financial point of view, the security was ample. But people had no faith in their government, and therefore no faith in the assignats.

Further issues of assignats kept coming (now non-interest-bearing) and inflation accompanied them. In 1792 war with Austria and Prussia helped prices shoot up.

By April, 1795, the total issue was 11,500,000,000 livres. The following month, when the assignats had plunged to 10 per cent of their face value, the government printing workers went on strike. They went back to work on being promised a loaf of bread daily instead of money.

Between May and November, 1795, the assignats went down in value to 8/10 of 1 per cent. The face value issued was now 20,000,000,000 livres — not to mention hordes of counterfeit notes!

Plate 138. **Silver 5 francs (1803).** ***Obverse:*** **Hercules group, symbolizing strength and union.**

In February, 1796, the Directory (the new five-man governing board) formally ended the issuing of assignats and had the plates destroyed. The government introduced a new coinage based on the franc.

Where did the metal come from? Some coins came out of hiding. Napoleon Bonaparte, assigned by the Directory to invade Italy, "requisitioned" every piece of gold and silver he could lay his hands on. In three months he extorted no less than 53,000,000 francs worth of coins in Italy; somewhat later, he even pillaged the magnificent Vatican collection of coins and medals, as well as many priceless art treasures.

Man of Destiny

Napoleon Bonaparte, the most famous man in French history, came of Italian stock and hailed from the Mediterranean island of Corsica. He was sent to a military academy in France at the age of 10; the other boys made fun of him because of his poverty and Italian accent. His small stature earned him the nickname "the little Corporal." Commissioned a lieutenant and then a captain in the closing days of the French monarchy, he was lonely but ambitious, and dreamed of having grand opportunities to make a name for himself.

His promotion to brigadier-general after the capture of Toulon from the British in 1794, seemed to be a dead end. Kept off active duty and forgotten during the Terror, he grew poorer and shabbier until he had to pawn his watch and forego his daily game of chess at a café because the coffee would have been an extravagance.

Napoleon was seriously thinking of signing up for military service with Turkey, when at last, in October, 1795, he got his chance: he was assigned command of troops guarding the Convention in Paris. As an unruly mob advanced, the contemptuous young general scattered it with a "whiff of grapeshot"—a whiff which killed 100 insurgents.

By way of reward, the Directory gave him the command of the army to invade Italy, then held by Austrian forces. It was a ragged, starving army, but Napoleon quickly transformed it into a first-class fighting unit. His methods were to free the army from dependence on the penny-pinching Directory by having them feed and supply themselves from the land; his magic influence on his men's morale led them to incredible feats. When his army seemed about to run away at the battle of Lodi, he rushed into the thick of the fight and rallied his men to win a brilliant victory. In three short months, Napoleon defeated numerically superior forces in a series of lightning-quick maneuvers.

Napoleon's head was turned by rapid victories in Italy, the adoration of his soldiers and the wild cheers that met him everywhere in France. Next he tried to strike at the British Empire by conquering Egypt, with the idea of marching on to India. His victories in Africa were made useless, however, because his fleet was smashed by the great Nelson, commander of Britain's Mediterranean fleet. Finally Napoleon deserted his army in Egypt, sneaked back to France which had meanwhile lost Italy and was facing domestic bankruptcy. (It took two years to repatriate his stranded army.)

Welcomed as a conqueror, nevertheless, he had an easy time disposing of the incompetent and graft-ridden Directory. He surrounded the meeting hall of the Directory with armed guards and chased out the members. Soon France had a new government—the Consulate. Napoleon was First Consul, and there were two more Consuls as "window dressing." In 1802 he became Consul for life, and in 1804 he had himself crowned Emperor of the French. Each step was ratified by overwhelmingly favorable votes.

Napoleon the Man

Napoleon was a dynamo in action. Words poured from him like a torrent. He could read a document at a glance, and he dictated to several secretaries simultaneously. Working 18 hours a day meant nothing to him; he remarked once, "In the future I may lose a battle but I shall never lose a minute."

As a general, he was extremely painstaking, studying maps and terrain and seeing possibilities undreamt of by his opponents. But he was also quick as a flash to improvise as the need arose. His insistence on mobility baffled his cumbersome enemies, as when he crossed the Alps through the St. Bernard Pass and defeated the Austrians with 15 cannon to their 200.

Napoleon's mind was clear, logical and forceful. Always scheming and ruthlessly ambitious, he looked on other men as mere instruments. Though he was arrogant, he had tremendous charm and knew how to make use of it: he could wheedle and flatter, and he was a master of catchphrases about Liberty and Freedom.

Napoleon's soldiers adored him, and not merely for his victories. He had a fantastic memory, and knew about 20,000 of them by sight. What could be more flattering? He displayed a deep interest in their welfare, even to checking on whether they had buttons for their underwear.

But this public solicitude masked a private heartlessness. Once he told the Austrian Prime Minister: "You cannot stop me; I spend 30,000 men a month."

To the people of Europe, Napoleon presented himself as a liberator and apostle of freedom. Thus, after his Italian victories in 1796, he proclaimed, "People of Italy! The Army of France has broken your chains!" A few days later, he demanded from Milan 20,000,000 francs, thousands of horses, huge stores of provisions; he seized works of art, burned towns, and massacred people at random when the spoils did not turn up rapidly enough.

He promised France peace and order, and left her well over 2,000,000 war dead. Calling himself "a child of the Revolution," he created a regime that was in some ways more repressive than the old monarchy. Spouting democratic talk, he put members

Plate 139. Silver 5 francs (1813). *Obverse:* crowned "N" separating value. *Reverse:* crossed guns. Necessity money issued during the 5-month siege of Cattaro, a Dalmatian seaport.

of his family on European thrones, and, after divorcing his first wife, Josephine, he married a Hapsburg princess, Marie Louise, grand-niece of Marie Antoinette.

Yet in one sense he was "a child of the Revolution." The people liked him because he had been born poor. His soldiers remembered that he had earned his promotions by his abilities, and that he promised a Marshal's baton in every knapsack. To everyone Napoleon offered something —the peasants had the confiscated lands, business was booming, brilliant careers were possible in the army and government service.

Plate 140. Gold medal (1811). *Obverse:* Napoleon and Marie Louise. *Reverse:* their son Napoleon II (1811-1832), King of Rome, Duke of Reichstadt and nicknamed *L'Aiglon* ("the eaglet"). The short life of Napoleon's heir was shrouded in mystery.

Napoleon the Statesman

Napoleon's work as an administrator is not as well known as his military victories. He gave France its first comprehensive body of law, the Civil Code, which is still in use. His reform of tax-collecting methods ended the abuses of centuries. He revamped the educational system, introduced metric weights and measures, brought back 100,000 émigrés to France, and assured the financial stability of the country by founding the Bank of France.

One of Napoleon's earliest (and most important) contributions was putting coinage on a sound basis with a five-franc silver piece. He introduced the decimal system of coinage and replaced the monarchy's louis d'or with a 20-franc gold coin. It was also Napoleon who fixed the fineness of the franc at 900 grains of silver in every 1,000 grains of metal.

Napoleon did not put his likeness on coins until 1803, when he was already scheming to become Emperor. His 1803 coins read "*Premier Consul*"; in 1804 the legend was "*Empereur.*" Coin scholars have expressed surprise that up to 1808 the reverses read "*République Française.*" The reason for this is interesting. When Napoleon became Emperor, he did not bother to change the Constitution of the Republic. He simply inserted a preamble: "The government of the Republic is confided to an Emperor."

In 1809 the pretense of a republic was dropped, and from then on France was frankly an empire, although Napoleon continued the Revolutionary calendar up to the Year Fourteen. The year 1807 is the first old-style date that appears on his coins.

Napoleon's Downfall

The curse of Napoleon's conquests was that he could not stand still. Every success required an additional effort. As he himself said: "My reign will not outlast the day when I have ceased to be strong, and therefore to be feared."

Napoleon was extremely conscious of his place in history. With his invasion of Egypt he was following in the footsteps of Alexander the Great; in winning his brilliant victories, he was matching himself with Julius Caesar; when he became Emperor, he compared himself to Charlemagne. The logical goal of his ambitions was a United Europe, under French domination.

What this meant was war to the death with England; a Continent controlled by

Plate 141. **Silver 5 francs (1804-1807).** ***Obverse:*** **Napoleon with inscription** ***Empereur.*** ***Reverse:*** **value in wreath with inscription** ***République Francaise.***

Napoleon would reduce England to the status of Sicily. For two years Napoleon assembled a great invasion force on the Channel coast; but England was master of the sea. In 1805 Nelson's defeat of the French and Spanish fleets off Cape Trafalgar on the Spanish coast meant that Napoleon was confined to the Continent for good.

The only other way to crush England was to stifle her trade. Napoleon forbade all European countries to do business with England. To enforce this Continental blockade, Napoleon had to invade every country with a coastline—Portugal, Spain, Italy, Holland, Belgium, northern Germany, eventually Russia. In the end, his armies were spread too thin and his casualties became too great.

After his disastrous Russian invasion, Napoleon's armies were pathetically weak. An alliance of Prussia, Russia, England, Sweden and Austria undertook a "War of Liberation" against him. Napoleon's pathetic armies of 1814 were made up largely of untrained youngsters, outnumbered 2 to 1 and worse. In March, 1814, his enemies entered Paris, and eleven days later he abdicated and threw himself on the mercy of the British. They exiled him to Elba, a small island near his native Corsica.

While the victorious powers were still arguing about how to divide the map of Europe at the Congress of Vienna, Napoleon escaped from Elba and landed on March 1, 1815 at Cannes, where the remnants of his former army joined him. There followed the famous "Hundred Days" of a new lease of power for the Emperor until he met defeat at Waterloo (Belgium) on June 18. This time he was banished to St. Helena, a desolate island in the south Atlantic, where he died in 1821.

After Napoleon's exile to Elba, the Bourbon dynasty returned, with Louis XVIII (brother of the guillotined Louis XVI) as King. A shrewd and level-headed man, Louis XVIII knew how to steer a cautious course between the excitable royalist and republican factions of his constitutional monarchy. He reigned from 1814 to 1824 and was succeeded by another brother, Charles X, who was anything but tactful. The three-day July Revolution in 1830 forced him out and refused to make his grandson King. His descendants became the Bourbon pretenders (claimants) to the throne of France.

Plate 142. **Silver 5 francs (1809-1815).** ***Obverse:*** **Napoleon with inscription** ***Empereur.*** ***Reverse:*** **value in wreath with inscription** ***Empire Francais.***

Plate 144. Silver 2 francs (1815). *Obverse:* Napoleon. A coin of the greatest historical interest, issued during the "Hundred Days."

Plate 145. Silver 5 francs (1816-1824). *Obverse:* Louis XVIII, first Restoration King of France after the downfall of Napoleon.

Plate 146. Silver 1 franc (1831). *Obverse:* Henry V, Duke of Bordeaux, pretender to the French throne. *Reverse:* crowned shield with lilies.

Plate 147. Silver 5 francs (1830-1831). *Obverse:* Louis Philippe, who lost his throne in the revolution of 1848.

To succeed Charles, a "liberal noble," the Duke of Orleans, was crowned as Louis Philippe, and called "King of the French" (significantly not of "France"). He had been an opponent of the Bourbons; but over the years he rejected the constant demand of the common people to vote, and he became less and less popular. Finally in 1848 he was forced off the throne and spent the rest of his life in England.

Another Napoleon

Unfortunately, the Second Republic, proclaimed after the abdication of Louis Philippe, was no improvement. The new President was Louis Napoleon Bonaparte, nephew of the Emperor, who had returned from years of impoverished exile to trade on his name. After three years as President, this shabby and incompetent adventurer put an end to the Second Republic in 1851 and declared himself Emperor Napoleon III.

He gave France a glorious façade which masked shocking weakness inside. To distract his subjects from unsatisfactory conditions at home, Napoleon dabbled in the affairs of Turkey, Italy, and Poland, bungled a war with Austria, talked the Archduke Maximilian into a futile attempt to seize Mexico, and allowed himself to be thoroughly fooled by the wily Prussian prime minister, Bismarck.

Plate 148. Silver 5 francs (1861-1870). *Obverse:* Napoleon III, who tried to live up to his famous uncle's reputation—with disastrous results for France.

This last blunder proved fatal to Napoleon III. France declared war on Prussia on July 19, 1870 and on September 2, Napoleon III surrendered with his army at Sedan. Two days later he was deposed and the Third Republic was proclaimed. Continuing to put up a heroic but futile resistance, Paris admitted defeat in January, 1871. The treaty of peace obliged France to give up Alsace and part of Lorraine, and to pay an indemnity of five billion francs.

The Third Republic, which was born in the hour of France's deepest humiliation, its loss of the Franco-Prussian War, is still in existence, after having weathered innumerable crises and survived German aggression in two World Wars.

After World War I, the franc went down disastrously in value. Since 1914 it has never risen near its former value of approximately 20 cents.

In 1932 the government issued a five-franc nickel piece, which was at once counterfeited very skilfully. The counterfeiters, when arrested and brought to trial, offered the defense that nickel was not included among the metals specified in the law prohibiting counterfeiting! The judges granted the soundness of the argument and freed the counterfeiters.

The law was made foolproof, but the counterfeit coins still pass freely—or did some years ago.

During World War II, the Vichy Government issued coinage with German permission. Significantly, the old republican motto of "Liberty, Equality, and Fraternity" disappeared in favor of "Work, Family, and Fatherland." Subsequent coinage of the Third Republic has restored the old motto.

Plate **149.** **Silver 5 francs (1871). Satirical version of Plate 148, one of many made by infuriated Frenchmen after their crushing defeat by Germany in 1871.**

Plate **150. Silver 5 francs (1870).** ***Obverse:*** **Ceres head. The first coin struck by the newly formed Third Republic, which replaced the regime of Napoleon III.**

Plate **151. Silver 2 francs (1899).** ***Obverse:*** **The Sower, one of the characteristic devices of republican coinage.** ***Reverse:*** **value and characteristic motto ("Liberty, Equality, and Fraternity").**

Plate **152. Vichy state, aluminum 1 franc (1942).** ***Obverse:*** **double ax between two wheat-ears;** ***Etat Francais*** **replaces** ***Republique Francaise.*** ***Reverse:*** **value between oak leaves, with a change from the republican motto.**

Great Britain

English coinage is a book-length subject in itself. English history covers over 2,000 years, and much of that history is reflected in a fascinating way in the coins issued.

The early coins of Britain which appeared about the beginning of the Christian Era, were often based on Greek designs. Sometimes the designs changed considerably for the worse, when they were copied from worn Greek imitations. Some of the island coins were particularly good, as in the case of two that remind us of the coinage of Corinth and Metapontum.

About the first century B.C., Roman coins were finding their way into Britain more and more frequently. Discoveries of Roman coins are an everyday occurrence in modern England. In these hoards we generally find coins of the Republic as well as the more common ones of the Empire, mixed with native coins of Britain.

Once the Romans occupied the country in force, beginning in 43 A.D., their sestertius (bronze), denarius (silver), and aureus (gold), became the official coinage of Britain as a part of the Roman Empire. Hence it is not surprising that hundreds of thousands of Roman coins have been dug up in Great Britain.

The ninth century saw the start of the invasions by the Norsemen, those "Commandos" of the Middle Ages. For two centuries—and more—these Danes harried England, and even ruled it a great part of the time. Among the native Saxon Kings, Alfred the Great (871-900) stands out.

Alfred was a many-sided man with wide-ranging interests and abilities. Deeply convinced of the importance of learning and education, he was also an outstanding general and lawgiver. It is to him that the mighty British Navy owes its first faint beginnings. In fact, his navy defeated a Danish fleet in 899.

Alfred's weak successors tried to buy off the Danes with an annual tribute called the "Danegeld." They struck a special coin to pay this tax. At its height, the tax reached a total of 48,000 pounds of silver, an enormous figure for those times. Later, when there was no more need for the tax, the Kings continued to collect it. Even in those days they knew that it is easier to levy a tax than to get rid of it.

In 1016 the Danes took over all of England, with the 22-year old Canute as the country's ruler. Canute was an exceptionally able monarch, and did much to improve conditions. It was Canute who established London as the capital. Called "the Great," he was King of England, Denmark, and Norway; but England was his favorite, and he spent the rest of his life there.

There is a legend that Canute's courtiers, in their efforts to flatter him, told him he

Plate 153. Ancient Britain, gold stater (about 10 B.C.). *Reverse:* galloping horse. See Plate 42.

Plate 154. Ancient Britain, gold stater (about 20 A.D.). *Obverse:* ear of wheat. See Plate 35.

was so mighty that he could make the waves stand still. To prove them liars, he is said to have tried out the idea for them. He had his royal chair placed on the beach and commanded the waves: "Rise thus far and no farther." Of course, the tide rose and wet his feet.

The coins of the chaotic period following the departure of the Romans, are crude and of little interest. About 700 or so, the style of these coins improved considerably, and the coins of Alfred the Great (871-900) are quite presentable by modern standards. They feature his portrait in the manner of the Roman Imperial coinage, from which they are doubtless copied.

It is interesting that the coins of Aethelred "the Unready" (978-1016), one of Alfred's feeble successors, are found in much greater quantity in Denmark than in England. The reason is simple—these coins were used to pay the annual tribute to the Danes (the "Danegeld").

The coins of Danish Canute the Great and Harold, the last Saxon King, have great historical interest, but not much artistic beauty.

Plate 155. Silver penny (871-900). *Obverse:* Alfred the Great. Note the similarity in style to that of Roman Imperial coins.

Plate 156. Silver penny (978-1016). *Obverse:* Aethelred. *Reverse:* cross. A "Danegeld" tribute coin.

The Norman Conquest

Canute's early death in 1035 led to a confused situation, with Saxon Kings once more on the throne. It was during this period that the construction of Westminster Abbey was started (1055). Finally William the Conqueror, Duke of Normandy, leading an army of 12,000 warriors, carried out a conquest that was as easy as it was thoroughgoing. Since that time (1066) neither fleets nor buzz-bombs have succeeded in conquering England.

The Normans, descendants of the bold Norse marauders, were formidable fighters, vigorous, ruthless men. Once in England, the Norman nobles lost no time carving out vast estates and building imposing castles on them. The new monarchy was tightly centralized, tax collections were grimly efficient and the jury system was improved. The English language began to take shape with the addition of many thousands of French-Latin words. In time, the Englishman replaced the Norman and the Saxon.

Plate 157. Cricklade silver penny (1016-1035). *Obverse:* helmeted bust of King Canute with scepter.

Plate 158. Canterbury silver penny (1066). *Obverse:* Harold II, the last Saxon King of England, defeated at Hastings by William the Conqueror.

For 400 years after the Conquest, the English Kings tried to gain control of France. They fought many a war, including the famous Hundred Years' War, with seesaw success. Not until 1453 did the English finally give up these futile attempts. England was slow indeed to realize that her destiny lay on the seven seas.

For a man who had a lifelong passion for collecting taxes in every nook and cranny, William the Conqueror paid surprisingly little attention to his coinage. Most of his coins—and those of the next 300 years—are full-face instead of profile. This was curious, for the coin designers of the ancient world realized very early that full-face coins neither look good nor wear well.* For a long time William's coins were quite rare, until a hoard of 6,000 of them turned up in 1833.

Incidentally, as we read about the difficulties that one English King after another had with his coinage, we must remember that the prosperous nineteenth century was the first in which there was enough metal for all kinds of coinage. It was also the first in which there was not an enormous amount of counterfeiting and clipping the edges of coins. Aside from the desire of some people to turn a dishonest penny, there is little doubt that the shortage of coins greatly stimulated counterfeiting.

Because of the shortage of coins, especially in the very small denominations, many tradesmen issued private tokens. It is significant that this private coinage also disappeared in the nineteenth century.

As we have seen, the coinage of William the Conqueror was undistinguished, and the same comment applies to the coins of his successors. In the twelfth century the coins were so debased that people formed the habit of slashing through a coin to check its content. These cut coins were not accepted by the public. To get them circulating again, the Mint cut *all* coins as they were newly issued!

Generally the King's head appeared on the obverse, and a cross on the reverse. The Englishmen of those days often disregarded the meaning of this cross, using it, for example, as a convenient pattern for chopping up pennies into halfpennies or farthings ("fourthlings"). Cutting the coin for checking its quality followed these same lines. Clipping the edges was so widely practiced a crime that the standard penalty was to chop off the culprit's right hand.

During the twelfth and thirteenth centuries the English penny came to be known as the *sterlingus*. It had an imitation in the base silver coins known as *esterlings*. The latter came mostly from Bruges and Luxembourg, arriving in England as payment for cloth. (Even in those early days, England was famous for the fine quality of its wool.)

It was Edward III (1327-1377) who issued the first really distinguished coin, the gold "noble." This large, handsome piece is thought to have commemorated a great

* One notable exception is the remarkable lion's-scalp coin of Rhegium (Plate 16).

Plate 159. Salisbury silver penny (about 1087). *Obverse:* William the Conqueror. *Reverse:* Cross. The full-face portrait reflects the influence of Byzantine coinage.

Plate 160. Silver groat (about 1356). *Obverse:* Edward III. *Reverse:* cross in circle, pellets in angles.

Plate 161. Edward IV, gold angel (1471-1483). *Obverse:* St. Michael killing the Devil (dragon). *Reverse:* ship with cross and English shield.

naval victory at Sluys in 1340, when an English fleet, commanded by the King, completely demolished the French.

This coin had texts from the New Testament inscribed around the edges, perhaps to discourage clipping. A "noble" of Henry VI (1422-1461) is a fairly close copy of this famous coin.

Plate 162. Edward IV, gold "rose" noble (ryal, 1465-1470). *Obverse:* king in ship, banner at stern, rose on side. *Reverse:* rose over sun on floriated cross.

Plate 163. Henry VI, gold noble (1422-1425). *Obverse:* king in ship, with sword and shield. Note similarity to Plate 162.

Wars of the Roses

The end of the French wars brought no relief from bloodshed. Two years later, in 1455, the terrible Wars of the Roses broke out. These were a series of civil wars with the British throne as the prize. In the ensuing 30 years of struggle between the houses of Lancaster (red rose) and York (white rose), there was frightful carnage among the feudal lords of England.

The Wars at last came to an end in 1485 when the Earl of Richmond, a Lancastrian, defeated Richard III at Bosworth Field. (This is the battle at which Shakespeare has the fleeing monarch exclaim desperately: "A horse! A horse! My kingdom for a horse!") The victor became Henry VII.

The first of the Tudor line, Henry VII was an outstandingly able ruler, working unceasingly to unite his devastated land.

For centuries English coinage had been plagued by a shortage of gold and silver. Yet during the reign of Edward IV (1461-1483), some very attractive coins appeared, including the "angel" and the rose noble (the "ryal"). The reigns of both Henry VI and Edward IV were broken up by the devastating Wars of the Roses. Some scholars believe that the design of the angel celebrates the temporary victory of the York faction in the Wars of the Roses. The angel

Plate 164. Henry VII, gold sovereign (1489). *Reverse:* shield on Tudor rose. One of the most beautiful of all English coins.

Plate 165. Henry VII, gold sovereign (1489). *Obverse:* king on throne. The *reverse* appears on Plate 164.

gets its name from the obverse design of the archangel St. Michael slaying a dragon.

Good-looking as these coins are, there is often noticeable variation in the quality of specimens of the same coin. There is a reason for this. The best dies were kept in London. With rival gangs infesting the roads during the Wars of the Roses, it was too risky to send the dies to the provincial mints. As a result, the mints in the smaller towns worked with cruder dies.

As you have seen, Henry VII was an exceptionally able ruler who succeeded in his task of repairing the damage caused by the Wars of the Roses. He took great interest in coinage, which made considerable progress during his reign.

One of his innovations was a magnificent new gold coin, the sovereign. It is one of the masterpieces of British coinage. On the elaborate reverse design we see the famous Tudor rose—combining the roses of Lancaster and York and representing the coming of peace after the Wars of the Roses. Like the noble, this coin had Biblical texts around the edge to discourage clipping.

Henry VII also introduced the shilling, a silver coin often called a "testoon" in the old days. The name comes from the Italian *testa* ("head") and reflects the influence of the Italian Renaissance in England. Toward the end of the fifteenth century some of the most famous Italian artists, such as Leonardo da Vinci and Benvenuto Cellini, were trying their hand at designing coins. The work they turned out was so masterly that other countries were spurred on to produce coins of superior quality.

Henry VII's shilling is worthy of this tradition, and it is also, by the way, the first English profile coin in about three hundred years. From this time on, practically all British portrait coins employed the profile style.

Henry VIII

Most people remember Henry VIII for his six marriages, but he has less sensational claims to fame. Continuing the work of his father (Henry VII), he solidified the power of the Crown by opposing the attempts of the great nobles to increase their power. He also drew England away, to a certain extent, from European problems and influences. Thus he laid the groundwork for later overseas expansion.

Henry had a great love for the sea. He enlarged the Navy, built extensive dockyards, founded a school for pilots and interested himself in improved ship design. When the *Princess Mary* was launched in 1519, he had his whole court attend the ceremony; he "acted as pilot and wore a sailor's coat and trousers made of cloth of gold, and a gold chain with the inscription *Dieu et mon droit,* to which was suspended a whistle, which he blew nearly as loud as a trumpet."

He had other interests too. An accom-

Plate 166. Silver groat (1526-1544). *Obverse:* Henry VIII. This coin shows the King as a young man.

Plate 167. "Silver" shilling (1544). *Obverse:* Henry VIII. The sadly debased coin that gave Henry the name of "Old Coppernose."

plished musician, he spoke French and Latin, and was keenly interested in theology. In 1521 he wrote an attack on Martin Luther for which the Pope rewarded him with the title of *Defender of the Faith.* To this day, the phrase is included in the formal titles of English monarchs.

The coinage of Henry VIII is chiefly famous, or notorious, for the steady debasement of the metal in his coins. At first this debasing had some point, as English coins had a higher bullion value than similar coins on the Continent. But once the King realized that debasing was quite profitable in itself, his coinage deteriorated steadily. The famous coin which earned him the nickname of "Old Coppernose" was one-third silver and two-thirds copper alloy—a shabby combination indeed.

We are told that Sir John Rainsford, on meeting the man who was said to be responsible for recommending the debasing of the coinage, threatened to break his head "for that he had made his Soveraigne Lord, the most beautiful Prince, King Henry, with a redde and copper nose."

It was in the reign of Henry's successor, Edward VI (1547-1553), that English coinage reached the lowest point of debasement prior to 1947. At one time the amount of silver in the shilling was one-fourth, the rest being alloy. Shortly before the death of this boy-king at the age of 14, there appeared the "fine" sovereign and the "fine" shilling. In these the metal content is again first-class. The shilling, for example, has 11 parts of silver to one part of alloy.

Elizabethan Sea-dogs

It was during the reign of Henry VIII's daughter, Queen Elizabeth I, that English sea power first revealed its magnificent qualities. Britannia did not always rule the waves, and up to the time of Elizabeth, the British were too occupied with internal problems to pay much attention to the sea. They had no glorious achievements to compare with the Portuguese, Spanish, and Italian navigators. True, five years after Columbus' first voyage, Henry VII sent John Cabot to the New World. It was on this trip that Cabot discovered Newfoundland, but the English failed to follow up this initial success.

With the coming of more peaceful times in England and the opening up of great foreign markets, it was inevitable that the British should take to the sea. From the very first they were noted for their unexampled daring and superb seamanship.

It was in 1577 that Francis Drake carried out the grandest coup of this period. The Spaniards used to ship the vast produce

Plate 168. "Fine" silver shilling (1550-1553). *Obverse:* Edward VI. *Reverse:* cross over shield in circle.

Plate 169. **Bronze halfpenny (1937-1948). *Obverse:* the *Golden Hind.* A modern coin that recalls the glories of the Elizabethan Age.**

Plate 170. **Silver sixpence (1567). *Obverse:* Elizabeth I. One of the most striking of all coin portraits.**

of Peru's gold mines up the Pacific to the Isthmus of Panama. There it would be unloaded, carried by land to the Atlantic coast, and then reloaded for the long voyage.

Drake's plan seemed simple; taking only a few ships, he sailed down to the southern tip of South America and entered the Pacific via the Straits of Magellan. The passage through the stormy straits, always fraught with danger, proved costly to the expedition. Drake emerged into the vast ocean with only one ship left, his flagship, the *Golden Hind.*

With no more than 100 men in this 75-feet-long vessel, Drake did not dream of giving up his plan. He ravaged the Spaniards' long Pacific coast, assembling a fabulous amount of booty. Sailing as far north as Drake's Bay, somewhat north of the present site of San Francisco, he gave the California region the name of New Albion. Some scholars believe that the California voyage may have been the first part of a grandiose plan for colonizing America from ocean to ocean. Such dazzling ideas came very easily to Drake!

At last ready to leave for home, Drake executed the final interesting phase of his plan. Instead of retracing his course, he sailed *west,* crossing the Pacific. When he reached the Cape of Good Hope, he had but 57 men left, and water was running desperately low.

Nevertheless, the intrepid voyagers arrived home in Plymouth harbor in England on September 26, 1580. (He had left on December 13, 1577.) Thus Drake was the second to make a continuous circumnavigation of the globe (Magellan's historic voyage had been some 60 years earlier.) "As a seaman Drake had few rivals; but it was in the leadership of men, in the originality of his designs, and in the superb brilliance with which he executed them, that the genius of the man shone at its brightest."

Drake's arrival created a problem for Elizabeth. The Spaniards had screamed belligerently over Drake's raids. "The colossal treasure disgorged from the hold of the *Golden Hind* was believed at the time to amount to a million and a half sterling, or between a quarter and a half of the whole annual produce of King Philip's American mines." Elizabeth was fearless, but she was also hard-headed: to indorse Drake's actions might risk open war. Finally she took the risk. Journeying to the coast, she dined on board the *Golden Hind* and knighted Drake.

In 1588 the Spaniards were at last ready to crush England by sending out the "Invincible Armada." Drake had contributed

Plate 171. **Silver sixpence (1567). *Reverse:* cross over shield. This is the *reverse* of the coin on Plate 170.**

Plate 172. British East India Company, silver half piece of eight (1600). *Obverse:* crowned shield with crowned ER (Elizabeth *Regina*). The first coins for use in the British Empire.

the crowning indignity the previous year by boldly sailing into the Spanish harbor of Cadiz, wrecking the shipping and sacking the city, thus greatly delaying the departure of the expedition. (Ten years later he repeated this feat, which he called "singeing the beard of the King of Spain.")

The Armada was indeed formidable—on paper, anyway. It was made up of 132 ships with 3,165 cannon. It carried a large army and, once in the Channel, it was to pick up another invasion force from the Spanish Netherlands.

Once the fight started, the dashing English forces outplanned, outmaneuvered, and outfought the enemy all the way. The soldiers were of no use to the Spaniards, merely cluttering up the decks and getting mowed down in great numbers. The English made wonderfully skillful use of their numerically inferior fire-power.

Part of the Spanish fleet fled, but, in their haste to escape the light English fireships, they slashed their cables and left their anchors behind. The battle clearly lost, the battered Armada headed for the North Sea, hoping to escape into the Atlantic by sailing around Scotland.

Unfortunately for them, a mighty storm came on; powerless to ride out the tempest without their anchors, many ships were lost. One of the ships that went down was the *Florenzia,* with a cargo of $15,000,000 in gold. More than one attempt was made to salvage this rich haul, apparently without success. Eventually about a third of the "Invincible Armada" managed to limp home ingloriously.

From this famous battle dates the ascendancy of England as a world power.

Machinery Appears—and Disappears

The reign of Elizabeth (1557-1602) was notable for a variety of interesting coinage. The most important event in the field of coinage, however, was the introduction of machinery. Eloye Mestrelle, a Frenchman, produced coins with a mill that rolled metal to the desired thickness, cut out the blanks, and stamped them.

The engraving on the dies was of a very high order, and the appearance of the machine-made coins was naturally a vast improvement over the old hand-hammered coins. Another important improvement was that some of these coins had grained (corrugated) edges to discourage clipping.

To be sure, Mestrelle's machinery appears amateurish compared to our modern equipment. Introduced 200 years before the steam engine was available, its power was horse-driven or depended on water pressure. Rudimentary as this contraption was, it was too revolutionary for its time. The Mint workers feared that Mestrelle's ma-

Plate 173. British East India Company, silver half piece of eight. *Reverse:* crowned portcullis. The *reverse* of the coin on Plate 172.

chinery would put them out of work, and their intrigues led to his discharge.

Mestrelle's story has a sad ending. In 1578 he was hanged as a forger. Whether he was really a criminal or whether he was "framed" by his enemies, we do not know. Almost a whole century passed before the Royal Mint finally adopted machinery.

King vs. Parliament

The whole seventeenth century was a period of struggle between the Crown and Parliament.

During her long reign, Elizabeth had enjoyed enormous personal popularity. Though a strong-willed woman, she had one of the prime qualities of a first-class ruler—she knew when to give way, and she knew how to do it gracefully. Thus she either carried Parliament along with her, or avoided serious conflict by surrendering before tempers became frayed and hostility became venomous.

The first Stuart king, James I (1602-25), was not similarly gifted. Called "the wisest fool in Christendom," he could be highly intelligent about trifling matters, and stupidly pigheaded at the wrong time. A strong believer in the "divine right" of Kings, he resolutely refused any compromise with Parliament. They were continually at odds on the vital subjects of religion, foreign affairs, and taxation. In each of these fields, James insisted that the King had the right to shape the nation's policy; he viewed Parliament's role as merely an advisory one.

The religious persecutions during the reigns of James I and his son, Charles I, led to the emigration of thousands of Englishmen to the New World, beginning with the pioneer voyage of the *Mayflower* to Massachusetts in 1620. In foreign relations, James followed a policy of friendship with Spain which was loathed by the members of Parliament and the rest of the country.

Plate 174. James I, silver crown (1603-1604). _Obverse:_ King on horseback. James I was the first English King of the Scottish Stuart family. He also reigned over Scotland as James VI. Scotland became part of the United Kingdom in 1707. This resulted in the adoption of the Union Jack, made up of the English cross of St. George and the Scottish cross of St. Andrew. The Scots have played an important role in British history, with valuable contributions to the development of the Empire. Many Scots have distinguished themselves in public life, in science and invention, in literature and the arts.

But taxation was the crucial point of the struggle. He had no sympathy with the view that Parliament had the right to refuse financial support to the policies he favored. When Parliament drew up The Great Protestation, affirming its legislative rights, James was so infuriated that he ripped the page from the journal of the House of Commons.

On coming to the throne in 1625, Charles I inherited these conflicts in sharpened form; he was even more headstrong

Plate 175. Ireland, silver sixpence (1643). _Obverse:_ crowned CR (_Carolus Rex_). _Reverse:_ value ("D" stands for denarius, or "penny"). Emergency coinage issued during the Civil War.

than his father. Matters came to a crisis in 1629 when, during a turbulent session, Charles dissolved Parliament and ruled without it for 11 years. Eventually the argument became a civil war, and the King's army was no match for Oliver Cromwell's Puritan troops. Charles was defeated, captured, tried, and beheaded. A Commonwealth was established with Cromwell as its Lord Protector (1653-58).

The Great Rebellion and the Commonwealth Coins

During the Great Rebellion against Charles I, there was a great deal of "necessity coinage." Siege pieces made their appearance when the King had to pay his troops at a time when the Mint was in the hands of the Puritan rebels. Like the later Irish "gun-money," these coins are well above the usual crude level of necessity money.

From 1649 to 1660, the period of the Commonwealth, England had no King. The Commonwealth coins are quite plain, in keeping with the familiar Puritan sternness in such matters as dress, luxuries, and behavior. However, the coins are not without a certain elegance. Portraits are absent, but the Puritan arms (featuring the St. George's cross) make an attractive and picturesque design.

An interesting feature of the Commonwealth coins is that they have English instead of Latin inscriptions—for the first time in the history of British coinage. The obverse reads, "The Commonwealth of England"; the reverse: "God With Us."

Shortly before the death of Oliver Cromwell, some beautiful patterns were struck with his portrait. Though Cromwell refused to have himself crowned King, the portrait appears in the laureated and draped style of the Roman Emperors.

Plate 176. Scotland, silver 12 shillings (about 1635). *Obverse:* Charles I and value behind head. This denomination was equivalent in value to one English shilling.

Enter Britannia

The Commonwealth was followed by the Restoration, when Charles II was recalled from France to assume the throne. A number of important "firsts" distinguish his reign.

It was in 1672, for example, that the first coin appeared with the figure of Britannia. More than one coin expert has traced the relation between the figure of Britannia and those on two famous reverses on the Imperial Roman coins of Hadrian (117-138 A.D.) and Antoninus Pius (138-161 A.D.); in fact, Britannia's pedigree goes even further back, to the image of the goddess Athene on the reverse of Lysimachus' Alexander the Great coin.

Interesting as it is to trace the classical origin of the figure, to an Englishman and

Plate 177. Commonwealth, silver crown (1656-1658). *Obverse:* Oliver Cromwell. Like the augustale of Frederick II (Plate 214), this coin shows strong Roman influence.

Plate 178. **Commonwealth, silver crown (1653).** ***Obverse:*** **shield of St. George in wreath.** ***Reverse:*** **shields of St. George and Ireland in wreath. A beautifully designed coin.**

to the world at large Britannia suggests the might of the British Navy and the courage and skill of its sailors.

Britannia usually appears holding a shield with the Union Jack; in earlier coins, she also grasps a spear. Later on, beginning with the famous "Cartwheel" coins of 1797, Britannia borrows Neptune's trident to replace the spear. (It was no empty boast to give Britannia this symbol of the mastery of the seas; only a year later, Nelson smashed Napoleon's fleet in the Battle of the Nile!)

It is rewarding to scrutinize coin reverses with the Britannia figure. Sometimes she holds an olive branch, the familiar emblem of peace. On some coins you can see a beehive and horn of plenty (meaning: "industriousness and plenty"). On other types, a lighthouse and ships appear in the background.

The first appearance of the Britannia design was part of an issue of small denominations in copper. These coins came out to relieve the shortage of small change, and to do away with the abuses resulting from the widespread use of private tokens.

The pattern for the first Britannia coin, designed in 1665, had the motto *Quattuor Maria Vindico* ("I claim the four seas"). But in 1667—before the coin had been struck—the Dutch won a resounding naval victory from the English. The proud claim disappeared from the coin.

Machinery at Last

At first, Charles II's coins continued to be hand-hammered in the good old style used century after century. Though the Italians as well as the French had devised improved methods of making coins, it was not until 1662 that these methods took hold in England. Here is how Peter Seaby* describes the new process:

"The early rolling mills were driven either by horse or water power, and the term 'milled money' was applied to any coin produced by machinery—coins made

* Peter Seaby: *The Story of the English Coinage.* London, 1952: B. A. Seaby, Ltd.

Plate 179. Charles II, copper farthing (1675). ***Reverse:*** **seated figure of Britannia with spear and shield, and holding a sprig of ivy. The first Britannia coin; note how it harks back to the Roman coin pictured on Plate 98.**

by the older method being known as 'hammered money.'

"After bars of metal had been dragged through the rolling mills, being reduced in the process to thin strips of the thickness of the finished coin, they were passed through the blank-cutting machine where a sharp punch with an inclined face tore out the circular blanks. As the blanks became curved in the cutting-out process, they were flattened again by a heavy drop-hammer.

"Blanks were weighed individually before being struck: if much underweight, they were rejected; but if too heavy, they were filed across their flat surface until within the required limits. These file marks can often be seen on the milled gold and silver coins of the seventeenth and early eighteenth centuries.

"While coins were made by the hand-hammering method, they were always liable to suffer from clipping. With the introduction of machinery for punching out the blanks, coins could be produced that were perfectly circular. The clippers were not finally defeated, however, until coins were made with graining or lettering around the edge."

Many of Charles II's coins have the words *Decus et Tutamen* ("Decoration and Safeguard") inscribed on the edges to prevent clipping. The detailed excellence of some of these coins may be gathered from the fact that when George Sanders played Charles II in the film *Forever Amber,* his wig was designed from a blown-up photograph of a 20-shilling piece picturing that monarch.

Plate 180. Silver crown (1668). *Obverse:* Charles II. *Reverse:* coat of arms of the United Kingdom, with interlaced C's.

The Guinea

The English guinea was a gold coin issued between 1663 and 1813. The earliest guineas were 20 shillings. Later on the value was generally 21 shillings, although there were changes from time to time.

We derive the name of this coin from the fact that the Africa Company supplied much of the gold from the region now known as the Gold Coast, in those days called Guinea. Coins made from this gold used the device of the elephant and castle, taken from the company's badge.

Even though the coining of the guinea ended in 1813, the term "guinea" continued in use, and we still come across it today. When an article is priced at a guinea, this simply means that it costs 21 shillings.

Plate 181. George III, gold guinea (1798). *Reverse:* spade-shaped crowned shield. Known as the "spade guinea."

Catastrophe in London

Despite the extensive coinage in Charles II's reign, money ran short in 1665, when the outbreak of the fearsome London Plague carried off as many as 10,000 victims in a single week during the worst stage. In September of the following year, the Great Fire of London raged for four days and four nights. In those days there were no fire engines or fire hoses worthy of the name; worse yet, practically all the buildings of the city were wooden. Over 13,000 houses and 100 churches went up in flames.

The Great Recoinage

In 1695, during the reign of William III, the government decided to call in all hand-hammered money that was in circulation. Some of these coins went back to the time of Edward VI (1547-1553); many were of course badly worn and faded; some had been clipped unmercifully. To put the exchange of old coins for new on a basis of equal weight would have meant a considerable loss—maybe as much as £2,000,000*—for the holders of the old coins. Also, it would have been a time-wasting process for the Mint.

Therefore the government decided to absorb the loss, making the exchange on the basis of value for value. However, there was a catch to this generosity. The government got its money back—and more—by putting a nuisance tax on all windows. Until this law was repealed, builders used as few windows as possible and this had a bad effect on the health of the English population.

* "£" is the abbreviation for *libra,* the Latin word for "pound." (The Roman *libra,* by the way, was made up of 12 ounces, not 16.) The abbreviation for "pence" is the mysterious "d." which comes from the Roman denarius!

Plate 182. **Silver shilling (1696).** ***Obverse:*** **William III. This coin appeared during the great recoinage of 1695-1697.**

Newton at the Mint

It is a fact not generally known even to coin collectors that Sir Isaac Newton was Master of the Mint from 1696 to 1727. We are told that Newton was extremely conscientious and active in his work for the Mint. His zealous hunt for clippers and counterfeiters seems a strange occupation for the man who was the greatest physicist and mathematician the world had produced!

Raids on the Treasure Galleons

The most interesting coins of Queen Anne (1702-1714) are those which bear the word VIGO under the Queen's portrait. The story behind these coins is a fascinating one.

In 1702, during the War of the Spanish Succession—known in Colonial America as Queen Anne's War—a combined English and Dutch fleet raided the Spanish cities of Cadiz and Vigo. In Vigo harbor they ran into Spanish galleons that had just arrived with the annual treasure shipment from Peru and Mexico. The raiders seized no less than 11,000,000 pieces of eight which were brought to England and melted down.

All coins made with this silver carry the name "VIGO." This applies also to guineas coined with gold that was part of these shipments. A few of the coins are dated 1702, the majority date from 1703.

But this is not the whole story! Helpless as far as resistance was concerned, the

Spaniards had the doubtful satisfaction of cuttling some of their galleons, sending $150,000,000 worth of gold, silver, and precious stones to the bottom of the sea. For all anyone knows, this vast treasure is still there.

During the reign of George II (1727-1760), Admiral Anson brought back another sizable haul in 1744. The scene of Anson's wartime exploit was the Pacific, where he relieved the Spanish galleons of some $3,000,000 worth of gold and silver. The vessels were loaded with shipments from Lima in Peru. The guineas and silver coins struck by the Mint from this metal contain the inscription "LIMA."

Picturesque Designs

Among the most picturesque reverses on English coins are those featuring the coat of arms of the United Kingdom. On some coins of Charles II, for instance, we find four shields surrounding the Star of the Order of the Garter. (This is the highest order of knighthood in England, dating back to 1348.) In the shields are three leopards (England), fleur-de-lis or lilies (France), a harp (Ireland), and a rampant lion (Scotland). One of the most famous George III coins is the "spade" guinea. The name comes from the spade-shaped shield on the reverse of the coin.

It was not until 1801 that the Kings of England gave up their ancient claim to the French throne. Consequently, from that year on, English coins no longer show the lilies of France on the reverses.

Plate 183. Silver shilling (1703). *Obverse:* Queen Anne with "VIGO" inscription.

Plate 184. Copper twopenny (1797). *Obverse:* George III. The famous "Cartwheel," so called because it was unusually large and heavy.

When George I became King of England in 1714, the reverses of his new coins included the Hanoverian coat of arms as a compliment to his native Electorate of Hanover in Germany. The obverses of some of his coins have the initials SSC (South Sea Company) for the organization that supplied South American silver to the Royal Mint.

Coin Shortages

The reign of George III was a very long one (1760-1820). The period includes two of the most crucial events in English history —the American Revolution and the Napoleonic Wars. Silver was scarce even before the beginning of George III's reign, and in wartime there is always an added need for money. (We have seen this to be true at least as far back as Rome's wars with Carthage.) Copper became so expensive that very little of it went to the Mint.

There was still another reason for this shortage of money. During the second half of the eighteenth century, more and more people were leaving the countryside and coming to the city in search of work. In the country these people had lived more or less self-sufficiently, with little use for money. In the city, they received wages and spent them for food and other necessities. Hence the need for a much greater supply of money.

Plate 185. William IV, silver crown (1831). *Reverse:* crowned shield. A rare coin, but the same magnificent *reverse* on a sixpence costs only about $1.00.

Unfortunately, England's home supply of silver was nearing exhaustion by the turn of the century. After the 1758 issue of silver coins, no new ones were to appear for 30 years. The large issue of shillings in 1787 was due to a temporary fall in the price of silver.

Despite the shortage of copper, the first halfpence of George III appeared in 1770. They were anything but handsome, and a coin collector named Pinkerton took it very much to heart. "The first halfpence present such a face as human being never wore, jutting out something in the likeness of a macaw," he fumed.

Coinage During the Napoleonic Wars

By 1797 the shortage of silver had become so desperate that the Bank of England began to buy large quantities of Spanish pieces of eight. Most of these coins, bearing the portrait of Charles III or Charles IV of Spain, came from the New World mints at Mexico City, Potosi, and Lima.

Plate 186. George III, silver Bank of England dollar (1804). *Reverse:* seated Britannia.

In England the Royal Mint countermarked these large coins with a tiny image of George III. This touched off the following peppery comment:

The Bank, to make their Spanish dollar pass
Stamped the head of a fool on the head of an ass.

Plate 187. George III, silver dollar (1800). *Obverse:* counterstamp on Spanish piece of eight (Charles IV).

For some reason, counterfeiters delighted in imitating these coins. To foil them, the Mint decided to completely overstrike the coin. The result was the famous Bank of England Dollar, issued in 1804. It pictures Britannia on the obverse, and instead of a royal crown the coin carries a wall design, reminding us of a chess piece—a rook or castle. Perhaps the wall was intended to suggest the solidity for which the Bank of England is famous.

For some years there was quite a bit of gold coinage. But by 1799, with the struggle against Napoleon in full force, it became too risky to bring in gold bullion from overseas. The Royal Mint stopped issuing guineas, breaking its rule for one exception—in 1813, when it struck enough guineas to pay the soldiers in the army fighting in Spain and Portugal.

Counterfeiting became a more serious problem than ever during this period. Counterfeiting gold and silver coins was treason, punishable by death or transportation to a colony with an unhealthy climate. But counterfeiting copper coins was only a misdemeanor. So the counterfeiters took to the copper coins with real enthusiasm.

They cleverly substituted their own mottoes and legends for the official versions used on honest coins. In this way they could even claim that their coins were not counterfeits! In an age when many people were still unable to read, their coins readily passed for the real thing.

The Industrial Revolution

We are often told that James Watt invented the steam engine. Of course, this is not true. It was Hero of Alexandria, who lived in the first century B.C., who invented what was probably the first steam engine. However, to the ancients, this marvelously ingenious device was just a toy. With millions of slaves at their disposal, they had no use for machinery.

Therefore, in the seventeenth century there was a real need for an engine that could turn wheels. Men were working on a steam engine not only in England, but in Italy, France, and Germany as well.

For years James Watt, a Glasgow instrument maker, had been working on a steam engine. There is a story that as a child he was fascinated by the sight of steam coming out of a teakettle. He held a spoon near it, and watched the steam condense—form into drops of water. Apparently it was an experience he never forgot. By 1769 Watt, hitting on the idea of separating the engine from the boiler, perfected a steam engine that was safer, more efficient, more reliable, and cheaper to operate than any other steam engine seen up to that time.

One more invention was needed for the

***Plate 188.* John Wilkinson, halfpenny token (1788). *Reverse:* man working at a forge.**

Age of Steam—steam-propelled vessels. We associate the steamboat with the name of Robert Fulton, but like Watt and Stephenson, he was only the man who came at the end of a long line of inventors. Fulton's *Clermont* proved successful in 1807; three years earlier, when Fulton was in Paris, he tried to interest Napoleon Bonaparte in his steamboat and in another invention of his that seemed altogether absurd—a torpedo. At that time, Napoleon was planning a Channel invasion of England, and both devices should have fascinated him. Instead, he foolishly turned them down, and thus saved England from a great disaster.

In all these uses of steam, coal was all-important. But coal had other applications. Before the Industrial Revolution, iron was used sparingly, because it comes out of the earth full of impurities. Coal made it possible to purify the iron ore in blast furnaces and thereby replace wood with iron to construct more accurate and more durable

***Plate 189.* Parys Mines Company, halfpenny token (1791). *Obverse:* Druid in a wreath of oak. In olden times Anglesea, where this token was issued, was famous for its Druids (ancient Celtish priests).**

machines. How long it took for iron to come into general use may be seen from the fact the first iron plow was not patented until 1797.

Coal also made it possible to give cities adequate night lighting for the first time in history. Gas light using illuminating gas, which is a by-product of coal distillation, was introduced in London in 1807.

Coinage and the Industrial Revolution

It is no wonder that in view of the difficulties of obtaining metals on a large scale, the British began to rely to a considerable extent on paper money. However, the process of coining was greatly improved during the Industrial Revolution.

During the early part of the eighteenth century, the Royal Mint had used a hand-operated screw-press. As Peter Seaby explains, "the screw-press had the lower die fixed to its base, while the upper die moved up and down in guide plates at the lower end of the screw shaft. Two arms with heavy weights at the ends were fixed to the top of the screw. A team of laborers heaved on the thongs attached to the ends of the arms, thus spinning the loaded screw and trussel* down on to a coin blank which was placed on the lower die by a boy crouching in a well on the floor.

"The screw was taken back to the top of the press by the force of the rebound, and this gave the boy time to flick the coin away and to center another blank on top of the lower die. The manually operated screw-press could strike between 20 and 25 coins a minute."

* Reverse die.

Plate 190. Halfpenny token (undated): *reverse.* This beautiful lettering appears on one of the many tokens issued during the eighteenth century by a London coin dealer named Skidmore.

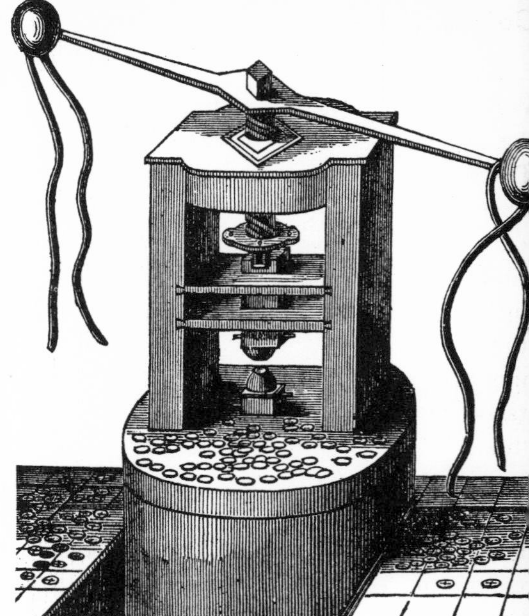

Plate 191. This drawing of an eighteenth-century screw-press appears in Peter Seaby's *The Story of the English Coinage.*

In 1774, as we have seen, James Watt began manufacturing his steam engine. Power from steam greatly speeded up the output of coins; it also struck them more accurately.

Watt worked with Matthew Boulton to make the first steam-driven coin press. By 1790 they were able to work eight presses with a single steam engine, producing 50 large or 150 small coins per minute.

Once more the Mint officials were slow in admitting the value of new techniques. Not until 1797 did Boulton get his contract for striking new coins for the Mint. His first efforts were the famous "Cartwheels" mentioned earlier. These coins got their nickname from their unusual size and weight.

;oinage Reform

Finally, at the end of the Napoleonic Wars, there was a thorough overhauling of he coinage system in the years 1816-1818. The Royal Mint at last adopted steam-lriven presses for all its coinage. Private okens were outlawed. The "sovereign" (20 hillings) replaced the guinea (21 shill-ngs). The country went on the gold tandard. This meant that only gold coins ıad the full metal content equal to their tated value. Silver coins became mere 'token" coins, with less metal than their tated value.

New coins appeared in all denomina-ions. The most famous feature was the new everse of St. George and the Dragon, lesigned by Benedetto Pistrucci. St. George s believed to have been a soldier of the Eastern Roman Empire who was executed n 304 during the persecutions of Diocle-ian. He was revered as the patron saint of oldiers, and later adopted by the Crusaders

'late 192. George III, copper twopenny (1797). *Reverse:* seated Britannia. This is the everse of the coin pictured on Plate 184.

'late 193. George IV, silver shilling (1825). Reverse: lion upon crown, with rose, thistle, ınd shamrock below. A very handsome coin.

Plate 194. Gold 2 pounds (1902). *Obverse:* Edward VII. *Reverse:* St. George slaying the dragon (a copy of Benedetto Pistrucci's famous design of 1816).

as their saint. He became the official patron saint of Britain in the fourteenth century.

The Victorian Age

The English were shamefully slow—almost as slow as we Americans—to give women the right to vote. Yet the two greatest ages in British history were when queens ruled England—the Elizabethan Age and the Victorian Age.

It was in the nineteenth century that England attained her greatest prosperity and prestige, and the British Empire its greatest power. The British Navy was supreme; England was "the workshop of the world," her foreign commerce and investments exceeded those of any other country.

During Victoria's remarkably long reign of 65 years some interesting coins appeared. In 1839, two years after she came to the throne, the charming "young-head" coins were struck. William Wyon, the Mint engraver, prepared a pattern for the five-pound gold piece, but this coin was never issued. A rare item, it is famous for the interesting reverse which pictures the Queen as a graceful young girl guiding the British lion with her scepter.

In 1847 a new crown (five-shilling piece) was struck to celebrate the tenth year of Victoria's reign. This coin, known as the "Gothic" crown, is considered one of the handsomest examples of English coinage.

Many collectors are familiar with this coin, but may not know how it got its name. In nineteenth-century England, business and trade were all-important and life seemed humdrum in comparison to the romantic days of the Middle Ages. People of the Victorian Age delighted in reading about the glamorous past, in such novels as Sir Walter Scott's *Ivanhoe*.

"Gothic" was the key-word for everything medieval, hence the name of this coin. Its inscription is in the old Gothic script, and the Queen's gown, elegantly jeweled and embroidered in the medieval style, is surrounded by an elaborately patterned edge. For the first time in almost 200 years, an English monarch appeared with a crown. (This pun on the name of the coin is repeated in later British coinage.)

In 1849, influenced by the example of France and the United States, England decided to experiment with decimal coinage. The result was a two-shilling piece called a "florin" (one-tenth of a pound or sovereign).

Despite its good-looking appearance, this coin created a minor scandal, and soon had to be withdrawn. It lacked the phrase *Dei gratia* or its abbreviation D.G. ("by the grace of God"). To the British, this omission was as disturbing as the omission of "In God We Trust" would be to Americans. Known as the "Godless" florin, it was replaced in 1851 by a florin with "D.G."

Although all these coins portray the Queen as a young woman, they were not replaced until 1887 (her Golden Jubilee) when she was close to 70. In that year the "Jubilee Head" coin appeared, a portrait that is gloomy but impressive—a fine character study. Some coins of this issue have Pistrucci's famous St. George and the Dragon on the reverse.

Plate 195. **Gold medal (1887). *Obverse:* Queen Victoria. *Reverse:* Victoria enthroned before allegorical figures representing the arts and sciences. Issued to commemorate the fiftieth year of Victoria's reign.**

It was during Victoria's reign, as we have seen, that England and the British Empire reached their highest stage of power and prosperity. It is significant that during this period there was no talk of shortages in metal or coinage. Even gold was in more than ample supply.

Plate 196. Silver crown (1845). *Obverse:* Victoria. The "young head" crown.

Plate 197. Silver crown (1847). *Obverse:* Victoria. The famous "Gothic" crown.

Plate 198. Silver crown (1887-1892). *Obverse:* Victoria. Issued to commemorate the fiftieth year of her reign.

Plate 199. Victoria, gold 5 pound pattern (1839). *Reverse:* Una and lion. Una (literally "the one") representing Truth, is the heroine of the first book of *The Faerie Queene* written by Edmund Spenser and published in 1590.

Plate 200. Silver florin (1849). *Obverse:* Victoria. The famous "Godless" florin, lacking the inscription *Dei gratia* or its abbreviation "D.G."

Twentieth-century Coinage

In the present century, war and its aftermath have considerably influenced British coinage. Since 1914, for example, the Mint has issued no gold coins for general circulation; maintaining the country's gold reserves has been a vital problem. During World War I the Treasury withdrew gold coins from circulation and replaced them with currency.

Silver was also scarce. As a result of wartime shortages, the price of the metal rose to a point where bullion was more valuable than the same amount of silver in a coin. There was only one way out—a radical debasing of the shilling. The traditional sterling silver ratio—925 grains of silver to 75 grains of copper—was reduced to 50 grains of silver to 50 grains of copper.

For the crown issued on the occasion of George V's Silver Jubilee, British coinage went "modern"—a sleek, streamlined St. George in armor crushes a modernistic dragon. It is a very pleasing coin, interesting to compare with Pistrucci's St. George and with the mounted figure of James I issued more than 300 years ago.

One of the great rarities of modern British coinage is the 1933 penny. Only six of these coins are supposed to have been issued, and according to official sources they are all accounted for—three are in museum collections, the rest under the foundation stones of public buildings. But of course collectors can always hope that somewhere, some time, more of these coins will turn up!

World War II brought a further debasement of the silver coinage—in fact, its complete disappearance. In 1947 the "silver" coinage was changed to 75 per cent copper, 25 per cent nickel. The postwar coinage has some interesting motifs—Sir Francis Drake's *Golden Hind*, for example, on the threepenny piece. The splendid commemorative crown for the 1951 Festival of Britain featured a fine head of George VI and for the reverse, the Pistrucci St. George. Equally attractive are the 1953 Coronation coins for the reign of Elizabeth II.

Plate 202. Copper-nickel (1953). *Obverse* Elizabeth II. Coronation crown.

Plate 201. Silver crown (1935). *Obverse:* George V. *Reverse:* St. George slaying the dragon. Issued for the twenty-fifth year of the King's reign.

Maundy Money

We are told that on Maundy (Holy) Thursday—the day before Good Friday—Christ washed the feet of his disciples and commanded them to follow his example. ("Maundy" comes from the Latin *mandare*—"to order.")

Among pious Christians it became a custom for kings, nobles, and clergy to observe this day by washing the feet of beggars and poor people, and making them gifts of money, food and clothes. The first English King about whom we have reliable information as observing this picturesque custom is Edward II, who reigned early in the fourteenth century.

As time went on, more and more details dropped out of the ceremony. When George V presented the Maundy money in person in 1932, he was the first monarch to do so in well over 200 years. Maundy money is unusually small and comes in the following denominations: penny, twopence, threepence, and fourpence. The number of men and women receiving Maundy money equals the monarch's age. The amount of money also adds up to the monarch's age.

Plate 203. Edward VII, silver Maundy money (1902). *Reverses:* crown over value for fourpence, threepence, twopence, and penny.

Thus, at the Coronation of Elizabeth II in 1953 when she was 27, she gave 27 men and 27 women each 27 pence in Maundy money. The Royal Mint issues separate sets for collectors.

The Isle of Man

One of the British Empire's most curious coinages is that of the Isle of Man. Located in the Irish Sea, the island has an area of about 220 square miles and a population of some 50,000.

Among numismatists this island is famous for the device of the triquetra which appears on most of its coins. What is a triquetra? It is a "three-legged device of booted and spurred human legs bent at the knee as though running, and joined at the hip to form a radiating design."

Even more remarkable is the story of the design, which goes back to Athenian coins of 600 B.C. From Athens the triquetra spread to the Greek colonies in Sicily. When King Alfred III of Scotland became King of Man in 1266, his wife, sister of the Queen of Sicily, introduced the device to the island.

Plate 204. Isle of Man, copper penny (1839). *Reverse:* triquetra.

Before that time, Man had been under Roman, Irish, and Scandinavian rule. Subsequently the English annexed the island. In 1405, Henry IV of England made a present of the Isle of Man to his favorite, the Earl of Derby. Much later, in 1736, the island passed to the Duke of Athol. (The triquetra coinage had started in 1709.) In 1765 the British government paid £70,000 for a part interest in the island, and in 1829 took complete title with a further payment of £133,000.

Plate 205. London, farthing token (about 1780). *Obverse:* elephant. One of a series issued by Pidcock, proprietor of a London menagerie.

Tokens

As we have seen, English coinage was often plagued by shortages until after the Napoleonic Wars. From about 1600 to about 1815 there was quite a bit of private coinage in the smaller denominations to take care of the need for small change. Most of these tokens appeared in London, but we find them also in smaller cities, market towns—even in villages and poorhouses!

For tradesmen, these tokens had the advantage that the customer would have to return to the same store to spend the change received in tokens. Sometimes the tokens were issued for advertising or political propaganda; some were struck by coin dealers. In appearance and design they are usually crude, but occasionally we find picturesque motifs with fairly interesting designs.

Ireland

The early history of the Celts in Ireland is swathed in delightful legends of warrior kings and their battles and councils. Legend has it that a lawmaking group gathered once a year in each of the kingdoms (originally five, later seven). Once the serious work was over, there was a pleasant folk festival with minstrels, poetry, and games. As far back as we can go in Irish history, these gifted people have been famous for their harpists and storytellers.

Reasonably safe from invasion, Ireland was the outpost of learning in northern Europe during the Dark Ages. The numerous monasteries provided a first-class education; in fact, they taught the ancient Greek language which was not revived in most of Europe until 1400.

With the ninth century there began the frightful period of Norse invasions coupled with intermittent civil war. The plundering and killing went on for four centuries. Finally, in 1172, England conquered the island, but only in a military sense.

Irish "Gun-money"

During the 700 years or so of English rule, Irish resentment continued to simmer and boil over at the slightest opportunity. Thus, when the English threw out the tyrannical James II in 1688, Ireland welcomed him with open arms. His attempt to regain the throne, squelched speedily enough, produced one of the most interesting oddities of coinage, the famous Irish "gun-money."

Arriving in Ireland in June, 1689, James immediately set about raising an army. In need of coinage to pay his troops, he issued emergency money made from cannons, church bells, and anything else that was suitable. Remarkably well executed considering the circumstances, these curious coins can be obtained at quite reasonable prices.

Plate 206. Silver penny (989-1029). *Obverse:* Sihtric III. *Reverse:* cross with pellets in the angles. This is an imitation of the Saxon coin that appears on Plate 156.

Plate 207. Brass shilling (July 1689). *Obverse:* James II. *Reverse:* crown over crossed scepters. A coin of the fascinating "gun-money" series.

A strange feature of the "gun-money" coins is that they show not only the year, but the month of issue as well. In those days the year did not begin on January 1 but on March 25; consequently the coins dated March, 1690 were issued only a few days after the coins dated March, 1689! (The calendar we use now came into existence in the eighteenth century.) Here is the complete list of dates of "gun-money," in chronological order:

July, 1689
August, 1689
September, 1689
October, 1689
November, 1689
December, 1689
January, 1689
February, 1689
March, 1689
March, 1690
April, 1690
May, 1690
June, 1690

Modern Ireland

After the First World War, it became clear that England could continue her rule in Ireland only on a military basis. In December, 1921, following negotiations between the two countries, southern Ireland became the Irish Free State, while northern Ireland remained part of the United Kingdom.

Plate 208. Bronze halfpenny (1736). *Reverse:* crowned harp with figure of Hibernia (Ireland). Rarely does one find so lovely a design on a coin of the lower denominations.

Plate 209. Silver florin (1939). *Obverse:* harp. *Reverse:* salmon. One of the most attractive coins issued by Ireland.

Plate 210. Silver half crown (1928-1939). *Reverse:* horse. The Irish are noted for their keen interest in breeding fine horses.

About sixteen years later, the Free State became officially known as Eire. Its delightful coinage, as many collectors know, includes some of the handsomest coins of modern times. Here are the denominations:

Farthing	Woodcock	Bronze
Halfpenny	Sow and pigs	Bronze
Penny	Hen and chickens	Bronze
Threepence	Hare	Nickel
Sixpence	Wolfhound	Nickel
Shilling	Bull	Silver
Florin	Salmon	Silver
Half Crown	Horse	Silver

The above descriptions apply to the reverses. All the obverses display the famous Irish harp. Although the currency denominations were taken over from English coinage, Eire is no longer a member of the British Commonwealth.

Germany

William I, King of Prussia, was proclaimed Emperor of Germany in the famous Hall of Mirrors at Versailles in 1871. On that day Germany became a country instead of a loose confederation of Germanic states. For centuries these states had remained separate, with their own rulers, laws, taxes, armies, and coinage. The reasons for this split go far back in German history.

After Charlemagne's death early in the ninth century, his empire fell apart. The Kings of the Germans, in the eastern section of his empire, had a hard time maintaining their power over the feudal dukes who were technically their subordinates. A strong King was able to pass his rule on to his son or his designated heir. A weak King's death was followed by squabbles over the choice of his successor. Generally, this made for strong dukes and weak Kings. From time to time there were Kings of outstanding ability; but their successes were usually temporary.

One of these strong Kings, Otto I (936-973), revived Charlemagne's medieval Roman Empire in an attempt to give the German Kings more prestige. From 962 on, they had the title of Roman Emperor —*Kaiser,* the Germanized form of "Caesar."

For 300 years these Emperors fought with their nobles, wrangled with the Popes over state powers, and at the same time tried to subdue Italy, which was theoretically part of their Empire. The Emperors emerged from these struggles weaker than when they started. Their quarrels with the Popes left a lasting mark on German history and, some scholars feel, were one cause of the later German Reformation.

Frederick I (1152-1190), nicknamed Barbarossa (red beard), was the Emperor who changed the name of the Empire to *Holy* Roman Empire. He invaded Italy five times without success, but his conquests in Poland, Bohemia, and Hungary made him one of Germany's national heroes.

Generations of German children have been enthralled by the legend that Barbarossa, bewitched, sits in a mountain cave at a stone table, through which his beard

Plate 211. Brunswick, silver denarius bracteate (1142-1195). *Obverse:* Henry the Lion, Duke of Saxony and Bavaria, and a bitter rival of Frederick Barbarossa.

Plate 212. Frankfurt am Main, silver denarius bracteate (1152-1190). *Obverse:* Frederick Barbarossa, one of the most famous of the Holy Roman Emperors. He is idolized by German patriots.

has grown, ready to come forth to restore German greatness.

Bracteates

During the period 1120-1350 (the dates are approximate) coins later called bracteates were issued. The name of the coins comes from the Latin *bractea*—a thin piece of metal. The design on this paper-thin metal was incused—cut into the surface of one side. This created a pattern that pushed through to the other side. They were almost all of silver; a few, equally thin, were gold, debased silver, or copper.

Bracteates originated in Thuringia and Hesse in Germany. Though they were also issued in Bohemia, Hungary, Switzerland, Poland, and the Scandinavian countries, we associate the bracteates particularly with districts that were part of the medieval Holy Roman Empire.

At the time the bracteates were in use, they were known as denarii or pfennigs; it was not until the eighteenth century that they came to be called bracteates.

Though these coins were sometimes cut up into halves or quarters to make small change, they were too fragile to have been repeatedly used. Cities like Cologne, which had a large volume of trade, never issued bracteates. Another indication that the coins did not wear well is the fact that bracteate hoards usually have no more than a thirty-year maximum span between their earliest and latest date.

The figures on the bracteates are stylized—there is no attempt to produce a likeness of the person for whom the coin is named. For instance, the designers used a crown and a scepter to represent a King, a mitre and a crozier to indicate a bishop.

Barbarossa's grandson Frederick II (1211-1250), most remarkable by far of all the Holy Roman Emperors, was one of the truly fascinating figures of the Middle Ages. Through his Norman mother he also inherited the Kingdom of Sicily; this semi-tropical island and southern Italy were the two lands he loved best.

Frederick, called *Stupor mundi* ("the Wonder of the World"), was one of the most learned men of his day. Byzantine, Saracen, and Jewish scholars were welcome at his court, and he read widely in Arabic philosophy, science, mathematics, and literature. He spoke nine languages, including Greek and Latin. He wrote a treatise on hawking, one of the earliest scientific studies of animals, and he collected a menagerie of exotic animals that he took with him on his travels.

Despite all his studious interests, Frederick had time for brutal campaigning and

Plate 213. Nordhausen, silver denarius bracteate (1211-1250). *Obverse:* Frederick II (Barbarossa's grandson) and his Queen, Constance of Aragon. The stiff attitude of the figures may well reflect Byzantine influence dating from the Crusades to the Holy Land.

Plate 214. **Holy Roman Empire, gold augustale (1228).** ***Obverse:*** **laureated bust of Frederick II with draped tunic, in the style of the Roman Emperors.** ***Reverse:*** **the imperial Roman eagle, a symbol borrowed from the Greeks and later the most popular motif on American coins.**

devious diplomacy. His lifelong ambition to unite Italy and Germany into a stable Empire was defeated by the opposition of the Popes, the Italian towns, and the German nobles.

In Frederick's Italian realm the State managed most enterprises, including industries, large farms, and foreign trade. Southern Italy prospered, and Frederick's coinage was notably sound. His gold augustales picture Frederick as a Roman Emperor of ancient times. Experts consider these the finest examples of medieval coins.

At Frederick's death, Germany split again into many fractions. One hundred years later, Emperor Charles IV issued a proclamation (the Golden Bull of 1356) by which a constitution was established and the Empire became a federation of independent states. The Emperor was to be chosen by seven Electors: the Archbishops of Mainz, Trier, and Cologne; the Elector Palatine; the Duke of Saxony; the Margrave of Brandenburg; and the King of Bohemia. The Electors had the right to have their own courts and issue their own coinage.

The Holy Roman Empire endured until 1806, when it was swept out of existence during the Napoleonic wars. For a time, the Counts of Luxembourg provided several Emperors, but from 1438 on, all the Emperors were members of the Hapsburg family (see page 113).

The Hanseatic League

The numerous divisions of the Holy Roman Empire included "free cities." These communities paid the Emperor a handsome sum for the privilege of self-government and freedom from the control of envious princes. The free cities were extremely proud of their status, and were permitted to continue their coinage even after the unification of Germany.

One of the famous free cities was Lübeck, founded on the shores of the Baltic during the twelfth century by a group of German grain merchants. Lübeck prospered, for its port had a strategic location for handling east-west traffic along the Baltic. The city prided itself on the excellence of its coinage; we are told that only the coinage of Florence rated comparison.

In the thirteenth century, Lübeck began to band together with other cities to form the Hanseatic League, or Hanse. At its height the League had ninety member-cities, the majority of them German; it endured well into the seventeenth century.

Plate 215. **Lubeck, silver taler (1537).** ***Obverse:*** **knight kneeling with shield.** ***Reverse:*** **Charles V (Holy Roman Emperor).**

Plate 216. Luneberg, silver taler (1547). *Obverse:* city gate. *Reverse:* "man in the moon." Note the pun on the city's name and the Latin word for "moon" (luna).

The main job of the Hanseatic League was to control the exchange of raw materials from the north and east for finished goods from the south and west. It established codes of fair business practice which were binding on all Hanseatic merchants. Wherever necessary, the League brought suit in foreign countries for damages suffered by its members. It sent agents to study favorable possibilities for new markets. And—perhaps most important of all—it came to the aid of members in case of attack, and raised fleets to clear the Baltic of pirates.

The Hanse had branch offices all over Europe—including London, Venice, Bruges (Flanders), Bergen (Norway), Visby (Sweden), and Novgorod (Russia). The chief cities of the League, besides Lübeck, were Hamburg, Bremen, and Danzig.

The slow decline of the Hanse dates from the fifteenth century. The discovery of the New World, the growing importance of trade with the Indies, and England's steadily improving ability to process her own raw materials, all contributed to deprive the Hanse cities of a substantial part of their commerce.

Plate 217. Nuremberg, gold 6 ducats (1698). *Reverse:* view of Nuremberg, surmounted by the all-seeing eye of God, with the name "Jehovah" in Hebrew letters. *Obverse:* allegorical figure of Peace; cherubs below.

Plate 218. Cologne, silver taler (1516). *Obverse:* The Three Magi ("wise men of the East" who visited the Christ-child in the manger).

Martin Luther and the Reformation

In the days when Martin Luther was growing up (he lived from 1483 to 1546) the Church and the Popes were losing some of their influence. There were a great many reasons for this. There was the growing worldliness of some of the clergy. The rediscovery of the philosophy and literature of the ancient Greeks and Romans also played a major role in stimulating imaginations of scholars and teachers as it widened their horizons. Trade with distant countries, travels in strange lands, the exploration of the New World, a host of new inventions—all these had the same exhilarating effect. In Germany there was an additional reason: Germans were hostile to Rome—an attitude older than Christianity itself.

Luther had been an Augustinian monk for several years when he was sent on a mission to Rome in 1510. There he was horrified by some of the customs that had developed in the Church, such as the sale of Indulgences. These were Church documents granting the buyer forgiveness for his past sins. The money collected from the sale of Indulgences was used for building cathedrals, for running charities, and other worthy projects of the Church.

Whatever their purpose, Luther objected to Indulgences. He was a man of deep religious convictions, fervent in his faith, and not afraid to attack men in high places. He felt that a sinner had to do penance—submit to discipline and punishment for his misdeeds. Indulgences, said Luther, made the sinner's life too easy.

Plate 221. Saxony, silver taler (1717). *Reverse:* all-seeing eye of God, with forest below. Commemorates 200th year of the Reformation.

Plate 222. Saxony, silver taler (1717). *Reverse:* Martin Luther. Commemorates 200th year of the Reformation.

But it was not until 1517 that Luther's anger really exploded, and he brought his attack out into the open. A Dominican monk named John Tetzel was traveling through Germany selling Indulgences in order to raise money for the rebuilding of St. Peter's in Rome. Tetzel's methods infuriated Luther, who, in addition to his religious objections, saw no reason why Germans should pay for a cathedral located in Rome.

In his famous 95 Theses, Luther attacked the whole practice of Indulgences, and nailed the document to the door of the court church at Wittenberg. The following year, 1518, Luther was summoned to Augsburg and ordered to recant. He refused. As a result, his books were publicly burned in Cologne by order of the Holy Roman Emperor. The Church denounced him as a heretic and excommunicated him. In reply, Luther burned the Pope's bull (proclamation), as well as the volumes of Canon Law which set forth the supreme power of the Pope.

Plate 223. Worms, silver taler (1617). *Reverse:* open Bible, candlestick above. *Obverse:* lighthouse, city shield below. Commemorates centenary of the Reformation.

Charles V, the new Holy Roman Emperor, was deeply troubled by the daring of Luther's views and the extent of the support he was receiving in Germany. The Emperor ordered Luther to appear before the Diet (legislative council) which was to meet in the city of Worms, and gave him a safe-conduct pass which was scrupulously respected. Though well aware of the danger he was in, Luther resolutely stood his ground at the Diet session. He concluded, "I cannot do otherwise!" Thereupon he was declared an outlaw in all the domains of the Holy Roman Empire.

Now excommunicated and outlawed, Luther set out for home (his safe-conduct still had 20 days to run). On the way, he was "kidnaped" by Duke Frederick, the Elector of Saxony, and safely hidden away in one of the ducal castles. This duke, known to history as Frederick the Wise, was a pious man who had complete faith in Luther. Frederick not only sheltered Luther, but gave him a post at his university at Wittenberg where he could teach his doctrines. After Frederick's death, he was succeeded by his brother John the Constant, who also protected and aided Luther.

Luther wrote many pamphlets explaining his views and devoted ten years to translating the Bible into German. The translation gave his people their first chance to become thoroughly familiar with the contents of the Bible. Luther won a wide audience for his doctrines, and the beauty of his writing had a lasting effect on the development of the German language.

Reformation emphasis on Bible study was a powerful force for widening education. Without the existence of the printing press, the Reformation might have failed. It was the invention of printing that supplied the Bible for Luther's faithful followers and enabled Luther to make his views known to a wide audience.

Plate 224, left. Saxony, silver taler (1514).

Plate 225, above. Saxony, silver 3 marks (1917). Two vividly contrasting portraits of Luther's faithful friend and protector, Duke Frederick of Saxony.

Plate 226. Magdeburg, silver taler (1638). *Obverse:* Virgin Mary over the city gate. *Reverse:* Imperial eagle with bust of Emperor Ferdinand III. Commemorates rebuilding of city after destruction in Thirty Years' War.

Thirty Years' War

The German phase of this disastrous war was to a great extent a religious struggle between Catholics and Protestants. It lasted from 1618 to 1648, and was fought with barbaric ferocity. The troops that invaded Germany pillaged the towns and countryside in raids that led to famine and even cannibalism in some localities. One of the most horrifying incidents was the complete destruction of Magdeburg, with the exception of its cathedral. It was the sack of this city that induced Gustavus Adolphus, the King of Sweden, to come to the aid of the German Protestants (see page 150).

Ablest of the generals opposing the Protestants was Wallenstein, a brilliant leader, but an intensely ambitious and money-minded man. Though of noble birth, he had hired himself out to the Holy Roman Emperor as commander of a mercenary army on the promise of plenty of booty. Eventually the Emperor had Wallenstein assassinated on receiving reports that he was negotiating with the enemy.

By the time the Peace of Westphalia was signed in 1648, half of the German population was dead and the country was so devastated that it took a century to recover. The political power of Germany was broken for years to come, divided as

Plate 227. Brunswick, silver "Parson's foe" taler (1622). *Reverse:* celestial arm with sword.

Plate 228. Erfurt, silver "Purim" taler (1631). *Obverse:* celestial rays with the word "Purim" in Hebrew letters. (The Reformation had popularized the Old Testament and ancient Hebrew stories of struggle against tyranny. Purim is a joyous festival which commemorates one such Biblical victory.) *Reverse:* inscription commemorating the brilliant victory of Gustavus Adolphus in the battle of Breitenfeld.

the country now was into 350 parts. The wretchedness of the people was multiplied by a staggering inflation during which coins were shortweighted or else debased with a large proportion of copper.

German Talers

Until about 1530, when vast amounts of gold and silver began to pour into Europe from the New World, Germany and the Austrian dominions were the chief sources of Europe's precious metals. Extensive deposits of gold, copper, and silver had been discovered in Germany. The increased need for metal led to many improvements in mining techniques, and soon boom towns sprang up in Germany. One of the largest metal orders of the period was a Venetian purchase in 1496 of 80,000 pounds of copper for cannon.

The gold florin of Florence, first issued in 1252, was copied in Germany in the fourteenth and fifteenth centuries in a coin called the gulden ("golden"). During this period, the archbishops of Cologne and Mainz and the cities of Frankfurt am Main and Nuremberg seem to have issued most of the guldens. (These coins are also known as Rheinische Goldgulden.)

As time went on, the coins began to be alloyed with silver in ratios that left less and less gold in the gulden. The gradual exhaustion of Germany's gold mines hastened this process. Then came issues of silver coins that seem to have been in experimental small quantities. By 1500, however, they were becoming established as regular coinage under the name of Guldengroschen.

Plate 230. Palatinate, silver taler (1624). *Obverse:* Wolfgang Wilhelm, who reigned as Count from 1614 to 1653.

Plate 229. Wallenstein, silver taler (1632). *Obverse:* Albrecht Wenzel Eusebius von Wallenstein, Duke of Friedland. *Reverse:* coat of arms within chain of the Golden Fleece.

The silver coins struck at Joachimsthal in Bohemia about 1518-1525 acquired an enormous vogue (see Plate 258). First known as "Joachimsthalers," the coins soon had their name shortened to "thalers." (The modern spellings are "Joachimstal" and "taler.")

The silver taler seems to have been just right as to size, weight, and metal content. It was copied all over Europe and in the New World, where it became the Spanish dollar ("Piece of eight"). Much later, after the United States came into existence, the American Dollar followed the taler tradition.

Plate 231. Brunswick, broad silver "Good luck" $1\frac{1}{4}$ taler (about 1630). *Obverse:* four fields with Neptune on dolphin, heron baiting, mine, alchemy. *Reverse:* Fortuna (goddess of good luck or chance) with sail.

Plate 232. Loewenstein, silver taler (1697). *Obverse:* tree with fruit and dead tree, each with ribbon. *Reverse:* coat of arms.

Plate 233. Brunswick, silver "Triple" taler (1617). *Obverse:* Duke Friedrich Ulrich on horseback. *Reverse:* coat of arms. One of the most impressive of the many distinguished coins issued by this duchy.

The German states are famous for the huge volume of their taler coinage. Many of these coins commemorate outstanding events, such as battles and peace treaties; others were issued for the weddings or deaths of minor princes. Quite a few were issued by petty states as a matter of local pride.

Collectors prize the talers for their generally admirable workmanship and masterly portrait heads. Some talers are notable for lavish showing of detail. In a few cases the artist designed outsize coins, much bigger than the taler, because he needed room for all the details that went into his composition.

Rise of Prussia

The heartland and the historical core of the Kingdom of Prussia was the province of Brandenburg, a flat, sandy region with no natural barriers against invasion. The centuries-long struggle of the Prussian Junkers with the peoples of eastern Europe developed the harsh spirit of duty and discipline for which the Prussians have always been noted. Under the rule of the Hohenzollern family from 1417 on, Brandenburg slowly expanded until, at the beginning of the eighteenth century, its rulers took the title of "King of Prussia."

It was Frederick II ("the Great") who made Prussia a great European power and transformed the Prussian army into a force feared by the rest of Europe. Inheriting a well-trained army and an ample treasury, he snatched Silesia from Austria in 1740 without any justification; invaded Saxony in 1756 without warning or provocation; and engineered the first partition of Poland in 1772. Thus Frederick set the pattern for later Prussian or German lightning invasions ("blitzkriegs") of nearby countries.

King George II of England described

Plate 235. Corvey (Westphalian abbey), broad silver taler (1683). *Reverse:* St. Vitus.

Frederick as "a mischievous rascal, a bad friend, a bad ally, a bad relation, and a bad neighbor, in fact the most dangerous and ill-disposed prince in Europe." He was all these things, but he was also a military genius, as he proved in the Seven Years' War when he held out successfully against a coalition of France, Austria, Russia, and Sweden. Paradoxically, Frederick despised the Germans and the German language—his preferred language was French and his favorite palace had a French name.

After Frederick's reign (1740-1786) the Prussian military machine weakened and was no match for Napoleon's armies. However, a great national revival soon revitalized the army, and with the help of other German forces it took part in the Battle of Leipzig in 1813—the "Battle of the Nations" which assured Napoleon's downfall.

In the period after the Napoleonic wars, Prussia was the leading power in the German Confederation, a loose group of 38 German states. Napoleon had not only aroused German nationalist feeling; he had stimulated the unification of Germany by wiping out a great many principalities. This unification took time, because Prussia wanted to be the supreme power in the new Germany. The other states did not want to lose their powers, and were fearful of coming under Prussian domination.

Plate 236. Saxony, silver "8 Brothers" taler (1610-1615). Duke Johann Ernst and his brothers (four facing figures on *obverse*, four more on *reverse*).

Plate 237. Brunswick, silver taler (1636). *Obverse:* Duke August holding helmet. *Reverse:* his brothers Frederick and George.

Plate 238. Brunswick, silver quadruple "Mining" taler (1685). *Obverse:* lute player on shell before city and landscape. Note celestial rays and all-seeing eye of God with Hebrew letters. *Reverse:* coat of arms with five crests. One of the most striking of the many ornate coins of this duchy.

Plate 239. Prussia, silver "Levantine" taler (1767). *Obverse:* Frederick the Great. This coin was intended for trading in the Levant.

After three quickly victorious wars, the Prussians had their way. In 1864 they took Schleswig and Holstein from the Danes; in 1866 they defeated Austria in seven weeks, removing their last rival for German domination; and in 1870-1871 they defeated France. All the German states took part in this war, under an agreement whereby they turned over their armies to Prussian leadership but retained their other powers.

At the end of the Franco-Prussian War, the various states formed the German Empire, with the King of Prussia becoming the German Emperor (Kaiser). From the beginning, the new Germany nursed plans of world domination which failed in two World Wars.

From 1919 to 1933 the Germans had a republic which was not destined for survival. The disastrous inflation of 1919-1923 wiped out the savings of millions of

Plate 241. Prussia, silver 3 marks (1913). *Obverse:* Kaiser Wilhelm II. Issued to commemorate the 25th year of his reign.

Plate 240. Saxony, silver 3 marks (1913). *Obverse:* Leipzig monument of the "Battle of the Nations." Centenary commemoration.

Germans; the world depression of the early 1930's created widespread unemployment, and political fanaticism did the rest. During its short life, the Weimar Republic issued some handsome commemorative coins which for the most part were refreshingly free of nationalistic themes.

Plate 242. Saxony, aluminum 1,000,000 marks (1923). *Obverse:* ironworker. *Reverse:* value and coat of arms of Saxony. Necessity coinage of the inflation period.

Plate 243. Saxony, gilded bronze, 5,000,000 marks (1923). *Obverse:* man representing Germany turns his empty pocket inside out while the other hand is extended to beg. *Reverse:* value with satirical mottoes. This incuse necessity coin was also issued during the German inflation.

Plate 245. Weimar Republic, silver 3 marks (1927). *Obverse:* two figures reminiscent of old bracteate style, as in *Plate 213*. Commemorates thousandth anniversary of the founding of Nordhausen.

Plate 246. Weimar Republic, silver 3 marks (1928). *Obverse:* medieval sculpture. Commemorates thousandth anniversary of the founding of Dinkelsbuhl.

Plate 247. Weimar Republic, silver 3 marks (1928). *Obverse:* Albrecht Durer, Germany's greatest artist. This coin commemorates the 400th anniversary of his death.

Plate 248. Weimar Republic, silver 3 marks (1932). *Obverse:* Johann Wolfgang von Goethe, Germany's greatest writer. This coin commemorates the centenary of his death.

In 1933 the National Socialist Party put an end to the Republic. The Nazis, under Adolf Hitler, replaced the Republic with a dictatorship. After six years of large-scale war preparations, threats, invasions, and persecutions, the Nazis were ready for World War II. Allied with Italy and Japan, they failed by a narrow margin to win worldwide domination.

Although Hitler appears on many postage stamps of the Nazi era, there are no coins with his likeness.

In 1953 Germany is again dismembered. The former East Prussia has been annexed by Poland and the Soviet Union, though the finality of this seizure is disputed by the Western Allies. Germany proper is divided into a German Federal Republic (made up of the American, British and French zones). The eastern portion, under Soviet influence, is called the "German Democratic Republic." Berlin is under the control of all four occupying powers.

Plate 249. Weimar Republic, silver 3 marks (1929). *Obverse:* President Paul von Hindenburg. *Reverse:* uplifted fingers pledging "loyalty to the Constitution." Struck for the tenth anniversary of the Weimar Constitution.

Plate 250. German Federal Republic, bronze over steel 10 pfennig (1950). *Obverse:* wheat ears.

Plate 251. German Democratic Republic, aluminum 50 pfennig. *Obverse:* factory, with plow in foreground.

The Austrian Empire

An obscure Swiss family, named Hapsburg for its home, Habichtsburg ("hawk's castle"), first appeared in history about 900. By a long-term policy of advantageous marriages to royalty, the family kept adding to its holdings.

Rudolf I was the first Hapsburg to be elected Holy Roman Emperor—in 1273. Thereafter the family rose steadily in power and prestige. Gradually the Hapsburgs joined together a number of districts to form Austria, of which they became the hereditary Archdukes. Some of them were elected Kings of Bohemia and Hungary, and in time the Hapsburgs incorporated both of these countries into their empire.

From 1438 on, the Holy Roman Emperor was always a Hapsburg. But the heyday of the Hapsburgs arrived when they intermarried with the ruling family of Spain. Through his Hapsburg father and Spanish mother, Charles V in 1516 inherited the rule of Spain, Austria, the Netherlands (modern Holland and Belgium), Burgundy, and parts of Italy, as well as colonies in Africa and the Mediterranean, and the enormous colonial empire of Spain in the New World.

He was also elected Holy Roman Emperor, in what has been described as "the biggest business deal of the century—in fact, of many centuries."

Never before had so much widespread power been concentrated in one man. But power can be a burden, and to hold together the top-heavy Empire taxed his abilities. Charles V is represented on many coins, and on all of them he looks weary.

Plate 252. Donauwerth, silver taler (1548). *Obverse:* Charles V, most powerful of all the Hapsburgs.
Plate 254. See frontispiece.

Plate 253. Holy Roman Empire, silver "Three Emperor" taler (1590). *Obverse:* starting from left, Maximilian I and his grandsons Charles V and Ferdinand I. *Reverse:* Imperial double eagle. Struck at Joachimstal.

Plate 256. **Salzburg, gold 24 ducats (1727-1744).** ***Obverse:*** **Archbishop Leopold Anton Eleutherius, Baron of Firmian.** ***Reverse:*** **amazingly detailed view of Salzburg. There are said to be only two specimens of this remarkable coin.**

As early as 1522, he placed his energetic brother Ferdinand I in charge of the eastern part of the Empire. For years Ferdinand led the Catholics in the early struggles with the Lutheran princes, and disputed the Turkish conquest of Hungary.

After forty years, in 1556, Charles V voluntarily gave up the throne, entrusting the Spanish Empire to his son Philip II and the Hapsburg domains to his brother Ferdinand I. After abdicating, Charles V, broken in health and in spirit, retired to a monastery where he died two years later.

For years the Hapsburg territories were menaced by the Turks. Suleiman the Magnificent, greatest of the Sultans, conquered a large part of Hungary in 1526, and the Turks were not driven out until 1699. Ferdinand I actually had to pay tribute to the Turks for the small part of Hungary left to him. But he had the satisfaction of repulsing Suleiman's siege of Vienna in 1529. As late as 1683, the Turks made another attempt to take Vienna; they might have succeeded but for Jan Sobieski, King of Poland, who saved the city. (Page 156.)

Plate 257. **Fugger, silver taler (1694).** ***Obverse:*** **family coat of arms.**

The Power Behind the Throne

Behind the Emperor's throne was the Fugger family of merchant princes, whose outstanding member was Jacob Fugger (1459-1525). As a young man Jacob had wanted to study for the Catholic priesthood, but went instead into the family business which he developed enormously. As a result, he eventually became the richest man in sixteenth-century Europe, and one of the most influential men of his day.

The Fuggers' business interests brought them an annual average profit of 55 per cent. Their wealth was estimated in 1546 at 6,000,000 gulden—roughly $100,000,000 in modern money. More powerful than royalty, the Fuggers had the right to issue their own coinage.

Their silver mines in the Tyrolean and Carinthian regions of Austria netted them 200,000 gulden a year. Their control of the Hungarian and Bohemian mines yielded another 30,000 gulden a year—at a time when a nobleman was considered well off if his income amounted to 4,000 gulden a year! It is said that the Joachimstal mines in Bohemia—the source of the famous

Joachimstaler—were part of the Fugger mining empire. So great was the power of the Fuggers that at one time they cornered the German market in copper. When the Hapsburgs inherited Spain, the Fuggers acquired that country's valuable quicksilver mines, which had enriched the Romans many centuries earlier.

Jacob Fugger was called *Rex denariiorum*—"the money-king." His powerful banking firm, with seventeen foreign branches, was indispensable to the Hapsburgs in their wars. The Fuggers had their own fleet, their own news-gathering service. The business was always kept in the family. The Fuggers owned castles, vast estates, and priceless art collections. They outfitted many of the expeditions of the Conquistadores to the New World, and their huge loans to Spain and Portugal gave them a "mortgage" on the Spanish treasure fleets from New Spain and Portugal's fabulously valuable spice shipments from the Indies.

Kings were poor indeed, compared to the Fuggers. When Charles V's grandfather, Maximilian I, arranged the weddings of his grandchildren, Jacob Fugger put up the dowries and lent his gold dishes for a state banquet; he even provided jewels for the members of the Hapsburg court.

It was also Jacob Fugger who raised huge funds for bribing the Holy Roman Electors to choose Charles V. And yet, for all his wealth and power, Jacob Fugger was never accepted as a social equal by "the best people" of Augsburg, his home town.

Plate 258. Counts Schlick, silver Joachimstaler (1525). *Obverse:* St. Joachim. This coin, the earliest taler, became the model for all taler or "dollar" coins.

In the early part of the eighteenth century, it seemed that the Hapsburg line would come to an end. Charles VI (1711-1740) had no sons, and his daughter Maria Theresa was excluded from the succession by law. To make it possible for her to inherit the throne, Charles VI had to get the approval of his fellow monarchs of Europe. With one exception (the Elector of Bavaria, a claimant to the Austrian throne) they solemnly agreed to recognize her as the Holy Roman Empress.

However, as soon as Maria Theresa became Empress, an alliance of France,

Plate 259. Holy Roman Empire, silver "Wedding" taler (1479). *Obverse:* Maximilian I, Holy Roman Emperor from 1493 to 1519. *Reverse:* his bride Marie of Burgundy, who brought extensive lands into the Hapsburg domain. This coin was struck to celebrate their marriage.

Bavaria, Spain, Saxony, and Prussia was formed to dismember Austria. Frederick the Great of Prussia seized Silesia as his share of the spoils. The French captured Prague, while Bavarians attacked Vienna.

Maria Theresa fought back with the help of her Hungarian subjects and drove out her enemies. Though her right to the throne was accepted, Silesia was permanently lost. Her reign lasted from 1740 to 1780.

Maria Theresa Talers

These talers, first issued in 1780, are among the most famous coins in the world, and their popularity has continued to the present day. They acquired a vogue all over the Levant, the Middle East, and north and east Africa, particularly Ethiopia.

They were so popular that up to recent times natives of these countries refused to accept any other coin.

The Austrian Republic continued to issue the Maria Theresa talers long after the abdication of the last Hapsburg Emperor, but, strangely, all Maria Theresa talers have been dated 1780 regardless of the year they were minted.

Some scholars have devoted an enormous amount of study to these coins. It is said that they can discern minute differences so accurately that they can readily determine the period of any taler.

Plate 261. Esterhazy, silver taler (1770). *Obverse:* Prince Nicolaus Esterhazy is remembered as the patron of one of the greatest of all composers—Joseph Haydn.

Production of these coins has also been credited to the mints at London, Brussels, San Francisco, and Bombay. Italy issued Maria Theresa talers for use in Ethiopia after its conquest of that country in the 1930's.

Decline of the Hapsburg Empire

Austria took heavy losses in the Napoleonic wars, and the Holy Roman Empire came to an end in 1806. Yet the Hapsburgs were still left with sizable domains. They controlled a large number of Magyars, Czechs, Italians, Ruthenians, Poles, Slovaks, Croats, Rumanians, and Slovenes.

To administer such a patchwork domain was a formidable task. Aside from the inner tensions, there were also outside pressures. France wanted to take the Italian provinces. Prussia's ambition was to exclude Austria from any participation in the

Plate 262. Austria, silver taler (1780). *Obverse:* Maria Theresa. *Reverse:* coat of arms. The coin illustrated here was struck in the twentieth century—despite its date!

affairs of the German states. Russia was the self-appointed protector of all the Slavs in the Austrian and Turkish Empires. Turkey, though a declining force, was tenaciously holding on to its Balkan territories.

The Austrian government was slow-moving, narrow-minded, and behind the times. The Hungarians, for example, had to clamor until well into the nineteenth century for the right to conduct their parliament sessions in Magyar instead of Latin. The nobility and civil service resisted reform because they feared that the slightest change might upset the delicate balance of the Empire.

Austria's loss of her Italian territories and her humiliating defeat at the hands of Prussia in 1866 placed a glaring light on the weakness of the Empire. The following year the Dual Monarchy came into existence, giving Hungary a separate government on an equal footing with Austria. Both continued under Franz Joseph, with joint departments for finance, foreign affairs, and war. But, in all other respects they were independent of each other.

The Empire contained millions of Serbs, Croats, and Slovenes who longed to be united with their kinsmen in Serbia. In time, Austria's relations with Serbia became more and more strained. The discon-

Plate 263. Austria, silver 2 gulden (1887). *Obverse:* Franz Joseph. *Reverse:* St. Barbara's Cathedral in Vienna. This exquisitely executed coin was struck to commemorate the reopening of the Kuttenberg silver mines, which had been worked at least as far back as the sixteenth century.

Plate 265. Austria, silver 2 talers (1857). *Reverse:* Lighthouse. This beautiful coin commemorates the completion of the southern Austrian railways.

Plate 264. Vienna Ornithological Society, gold medal (1886). *Obverse:* Crown Prince Rudolf, who died under tragic circumstances at Mayerling. *Reverse:* bird in flight.

Plate 266. Austria, gold 100 corona (1908). *Reverse:* figure reclining on clouds. Commemorates the sixtieth year of Franz Joseph's reign.

Plate 267. Austrian Republic, gold 100 schillings (1935). *Obverse:* Madonna of the famous shrine at Mariazell. (A rare coin, but the same design appears on the 1934-1936 five schillings, priced very reasonably.)

Plate 269. Austrian Republic, silver 2 schillings. *Obverse:* Walther von der Vogelweide, the outstanding German poet *(minnesanger)* of the Middle Ages.

tent of these Slavs was particularly strong in Bosnia, a province that Austria annexed in 1908. It was in Bosnia that Archduke Ferdinand of Austria was assassinated in 1914, setting off the spark that started World War I.

Austria's eagerness for war was sheer folly. The end of the conflict left Austria reduced to about the size of Maine, with all its former subject peoples established in independent nations of their own. The Hapsburg dynasty came to an end, and Austria, now little more than a hinterland surrounding Vienna, became a republic.

Inflation, famine, and threats of civil war added to Austria's misery. Finally it was annexed by Germany, in time to be on the losing side in World War II. In 1953, this pathetic remnant of a great empire is once more a republic, subject to the supervision of the four occupation powers.

Plate 270. Austrian Republic, silver 2 schillings (1928). *Obverse:* Franz Schubert, the outstanding song composer.

Plate 271. Austrian Republic, silver 2 schillings (1931). *Obverse:* Wolfgang Amadeus Mozart, most illustrious of Austria's composers.

Plate 268. Austrian Republic, silver 1 schilling. *Obverse:* Parliament building.

Plate 272. Austrian Republic, silver 2 schillings (1932). *Obverse:* Joseph Haydn, "father of the symphony."

Plate 273. Hungary, silver broad half-taler (1506). *Obverse:* St. Ladislaus on horseback. *Reverse:* crowned coat of arms, Polish eagle in center. Struck by Vladislav II Jagiello, who was King of Hungary, Bohemia, and Poland.

Hungary

Starting from the Russian steppes in the ninth century, the Magyars swept into Germany, France, and Italy as well as into the Balkan regions, eventually settling down in Hungary. King Stephen I (997-1038) played a great role in Christianizing the Magyars. He invited Benedictine monks to his kingdom, where they passed on to his unruly subjects their skill in farming, their craftsmanship, and their industrious habits. Stephen was declared a saint in 1087.

In the sixteenth century, part of Hungary became a prize of the Hapsburgs, and the rest was conquered by the Turks. Eventually the Turks were driven out, and all of Hungary was incorporated in the Austrian Empire. After World War I, Hungary gained its freedom, but its history since then has been an unhappy one—civil war, dictatorship, German domination, and then Soviet domination.

Plate 274 (above). Hungary, silver 5 pengo (1938), *Obverse:* St. Stephen. A beautiful coin struck for the nine-hundredth anniversary of his death.

Plate 275 (below). Hungary, gold 9 ducats (1603). *Obverse:* George Basta, King of Transylvania. One of the great masterpieces of coin portraiture.

Plate 276. Hungary, 100,000,000,-000,000,000,000 pengo note (1946). Issued during what was perhaps the most disastrous inflation ever known.

Plate 277. Hungary, silver 2 pengo (1936). *Obverse:* Franz Liszt, the famous Hungarian composer and pianist.

Plate 278. Czechoslovakia, silver 20 korona (1937). *Obverse:* Thomas G. Masaryk, who devoted his whole life to the cause of Czech freedom.

Czechoslovakia

In the late Middle Ages, the Bohemian Kingdom (including the Czech people) was a power in central European affairs, and the King of Bohemia was one of the Electors of the Holy Roman Emperor. In time, the Hapsburgs added Bohemia to their domains. In the old Austrian Empire the Czechs suffered doubly from discrimination by the German and Magyar elements.

A university professor named Thomas G. Masaryk (1850-1937) became the acknowledged spokesman for the cause of Czech independence in the early twentieth century. Masaryk, who married an American girl, was deeply influenced by American ideas of democracy. After World War I, Czechoslovakia was created out of the regions of Bohemia, Moravia, Slovakia, Silesia, and Carpathian Ruthenia. Masaryk became the republic's first President, and was repeatedly reelected until his retirement in 1935.

Under his enlightened leadership, Czechoslovakia was one of Europe's most democratic and prosperous countries. But its happiness did not last long; as the first victim of the Munich settlement of 1938, it was condemned to endure first German domination and then Soviet "liberation."

Italy

Modern coinage, stable in value and artistic in design, began in Italy; and it was here that the study and collecting of coins got their real start. The Italians, too, were the first to use machinery for making coins.

From the twelfth to the sixteenth century Italy was far ahead of France, England, and Germany, economically as well as culturally. The Italian cities had hundreds of banking houses, with branches in many parts of Europe and the East. Insurance, public loans, corporations, were all fields in which the Italians pioneered.

As early as the 1300's the Italians used division of labor and the manufacture of standardized parts. They became rich from the wool trade and they were the first Europeans to produce silk.

It was they who passed on to Europe many of the Arabic achievements in mathematics, navigation, and medicine. The Italians were the first Europeans to establish a university, open a public library, found a museum, and perform an opera. And, most important of all, it is to the Italians that we owe that rebirth of ancient learning and magnificent outpouring of artistic genius that we call the Renaissance.

The Italian cities, duchies, kingdoms and principalities were not united into a nation until the nineteenth century.

Italian Regionalism

The Italians have clung more tenaciously to local cultures than have any other people. The islands, Sicily and Sardinia, have their own traditions. On the mainland mountains divide eastern from western Italy. Up to 1870 the Papal States, extending across the peninsula, cut off northern from southern Italy.

But geography is not the full explanation of Italian regionalism. The ancient peoples of Italy who were conquered by the Romans remained loyal to their local customs and revived them in the days of the Empire's decay. Foreign influences, too, poured in on Italy from time immemorial. Among these were the religions of the East (including Christianity); the Germanic invasions; the Byzantine and Saracen cultures which were brought to Italy across the Mediterranean.

Italy produced upwards of eighteen regional dialects, virtually separate languages.

Plate 279. Mirandola, gold doppia (about 1520). *Reverse:* St. Francis of Assisi kneeling before dove. *Obverse:* Gianfrancesco Pico.

Italian itself, which is considered the most beautiful of modern languages, was originally the dialect of Tuscany in central Italy. Its use by Dante and other great writers helped its acceptance as the national language.

The division between north and south was noticeable even in ancient times. After serving as a setting for the brilliant Greek, Carthaginian, Roman, and Byzantine civilizations, Sicily was conquered in the ninth century by the Arabs. At that time the Arabs were culturally far more advanced than the Europeans, and the island flourished under Arab rule. The Saracens built hundreds of mosques, introduced silk cultivation, and practiced large-scale irrigation.

The Arabs never succeeded in gaining a foothold on the mainland. The Normans drove them from Sicily about 1100, and combined Sicily and the southern mainland into the Kingdom of the Two Sicilies.

The struggle for control of Italy between the Popes and the Holy Roman Emperors during the Middle Ages gave the Italian cities their chance to assert their independence.

Famous Italian Cities

Milan, located in the northern farming area, has long been a highly industrialized city with large textile and armaments plants. For centuries Milan and the surrounding countryside bore the brunt of Germanic invasions. After the disappearance of the Roman Empire, it was invaded by the Goths, the Lombards, and the armies of Charlemagne and the Holy Roman Emperors. Frederick Barbarossa destroyed the city, but it was quickly rebuilt. In the 1200's, Milan had a population of 200,000—perhaps ten times the population of London in those days. In 1447, Francesco Sforza, a famous Renais-

Plate 280. Milan, gold ducato doppio d'or (1481). *Obverse:* Giovanni Galeazzo Mari Sforza. *Reverse:* Sforza coat of arms. One c the masterpieces of Renaissance coinage.

sance tyrant, seized control of Milan, an the city continued to be ruled by his de scendants for some time. By 1500 the duch of Milan had the greatest population den sity of Europe and was the furthest ad vanced industrially.

Unlike Milan was Genoa, a port on th northwest coast of Italy, with an extensiv Mediterranean commerce. The hard headed Genoese fought many bitter trad wars with Venice. It was in 1298, durin one of these wars, that the Venetian Marc Polo, back from fabulous Cathay (China) was captured. He wrote the famous ac count of his travels in a Genoese prison.

During the 1500's Genoese bankers com peted with the mighty Fuggers in makin large loans to Spain and Portugal. Like th Fuggers, they siphoned off sizable shares o the cargoes of the Spanish treasure fleets bringing silver from the New World. Geno ese bankers financed the construction an

Plate 281. Mantua, silver testone (abou 1500). *Obverse:* Francesco II Gonzaga. *Re verse:* melting pot in flames. Another gem o Renaissance coinage.

utfitting of the Spanish Armada that iled against England in 1588. They also dvanced huge sums to the Spanish Crown cover the cost of trying to crush the utch revolt.

Founded by refugees from a Hun invaon about 600 A.D., Venice had become urope's richest city by 1300. The city was mous for its lavish entertainments and arnivals and the richness of Venetian lothing, ornaments, and furnishings. Vene is built on 118 small, marshy islands ff the coast. These are separated by 160 anals and linked by about 400 bridges. It as on the celebrated Grand Canal that e Venetian aristocracy had their palaces. ike the cathedrals of Venice, these palaces eflected the impact of Byzantine and Arab ulture on the Venetians.

Originally a fishing village, Venice early arted trading through Constantinople for he products of the East. Once a year the ity sent out the heavily convoyed Caravan f the Levant to bring back rich cargoes. he Spanish treasure fleets later were paterned on this system.

Venice's shipyards were kept so busy that hey were never able to fill orders from utsiders. Venetian vessels were constructed o a uniform size, with standardized parts. This made it easy to repair the vessels or to onvert them into warships.

From their contacts with Alexandria nd Constantinople, the Venetians learned usiness techniques that had been preerved from the days of ancient Rome; and hey added many new ones. Venice issued he first government bonds in 1157, and truck the first ducat (a famous gold coin) n 1284.

Although the coins of Venice never acked some sacred Christian symbol, the Venetians consistently put cash before reliion. (They had a popular saying: "We re Venetians first and Christians afterward.") Despite the Pope's displeasure, they continued to trade with the infidel Arabs—and even sold them arms during the Crusades.

Plate 282. **Venice, silver grosso (1289-1311). *Obverse:* Doge and St. Mark (the city's patron saint). *Reverse:* Christ seated. A coin that reflects strong Byzantine influence.**

In 1204, during the Fourth Crusade, Venice was assigned to ship Crusaders to the Holy Land. But the Venetians, having no quarrel with the Arabs there, sailed to Constantinople instead, where the Crusaders captured the city from fellow Christians and turned over three-eighths of it to Venice in payment for its services.

Venice was ruled by a Doge, elected for life, and the Greater Council. (The word "Doge," like "duke" and *Duce,* comes from the Latin *dux,* a leader.) Despite its official title of "Venetian Republic," the government was absolutist. It functioned smoothly, suffered from few breakdowns, and its first-rate diplomatic service kept it well informed on conditions in foreign lands.

Plate 283. **Venice, gold 15 ducats (1709-1722). *Obverse:* floriated cross. Issued by Doge John II Cornelius.**

Plate 284. **Venice, gold 50 ducats (1763 - 1778). *Obverse:* St. Mark blessing the kneeling Doge. *Reverse:* Christ with right hand raised in benediction.**

Propelled by three banks of oarsmen, the Doge sailed once a year on the *Bucentaur*, known as the "Golden Ship" because it was heavily overlaid with gilt scroll work. Seated on a throne under a crimson and gold canopy, the Doge was escorted by a gaily decorated fleet. To the accompaniment of music, gun salutes, and the pealing of church bells, the Doge tossed his ring into the sea—the famous "marriage" of Venice with the Adriatic. In 1799 Napoleon had the ship burned in order to salvage the gold from its ashes.

Venice's commerce was declining by the end of the fifteenth century; the Mediterranean lost its commercial importance to the Atlantic Ocean, which now provided a westward route to the New World.

Florence and the Renaissance

The people of Tuscany in central Italy are in large part descended from the ancient Etruscans, who are thought to have come to Italy from Asia Minor in ancient times. The Etruscans, who were notable traders and fine artists, were conquered at an early date by the Romans. Scholars have failed to this day to decipher the language of the Etruscans.

Florence, the chief city of Tuscany, fostered the noblest achievements of the Renaissance. This is the period, extending roughly from 1350 to 1550, that separates the Middle Ages from modern times. During those centuries men showed a deep interest in ancient philosophy and learning, experimental science, larger business enterprises, and exploration of unfamiliar regions.

The wooldressers and dyers of Florence made the city rich. They exported to Flanders, France, and England, and later to the East. By 1338 there were 300 textile plants in Florence, with 20,000 workers, annually turning out 100,000 pieces of cloth, worth approximately $3,000,000 in modern money. Later on, silk replaced wool as the popular product. Florentine satins, velvets, and brocades were prized all over Europe.

With the money made from textiles, the richest Florentines went into banking at a very early date. The Florentine florin, which appeared in 1252, was known for

Plate 285. **Florence, gold florin (about 1450). *Obverse:* lily, emblem of Florence. *Reverse:* St. John the Baptist, the city's patron saint.**

the purity of its gold and was one of the first European coins to be freely acceptable everywhere. It was widely imitated. A century later, Florence had more than 80 banking houses, some of them quite influential.

The Frescobaldis, for example, made large loans to the Kings of England during the 1300's. They charged the monarchs 260 per cent interest, because of the heavy risks involved. Another great family, the Bardis, financed France and England in their Hundred Years' War. The Bardis are credited with introducing insurance in the early 1300's.

The most famous bankers of Florence were the Medicis, the richest men in fourteenth- and fifteenth-century Europe. Their bank had branches in France, England, the Low Countries, and the Levant. The Medicis became the rulers of Florence in the early 1400's, and they held that position for several hundred years.

At the same time the Medicis, like other Italian bankers, exerted enormous influence in France. Two Popes came from this famous family, as well as two Queens of France.

Some writers are enthusiastic about the Medicis, praising their sagacity and statesmanship, while others describe them as cynical tyrants.

The most interesting of the Medicis was Lorenzo the Magnificent, who died in 1492 at the age of 43. In his short life he displayed an incredible versatility of talents. Carrying on the family's banking activities, he also waged wars and proved himself a master of the complex intrigues of the time.

But this was not all; he wrote lovely poems and devoted many hours to studying Plato. He planned all the colorful festivals of Florence, founded the first public library, and administered the affairs of two universities. He not only gathered together

Plate 288. Milan, silver testone (1476-1494). *Obverse:* Giovanni Galeazzo Maria Sforza. *Reverse:* Sforza coat of arms. Leonardo da Vinci designed similar coins for the Sforza family.

the leading humanists in Florence but also invited Byzantine scholars to teach Greek philosophy and literature there.

Above all, Lorenzo was the greatest art patron of the Renaissance. He was on the best of terms with the finest painters, sculptors, and architects of the age, treated them with understanding, and rewarded them generously.

However, to round out the picture of Lorenzo, it must be mentioned that some accuse him of having debased the coinage of Florence and having dipped into the city till to cover a shortage of his branch office in Bruges. It is also charged that he was just as efficient as earlier Medicis in disposing of his enemies in Florence—by fair means or foul.

Whatever the final verdict on Lorenzo the Magnificent, it is clear that he was a man of remarkable versatility. In the age of the Renaissance, men had a tremendous lust for life, sought eagerly for many kinds of knowledge, and displayed many kinds of skill.

We find these qualities in the two greatest artists of the Renaissance, who both worked for a time for Lorenzo: Michelangelo Buonarotti, famous for his sculpture and mural painting, and Leonardo da Vinci, as famous for his scientific findings as for his "Mona Lisa."

Coinage and the Renaissance

The Renaissance had a powerful effect on coinage and numismatics. Some of the great artists of the time, Leonardo da Vinci and Benvenuto Cellini, for example, designed coins.

Cellini (1500-1571), a Florentine who is more famous today for his lively autobiography than for his artistic creations, was unsurpassed in working with metal. He was the ideal man for designing coins, as he had the knack of turning out exquisite miniatures—jewel settings, medals, elaborate bindings for books, vases with figures in relief, salt-cellars, statuettes, and the like.

In his autobiography, Cellini tells us that he designed gold coins for Popes Clement VII (1523-1534) and Paul III (1534-1549), and also for Alessandro de' Medici, Duke of Florence. Cellini prepared his own dies for these coins.

The influence of the Renaissance is clearly seen in the beautiful Italian coins of the period. Donato Bramante, the celebrated architect, was responsible for the first machinery for making coins, in about 1500. Leonardo da Vinci improved on the original models. In time, other countries adopted this equipment. The invention came when it was most needed; the growth of commerce required a much greater volume of coinage than could be supplied by the old hand methods.

The Renaissance also had a profound effect on the study and collecting of coins. In that age, with its rebirth of a passionate interest in Greece and Rome, cultivated people were eager to possess ancient coins. This absorption in "living examples" of antiquity gave coin collecting a powerful impetus.

It is significant that the first printed book on the coins of ancient times appeared in

Plate 290. Papal States, gold medal (159 1605). *Obverse:* Pope Clement VIII. One c the finest Papal portraits on coins.

1489. Its author was Angelo Poliziano, Florentine humanist and poet and a frien of Lorenzo the Magnificent. The growt of coin collecting from then on is indi cated by a report that in 1747 the Con vent of St. Florian purchased the coi collection of Apostolo Zeno, a Venetia poet, for 2,000 florins. There were ove 10,000 items in the collection.

The Popes and Rome

The origin of the Papacy goes back to time about which we have little historica evidence. St. Peter is generally believed t have come to Rome from Antioch abou 55 A.D., and to have become head of th local church (Bishop of Rome). Ancien tradition tells us that, with his head down ward, he was crucified on the Vatican hi by Nero on the same day as St. Paul. St Peter's successors as Bishop of Rome wer recognized as the leaders of Christendom and, in turn, Rome became known as th Holy City.

It is thought that early in the fourth century, the Bishop of Rome took the title of "Pope." St. Sylvester I (314-335), wa the first Pope to benefit by Constantine the Great's conversion to Christianity. The Papacy has survived many crises, including the Great Schism with the Greek Orthodox Church in 1054 and the Protestant Reformation which began in 1517. During the

Iiddle Ages there were many struggles etween the Popes and the Holy Roman mperors for supremacy. Since that time ıe authority of the Pope has come to be mited to purely spiritual matters.

For many centuries, and right up to 870, the Popes were the rulers of the apal States in Italy. In 1870 the Italian overnment brought the Papal States un- er its sovereignty. By way of protest, the ope remained a voluntary prisoner in the 'atican.

This policy continued until the Lateran 'reaty of 1929 was signed by the Church nd the Italian government. The Pope re- eived a large indemnity, and was assigned 'atican City, an area one-sixth of a square ıile.

Vatican City has its own coinage and ostage stamps, as well as its own news- aper and broadcasting station. The Swiss uards of the Vatican Palace wear the olorful costumes which Michelangelo de- gned almost 400 years ago.

The Basilica of St. Peter's in Rome is the ırgest church in the world. Its piazza public square) holds 300,000 people. The resent church replaces an older St. Peter's, uilt by Constantine the Great in 326 and orn down in 1452 when it showed signs f structural weakness.

The cornerstone of the present St. Peter's vas laid in 1506 by Julius II; the church vas dedicated 120 years later, though it vas not yet completed at the time. Con- truction required 176 years in all, at an stimated cost of $48,000,000. In 1947 rcheologists discovered a crypt with coins rom very early days with inscriptions that o some degree bear out the traditional be- ief that St. Peter was interred on the spot vhere St. Peter's Church is today.

The Vatican Palace was started by Nicholas V (1447-1455). It has had many dditions since his day; its breathtakingly

Plate 291. Papal States, gold medal (1655-1667). *Reverse* (left): architectural scene. *Obverse* (right): Pope Alexander VII. Few coins can match this one for magnificent workmanship.

Plate 292. Papal States, silver scudo (1846-1856). *Obverse:* Pope Pius IX, who became a voluntary prisoner after the loss of most of the Papal domains.

Plate 293. Papal States, gold medal (1655-1667). *Obverse:* conclave of cardinals. Another example of superb workmanship.

Plate 294. **Papal States, si ver scudo (1829).** ***Obverse*** **coat of arms of Cardina Galeffi.** ***Reverse:*** **seated figur representing the Church.**

wide spiral staircase was finished as recently as 1932. The numerous additions have turned the Vatican into a bewildering but not unpleasing hodgepodge of buildings, offices, museums, libraries, apartments, and galleries.

The Vatican is famous for its dazzling collection of ancient and Renaissance art, precious manuscripts, and coins and medals. (The coin collection is said to contain 100,000 items.)

The outstanding feature of the Vatican is the Sistine Chapel, with ceiling frescoes painted by Michelangelo. He spent 4 years, mostly lying on his back, on an ingeniously rigged scafford, painting 343 figures in an area of 10,000 square feet. The theme of these paintings is the Creation of the World. Thirty years later, Michelangelo covered the Altar Wall with an equally awe-inspiring conception of the Last Judgment.

Papal Coins

Adrian I (772-795) issued the first Papal coins after getting permission from Charlemagne. Later on, when there were rival Popes, both issued their own coins; scholars believe the rival factions destroyed each other's coins.

Since Adrian's time the Popes have struck a great many coins. These are naturally rich in Christian symbols, pictures of the Saints, and texts from the Bible.

The Chrismon has already been shown and explained (see Plate 111). The lio represents Christ or (more often) St Mark. The most familiar emblem of th early Christians was a fish, used becaus the Greek word for "fish" (*ichthus*) t the early Christians stood for the Gree sentence *Iejous Christos, Theou Uios Sote* ("Jesus Christ, Son of God, Saviour").

Other interesting symbols are a ship representing the Church, and an anchor which stands for faith. The anchor appears, for example, on a gold scudo o Clement IX dated 1706. Crossed keys refe to "the keys of the Kingdom of Heaven," and allude to the Popes, Peter's successors

The familiar tiara symbolizes the Pope' threefold function—to act as teacher, law giver, and judge. Some Papal coins hav the phrase *Sede Vacante* ("vacant seat") The Papal Chamberlain has the power t

Plate 295. **Parma, silver scudo (1592-1622)** ***Reverse:*** **Mars and Athene lifting crown.**

issue these in the interval between the death of one Pope and the election of his successor.

Italy's Decline

The fighting between the city-states led them to employ large groups of mercenaries, whose hard-boiled leaders were known as *Condottieri*. Some of these generals amassed fortunes; Bartolomeo Colleoni, one of the roughest and toughest of the lot, bequeathed to the city of Venice an estimated 500,000 ducats (about $20,000,000 in modern money) at his death in 1474.

In time, these *Condottieri,* as well as other ambitious and ruthless men, made themselves masters of the city-states and actually founded dynasties. The wars between these despots eventually led to calls for foreign help. This was the end of Italy's Golden Age. Invasion followed invasion, and before the end of the 1500's most of Italy came under foreign rule. From time to time, Italian territories were swapped by foreign countries as part of a deal or peace treaty.

Italy's helplessness was grimly emphasized in 1527 when the mercenaries of the Holy Roman Emperor sacked Rome. They killed thousands of people, captured the Pope, and plundered homes, palaces, and churches alike. No barbarian invasion had ever wreaked so much damage.

Plate 297. Piacenza, gold quadrupla (1622-1646). *Obverse:* Odoardo Farnese. *Reverse:* wolf capped by crown (Farnese coat of arms).

The long domination of Italy by foreign masters was climaxed by the coming of Napoleon. But for the first time in almost three centuries, the Italians had a taste of reforms so badly needed that they outweighed all Napoleon's robberies.

The Congress of Vienna in 1815 again carved up Italy. Austria had the flourishing northern provinces; the Papal States were restored to the Pope; the Bourbons reigned over Sicily and the southern mainland. The House of Savoy, which ruled the island of Sardinia and the northwest corner of Italy, was destined to become the ruling house of Italy.

Plate 298. Lucca, silver 5 franchi (1805-1814). *Obverse:* Elisa Bonaparte (Napoleon's sister) and her husband Felix Bacciocchi.

Plate 299. Italian Republic, silver scudo (1802-1805). *Obverse:* wand of Aesculapius, god of healing and medicine.

Plate 300. Naples, silver 5 lire (1808-1815). *Obverse:* Joachim Murat, Napoleon's brother-in-law and one of his most brilliant marshals.

The efforts of four remarkable men finally freed Italy: Giuseppe Mazzini (1805-1872), a patriot who kept the revolutionary spirit alive with his organization called "Young Italy"; Camillo di Cavour (1810-1861), the enlightened prime minister of the Sardinian kingdom, whose supple diplomacy exploited the differences between more powerful European countries to further the cause of Italian freedom; Victor Emmanuel II (1820-1878), King of Sardinia, who became the first King of united Italy because of his steadfast backing of Cavour; and Giuseppe Garibaldi (1807-1882), the military liberator of Italy.

Garibaldi, perhaps the greatest master of guerrilla tactics in military annals, is one of the most colorful and attractive figures in Italy's history. An exile for many years, he freed Uruguay from the bloody despotism of Juan Manuel de Rosas, South America's most tyrannical dictator, and had once earned a wretched living in New York as a candlemaker.

Plate 303. **Venice, silver 5 lire (1848).** ***Obverse:*** **lion of St. Mark's.**

Once Italy was united in the 1860's, the Italians needed a change of pace from the enthusiasm of fighting against tyranny to the sobriety of rebuilding a new land. The greatest problem of recent years has been the poverty of the peasants of Sicily and the southern mainland. Neither the constitutional monarchy of the House of Savoy nor the recent Mussolini dictatorship solved the problem, which was aggravated by the devastation of World War II. In the present-day Republic of Italy, the poverty of the peasants still remains the chief problem.

Plate 304 (left). **Italy, gold 100 lire (1912).** ***Reverse:*** **Italia with plow.**

Plate 305. **Italy, gold 100 lire (1923).** ***Obverse:*** **Victor Emmanuel III.** ***Reverse:*** **ax and fasces, the ancient badge of office of the Roman lictors, adopted by the Italian Fascist movement. This coin commemorated the March on Rome.**

Plate 306. **Italy (Republic), silver 10 lire.** ***Obverse:*** **Pegasus, the winged horse of the Muses, and the symbol for poetic inspiration. A very beautiful coin, and a very inexpensive one.**

The Iberian Peninsula

Spain and Portugal both were part of the ancient Roman Empire. In the days when the Empire became powerless to hold on to its territory, the Iberian peninsula passed under Visigoth control. Then, early in the eighth century these "West-Goths" were conquered by the Moors and Arabs (Moslems), who invaded the peninsula from north Africa.

The grip of the Moslems on the peninsula was not removed for eight centuries, during which time they established a culture which was distinguished for its prosperity and artistic achievements. Only Italy can be mentioned as a near-rival of the Moslems in the arts of civilization at that time.

Spain

Spain finally conquered the Moors in 1492, the very same year that Columbus discovered the New World. Thus Spain was thrust upon the stage of world history while it was still consolidating its internal affairs. During the centuries of warfare with the Moslems, the Spaniards became used to religious fanaticism, and acquired a taste for military life, as well as a contempt for trade and industry.

Under the Moslems, Spain had been a great agricultural country. After 1500, Spain, like ancient Rome, depended on Sicily for grain. It was similarly dependent on the Low Countries for the processing of fine wool from the famous Spanish Merino sheep. The story is that Spain was so poor that Queen Isabella had to pawn some of her jewels to finance Columbus' voyage to the New World.

When Charles inherited the throne of the Spanish Empire as Charles I and took the throne of the Holy Roman Empire as Charles V, he became the ruler of a domain that was huge even in comparison with the Roman Empire of ancient times but not nearly so wealthy or powerful.

Spain's glory was deceptive from the start. The lands in the New World needed settling and developing. Charles V drained the homeland of men, revenue, and resources in order to fight for the interests of the Holy Roman Empire.

Plate 307. Spain, gold excellente (1479-1504). *Obverse:* Ferdinand and Isabella, who financed the voyages of Columbus.

Plate 308. Spain, silver testone (1556-1598). *Obverse:* Philip II, who sent the Armada against England.

Plate 309. **Spain, gold 7 ducats (about 1550).** ***Obverse:*** **starting from left, Maximilian I and his grandsons Charles V and Ferdinand I (compare with Plate 253).** ***Reverse:*** **coat of arms displaying the towers of Castile and the lions of Leon.**

Plate 310. **Spain, silver piece of eight (1793).** ***Obverse:*** **Charles IV (1788-1808), who was driven out by Napoleon. This coin was minted in Mexico.**

Spain was almost continuously at war with France from 1500 to 1560. Charles V felt he could not allow France to take over Italy and his Sicilian granary nor could he permit Spain to be isolated from Austria.

However, Spain could not possibly supply the funds for the long war. Accordingly, Charles V was compelled to borrow vast sums from German and Italian bankers, in effect mortgaging the riches of the New World for the loans. Spain was also threatened by Turkish domination in the Mediterranean.

Some writers think that Charles V abdicated in 1556 because he was appalled by his mountainous debts. In any event, his son Philip II (1556-1598) went bankrupt the following year for 11,000,000 ducats—a crash that set off further bankruptcies in Portugal, France, and the Netherlands.

But this was only the beginning of Philip's troubles. The huge shipments of silver coming from the New World (see the later chapter on Mexico) were not exactly a blessing. By greatly increasing Europe's supply of silver, they reduced the metal's value considerably and thus created an inflationary rise in prices. This inflation was particularly painful in Spain which was a heavy buyer.

In 1567 the Low Countries, now Spain's best revenue-producing provinces, revolted against Spanish rule. In addition to losing substantial income from these provinces, Spain had to embark on vast new loans in its attempts to crush the revolt. Meanwhile the English and Dutch were harrying Spanish ships, inflicting heavy losses of men and money. In 1575 the Spanish Crown went bankrupt again, this time for 37,000,000 ducats.

Spain made a momentary recovery in 1580, when Philip inherited the Portuguese Crown, making it possible for him to draw on the revenue of the profitable spice trade with the Indies. Still at war with the Netherlands, Philip obtained further loans to send the "Invincible" Armada against England. With the defeat of that expedition, the decline of Spain became inevitable.

By 1650 Spain was no longer a world power, despite its tenacious hold on its overextended empire. One-third of the population was in the service of the Church, which had no less than 9,000 monasteries in Spain. The population had declined considerably, partly because of sizable military losses, partly because of emigration to the colonies. The decline continued in the eighteenth century, when Spain had no merchant marine and two-

Plate 311. Gibraltar, copper 2 quartos (1810). *Obverse:* lion. *Reverse:* castle. A private token.

thirds of the land was no longer under cultivation.

In 1704, during the War of the Spanish Succession, England annexed Gibraltar. To this day the British have retained this valuable base where the Mediterranean meets the Atlantic. Gibraltar gets its name from the Moorish general Tariq who landed there in 711 to invade Spain. He carved his name on the rock, which became known as Gebel-al-Tariq—the Rock of Tariq. The Europeans shortened this to "Gibraltar."

When Napoleon's armies invaded Spain it stirred the Spanish peasants into waging guerrilla warfare with great savagery. However, Napoleon won and installed his brother Joseph as King of Spain. After the defeat of Napoleon, Joseph emptied the Spanish treasury and fled with his plundered millions to the United States, where he lived comfortably in Philadelphia.

Spain's difficulties with Napoleon stimulated a widespread series of revolts in the New World colonies. In time this led to Spain's loss of South America, Central America, and Mexico. Since then Spain's history has been a long series of civil wars alternating with uneasy periods of peace. Never has it been remotely near the position it had in the days of Charles V.

Plate 313. Spain, silver duro (1808). *Reverse:* incused place of issue (Gerona), date, and value. A necessity coin of the Napoleonic wars.

Plate 314. Spain, silver 5 pesetas (1896-1898). *Obverse:* Alfonso XIII at the age of nine.

Plate 312. Spain, silver 8 reales (1809). *Obverse:* Joseph Bonaparte, who tried (and failed) to keep the country under control of his famous brother.

Plate 315. **Portugal, silver 10 escudos (1926). *Obverse:* crusader. *Reverse:* coat of arms. Commemorates the Battle of Ouriques (1139), which resulted in the unification of Portugal under Alfonso I when he defeated five Moorish chieftains.**

Portugal

Portugal is a small country with a comparatively long Atlantic coastline. From medieval times Portuguese sailors and fishermen have been among Europe's best. The vision of one great man, Prince Henry the Navigator (1394-1460), made possible the founding of a huge empire.

Prince Henry was obsessed with the idea of sending ships down the west coast of Africa in an attempt to find a passage to India and the Spice Islands. Prince Henry's ambition was to eliminate the Arab and Italian middlemen, who up to that time were indispensable in bringing spices to Europe, and to concentrate this trade through Portugal's excellent harbors on the Atlantic.

To execute this grandiose conception required almost a century of Portuguese planning and perseverance.

Prince Henry retired to a lonely tower at Sagres, overlooking the Atlantic coast. Here he brought together a group of distinguished navigators, mathematicians, astronomers, and mapmakers in the hope of getting the best possible results. The Portuguese had developed the caravel, a tiny, flimsy vessel by our standards, but the most seaworthy ship in those days. It took skill and daring to maneuver these vessels in stormy seas.

Prince Henry planned expedition after expedition; every ship sent out to Africa between 1418 and his death in 1460 was under his supervision. The earliest voyagers crept along the coast for a short distance and then turned back, terrified by the tales of monsters lurking on the "Sea of Darkness." (This was about 60 years before Columbus sailed to the New World.)

But the voyages continued, the caravels became progressively larger and sturdier, more and more charts were prepared to show coastlines, shoals, tides, and other data. The Portuguese improved considerably on the early compass. There seemed to be no end to the quest. When Prince Henry died, the search for the route to the Indies was still going on. Ships were now

Plate 316. **Portugal, silver 10 escudos (1932-1948). *Obverse:* caravel. This was the type of vessel the Portuguese used to win a vast empire.**

Plate 317. **Portugal, silver 1,000 reis (1898). *Reverse:* cross with motto meaning "By this sign thou shalt conquer" (see page 57). Issued for the 400th anniversary of Vasco da Gama's voyage to India.**

sailing 4,000 miles and then turning back without coming to the end of the African coast.

At last, in 1487, the greatest of the Portuguese navigators, Bartholomew Diaz, finally came to the end of the west African coastline, rounded the Cape, and emerged into the Indian Ocean. The hardships of the voyage and threats of mutiny forced him to turn back, but now the exultant Portuguese knew they could reach India. They changed the name of the dangerous cape from "Cape of Storms" to "Cape of Good Hope."

For a while the Portuguese were downcast by the return of Columbus with his announcement that he had found the westward route to the Indies. (He did not know that he had discovered America.) It took time in those days to prepare an expedition, and not until 1497 were they able to send out Vasco da Gama with orders to go around Africa to India or perish in the attempt. After a long, adventurous voyage, da Gama arrived on the Malabar (west) coast of India in 1498, thus crowning the efforts of almost a century. A year later he was back in Lisbon with the good news.

Da Gama's round-trip distance was 24,000 miles, and his voyage was much more dangerous and difficult than that of Columbus. His success in opening up a direct trade route was valued much more highly at the time than it is today.

Plate 318. Portugal, bronze 3 reis (1734). *Obverse:* crowned shield. *Reverse:* value in wreath. Despite its crowded design, this coin is attractive because of its excellent workmanship.

The Portuguese lost no time developing the spice trade, and their overseas empire grew steadily: Ceylon, Malacca, the Spice Islands, and in the New World the enormous colony of Brazil.

Yet Portugal's age as a world power lasted no more than a few decades. Basically a poor country, it had to turn over a part of the spice trade to German and Italian bankers. The Portuguese captains were expert navigators and brave fighters, but so much sudden wealth led to corruption, envy, and mismanagement.

Portugal's amalgamation with Spain in 1580 was a misfortune for the Portuguese. Philip II of Spain immediately closed the port of Lisbon to English and Dutch ships. This reduced the Portuguese spice trade considerably, and also gave the English and the Dutch the idea of going straight to the source and seizing the Portuguese colonies, which were now part of the Spanish Empire.

During this period, Portugal lost Ceylon, Malacca, and the Spice Islands. Even after these painful losses, the Portuguese Empire remained the third largest, exceeded only by those of England and France. Today the Portuguese Empire has 11,000,000 inhabitants and includes an area of 800,000 square miles, including colonies in Africa, Asia, and Oceania.

The Napoleonic wars led to a long period of acute unrest in Portugal, which lost Brazil early in the nineteenth century. Portugal became a republic in 1910, after violent upheavals had racked the country. Though still a republic in a formal sense, Portugal has been ruled by the dictatorship of Antonio de Oliveira Salazar since 1928.

Switzerland

Switzerland is a country of wild, majestic mountain peaks, mile-long glaciers, fertile valleys, and lovely lakes famed for their vivid blue waters.

Thousands of years ago, prehistoric men lived in houses built on wooden piles driven into the ground on the bottom of the lakes. To the Romans, the natives of this land were the Helvetii, and Switzerland is still called Helvetia on coins. To this day, the country is rich in those typical Roman miracles of construction and engineering—roads, bridges, viaducts, forts, and amphitheaters.

Overrun in ancient times by three Germanic tribes, the Alemanni, Burgundians, and Franks, the country has four official languages—German, French, Italian, and Romansh—together with several German and French local dialects.

The Hapsburg dynasty, rulers of the Holy Roman Empire for centuries, had its beginning in Switzerland. In time, Switzerland came under Austrian rule. Rebelling against this domination, the Swiss won their independence in 1386.

Though historians have proved that William Tell never existed, the Swiss continue to revere him as their great national hero.

Plate 319. Switzerland, silver 5 francs (1931-1949). ***Obverse:*** **William Tell, the legendary hero of the Swiss.**

In fact, not so many years ago they issued a very attractive coin picturing Tell as he should have looked.

The Swiss have had a long-standing policy of neutrality, but neither their neutrality nor their mountains could protect them against Napoleon Bonaparte. In 1798 the coin-hungry French regime, still suffering from the effects of a disastrous inflation, sent an army which looted the gold in the treasury of Berne. And so Berne, which had the reputation of being the most prosperous city in Switzerland, paid for Napoleon's expedition to Egypt.

Berne, by the way, has had a bear on its picturesque coat of arms for 700 years. You will find the bear on many coins of Berne and other Swiss regimes. Berne's bear pit is one of the city's most popular attractions.

late 320. Appenzell (can-
n), silver 4 francs (1816).
bverse: bear in wreath. *Re-
erse:* warrior (mercenary).

wiss Alps

The mountains of Switzerland contain iany glaciers—huge frozen rivers of ice. he pressure of the icy top layers causes the ɔwer sections to crack and shift. The re-iarkable Mer de Glace (Sea of Ice) on he slopes of the Alps' highest peak, Mont ilanc, is 3½ miles long and moves 18 iches a day.

Other famous peaks are the Jungfrau nd the Matterhorn, and for years moun-ain climbers have come from all over the vorld to try to scale these lofty mountains.

You may recall that many centuries ago Iannibal crossed the Alps, not for the fun f it but for very compelling reasons—to lestroy the power of Rome. To cut their vay through, Hannibal's men heated the ocks until they were red hot, and then oured snow and ice on them. These swift hanges in temperature cracked the rocks.

During the Middle Ages, pilgrims and ther travelers crossed the Alps through the it. Bernard and St. Gotthard passes. The amous St. Bernard dogs rescued many a veary traveler who would otherwise have erished in the snow.

In springtime, the melting of the top layers of snow brings on avalanches. Later on, when summer comes, there is a new danger of avalanches—this time from melting ice. To break the force of the avalanches, the Swiss have built many stone walls and other barriers. Forests are so important for this purpose that no Swiss can cut down a tree—not even his own!—without getting permission from the government.

Not until the spring avalanches are over can cows be allowed to graze on the mountainsides. These cattle, nourished on the exceptionally fine Alpine grass, are the source of two great delicacies—Swiss cheese and Swiss chocolate.

Tunneling Through the Mountains

With the exception of England and Belgium, Switzerland has more railroad track per square mile than any other country in the world. The construction of the St. Gotthard line through the Swiss Alps is one of the greatest engineering feats of all time. Work on this project started in 1873 and was completed in 1880.

Plate 321. Berne, silver taler (1679). *Obverse:* city shield with bear. *Reverse:* 4 B's arranged in the form of a cross.

Of the 4,000 men who toiled on this dangerous assignment, 250 were killed and 600 hurt in the course of their work. One of the most maddening problems was that even a slight miscalculation in drilling pressure might cause huge interior chunks of mountain to move.

By the time this line was finished, it required more than 40 bridges and 5 viaducts —not to mention 53 tunnels totaling 26 miles in length. To prevent avalanches, the engineers had to shield the tracks with seven galleries. Twisting through the mountains with unbelievable corkscrew turns, some of these tunnels have to pass underneath themselves!

Swiss Mercenaries

One of Switzerland's monuments is the Lion of Lucerne, a mighty lion with a spear thrust in its side. This statue is a tribute to the memory of the Swiss Guards who died defending Louis XVI and Marie Antoinette in 1792.

You may wonder how the French army came to have Swiss soldiers, and this is their story. From the fifteenth to the early part of the nineteenth century, Swiss soldiers had a well-earned reputation as Europe's finest fighting men. In 1478, for example, 600 Swiss in the employ of the French routed a Milanese force of 15,000 men. Because their native land was poor, the Swiss often hired themselves out as mercenaries (men fighting for pay), making u whole regiments in the service of foreig countries.

Plate 322. Switzerland, silver 5 francs (1934). *Obverse:* Swiss guard. Issued for the Fribourg Shooting Festival.

Plate 323. Berne, silver 40 batzen (1815 *Obverse:* overstamp on a French ecu.

There was always a war going on some where, so these migratory workers were sur of a job. In those days, there was mor demand for Swiss mercenaries than fc Swiss cheese. Swiss coins, especially thos before 1800, often picture a warrior c knight.

About 4,000 Swiss fought in our ow Civil War, the bulk of them on the Con federate side. Today all that remains of th Swiss "foreign legion" is the famous Swis Guard of the Vatican. Limited to abou 100 men, this group is employed to len a colorful touch for purely ceremonia purposes.

The Swiss, who have always had a repu tation as superb marksmen, have bee holding sharpshooting contests since 1452 Some of the handsomest Swiss coins com memorate these festivals.

How the Swiss Make a Living

Switzerland's watchmaking industr dates from the arrival of large numbers o French Huguenot refugees at the end o the seventeenth century. Later on, this in dustry branched out into the manufacture of other precision instruments. Swiss watch makers are genuine craftsmen, famous th world over for the delicacy and accurac their workmanship. The United States ıports about 7,000,000 watch movements ·ery year from Switzerland.

Swiss cheesemaking techniques go back the days of the Romans. Although the ·ocess of making Swiss cheese is exactly ıe same in the United States and Switzer-nd, most people consider the European ıeese superior as the Alpine grasslands ıake all the difference. Incidentally, the ɔles in Swiss cheese are formed by bubbles : carbon dioxide that resist solidifying.

Switzerland's ravishing scenery brings ıousands of tourists to the country every ·ar. Some come for mountain climbing, ıany for skiing and other winter sports. 'he thin mountain air has also proved łeal for tuberculosis sanatoriums.

Despite the jokes about the Swiss navy, is true that Switzerland charters a few ıerchant vessels that operate out of Genoa ying the Swiss flag.

he Red Cross

As we know, Switzerland has enjoyed eutrality in many of Europe's most de-:ructive wars. For this reason international onferences have often taken place there, nd the League of Nations had its head-uarters at Geneva throughout its existence.

Switzerland's classic neutrality also made fitting that the International Red Cross, erhaps the world's outstanding humani-arian organization, should have its begin-ing there.

A Swiss named Henri Dunant founded he Red Cross in 1862. Three years earlier,

Plate 324. Switzerland, silver 5 francs (1881). *Obverse:* view of Fribourg. Issued for the Fribourg Shooting Festival. Note the Swiss cross inside the star.

Dunant had been an eyewitness of the terrible battle at Solferino between the French and the Austrians. One of the bloodiest combats of all time, it resulted in 33,000 dead and wounded in ten hours of fighting—55 casualties a minute. What made the battle seem even more horrible to Dunant was that it ended without either side achieving victory!

The symbol of the Red Cross is adopted from the Swiss flag, which appears on some Swiss coins and many Swiss stamps. There is this difference—the Swiss flag shows a white cross in a red field, and the Red Cross reverses the colors.

Swiss Government

Under the constitution of 1874, Switzerland is a confederation of 25 cantons. Some cantons are small enough to have all their laws passed at outdoor public meetings. In some districts, failure to vote is punished by a fine, but women do not have the right to vote.

Belgium

Wedged in by the North Sea and the Netherlands on the north, Germany on the east, and France on the south and west, Belgium has often been caught in the middle during the wars of powerful neighbors.

It was at a small Belgian town that Napoleon Bonaparte "met his Waterloo" in 1815. It was at another small Belgian town, Ypres, that the Germans introduced poison gas a hundred years later. And in World War II, the unexpectedly rapid collapse of the Belgian army caught the British in a trap from which they managed to free themselves by the "miracle" of Dunkerque.

In earlier times, Flanders, part of which is now western Belgium, was the scene of fighting during the wars of the Spaniards, British, French, and Dutch. For almost 200 years, Belgium was known as the Spanish Netherlands and then as the Austrian Netherlands. The Treaty of Vienna in 181 united Belgium with Holland. The comb nation, dominated by the Dutch, was a unhappy one for the Belgians.

Plate 325. Copper 10 centimes (1832-1856). *Reverse:* lion. The national coat of arms is a golden lion rampant on a black background. The national motto is: "In union there is strength."

In 1830 the Belgians revolted and set u their own government, a monarchy. Thi might have been disastrous for them, as i cost them their share of the rich Dutc colonial overseas trade. However, Belgiur is blessed with large coal and iron deposit and its people are noted for their industri ousness. The country is so thickly populate that it has over 700 people to the squar mile.

To make up for the lost commerce, Bel gium pioneered on the Continent in th construction of railways—an achievemen of which its people are naturally ver proud. In 1935 a handsome coin appeare to commemorate the centennial of the rail way system.

Belgium is a country with two basicall different racial stocks and religions. Th people of Flanders are mostly Protestant

Plate 326. Bronze 50 centimes (1952). *Re verse:* miner with helmet and lamp. Much o Belgium's wealth is in its mines.

**ate 327. Silver 50 francs, 1935. *Obverse:* building of the
ternational Exposition at Brussels. *Reverse:* St. Michael
nd the Dragon. This handsome coin was issued to com-
emorate the centennial of the Belgian railway system.**

Plate 329. Silver 50 francs (1948). *Obverse:* Mercury head.

nd speak Flemish, which is much like Ger-
an and Dutch. The Walloons in the south
re mainly Catholic and speak French or a
rench dialect. That is why the inscriptions
n Belgian coins and stamps are in two
nguages.

he World's Greatest Seaport

Belgium reached its peak in the late
Iiddle Ages. The city of Bruges had al-
eady become the cloth-weaving center of
urope, famous for its fine wool and lace.
o this day, the Flemish towns still contain
nany magnificent buildings constructed in
he days of their old-time prosperity.

Few of us are aware that in the sixteenth
entury Antwerp was the world's greatest
eaport, doing a volume of business that
taggers the imagination. At a time when
ts thriving rival, Amsterdam, was proud to
ave 500 ships riding at anchor in its har-
oor, Antwerp had five times as many ships
n its port.

No less brisk was the land trade of Ant-
verp, with a thousand freight loads and ten times as many peasant carts arriving in the city every week.

The trading in government securities was so great in Antwerp that the annual turnover amounted to a good 40,000,000 ducats. When Spain went bankrupt in 1557, the bottom dropped out of the great Antwerp boom.

Belgium was a pawn in the hands of the powers during the next three centuries, governed by the Spanish, French and Austrians alternately.

Belgium's neutrality in case of international war was guaranteed by a treaty signed in 1839. At the beginning of World War I, Germany invaded the country, dismissing the treaty as "a scrap of paper." After the war, Belgium's neutrality was again guaranteed by the Locarno treaties. Germany violated this pact as well in its 1940 lightning invasion of the Lowland countries. Both invasions were costly to the Belgians: their country was devastated and they had to exist under miserable conditions during the German occupation.

late 330. Silver 5 francs (1880). *Obverse:* Leopold I and Leopold II. *Reverse:* a figure holding a tablet. At her left is the Belgian lion, and in the background we see a monument and a building. (Issued to commemorate the fiftieth year of the Belgian monarchy.)

The Netherlands

There is no other country in the world like Holland. The Dutch have a genial saying—"God made the world, but the Dutch made Holland." For centuries these methodical, practical, resourceful, and tenacious people have been rolling back the sea. Some 10,000 years ago, Holland ("hollow-land") was nothing but slippery, slimy muck and ooze. Today the country supports a population density of close to 850 people to the square mile.

Half of Holland has been "stolen" from the sea. You can get an idea of the labor involved in keeping Holland dry if you consider these figures: half of the land surface is below sea level, and half of this is from 10 to 25 feet below sea level!

Dangerous Rivers

Holland's worst flood came in 1421, not from the turbulent North Sea, but from the Maas River which burst its banks, destroying 72 villages and killing 100,000 people in a short time.

Three of Europe's great rivers, the Maas, the Scheldt, and the Rhine, all pass through Holland on their way to the North Sea. In springtime, swollen by melting snow, they rise to dangerous levels. For centuries they brought along vast quantities of mud and dumped it out on the land during their overflows.

***Plate 331.* Zeeland, bronze doit (1758). Ob** ***verse:* crowned shield with motto: *Luctor emergo*—"I struggle and I survive." *Revers* name of issuing province.**

Here and there slight hills piled up, an these were the sections where people of th Stone Age lived. When Julius Caesar legions came to Holland, they found th Batavii, primitive tribesmen but brav fighters.

Many centuries passed before the peopl of Holland built dikes strong enough t hold back the river overflows. But even th dikes were not enough. So they put u hundreds of windmills to pump the wate out 24 hours a day.

It was an unbelievably laborious proces They built windmills which used the Nort Sea gales to pump the water up throug a series of levels, each higher than the on before. The water was led into a networ of canals, and finally emptied into the se at low tide. In the twentieth century th windmills gave way to electric stations wit a pumping capacity of over 6,000,000 ton of water in a single day.

ate 332 (*left*). Utrecht, ver ducatoon (1760). *Obrse:* knight on horseback.

ate 333 (*right*). Amsterım, silver ducatoon (1673). *everse:* two lions supporting oat of arms. Struck during ı invasion of Holland by ouis XIV of France.

ilting Over Windmills

The wind has not always been free in Iolland!

Windmills came into use about the year 00. At first the feudal lords of the Middle ıges carried on endless disputes about who wned the wind. They claimed the right o collect fees from anyone who had a vindmill on his land. As late as the foureenth century, the Baron of Woerden and he Bishop of Utrecht quarreled about the ight to collect windmill taxes.

The early windmills worked only when he wind was blowing in the right direction. Later, the Dutch made mills with movable ops. In this way, the owner of a windmill could turn the roof around, keeping the ails in constant motion depending on the lirection of wind currents. Still later, the Dutch put their windmills to many other uses—to saw timber, to turn rags into paper pulp, to polish rice, to manufacture gunpowder, and the like.

Holding Back the Sea

For centuries the all-important task of flood prevention has been entrusted to the *Waterstaat,* which we might translate as the Department of Water Control. Dutch hydraulic engineers are the world's best—they have to be. The people call them the "Water Wizards."

The northern part of the Dutch coast is protected by sand dunes over 30 feet high and 4,500 feet wide in some places. To make these a really effective barrier, the Dutch have planted a grass called *helm.* Famous for its toughness, this grass helps to hold the sand together, making it sturdily resistant to wind and water.

In the great flood of February, 1953, these dunes kept the engulfing waters out, although the dikes further south gave way. This disastrous flood killed about 1,500 people, while 40,000 more lost their homes. Property damage amounted to well over $300,000,000 as 400,000 precious acres disappeared under water. Such appalling figures give us some idea of the crucial problems that confront the Water Wizards. And consider the terrain they have to work with! The great city of Amsterdam, for example, is built on land completely reclaimed from the sea. Every house in Amsterdam rests on tree trunks. The Royal Palace was built on no less than 13,659 tree trunks.

Dutch History

In an 80-year war against the mighty Spanish Empire (1568-1648) this little country had certain advantages: a great navy with which they defeated Spain on the sea again and again; then, too, they received support from time to time from the English. (You can see from some of their old coins how grateful they were for this aid.)

It was in 1568 that Philip II, the fanatical King of Spain, decided to bend the

Dutch to his tyrannical will. As commander of his army he chose the Duke of Alva, who imposed a crushing 10 per cent sales tax and hanged shopkeepers on their doorposts if they did not pay it. He buried other victims alive, introduced the Inquisition, confiscated estates right and left, and had thousands put to death after cities surrendered on his promise of merciful treatment.

William the Silent

These horrors made the Dutch stubborn. They were lucky in having a great leader, William of Orange, generally known as William the Silent. The story is that he received this nickname when, on being told of the Spanish plans, he gave no sign of indignation and kept his own counsel. Of German origin himself and possessing the principality of Orange in southern France, William could easily have steered clear of the Dutch revolt. Instead, he placed himself at the head of the revolt, uniting the seven northern provinces of the Netherlands into the Dutch Republic.

There is much about William the Silent that reminds us of George Washington. William was a man of moderation; he attracted followers by his obvious integrity; he declined the kingship of Holland when it was offered to him. "You can launch out when it is hopeless," he remarked characteristically, "and you can persevere even when there is no hope of success."

William gained nothing from the revol He lost several members of his family; a his estates were confiscated; the King Spain declared him an outlaw and put price on his head, as an encourageme to assassins. In 1584 William was murdere by a fanatic whom he had befriended.

Sea Beggars

The Low Countries were Spain's be source of revenue in the Old World. Y Alva went about the task of "pacifying the Netherlands as if he wanted to r duce the people to beggary. In the end, h was the architect of Spain's defeat, for h left the Dutch no choice but to escape b sea, where they took over the herring an whaling fleets.

These "Sea Beggars"—as they proudl called themselves—fought with the fury men who have nothing more to lose. Fierc hand-to-hand fighters, they boarded th Spanish galleons, overpowered the Spar iards, often tossed them overboard, an then, after plundering the ships of anythin useful, scuttled them.

On their coat of arms, the Sea Beggar defiantly displayed the beggar's proverbi wooden spoon. By harrying Spanish ship ping in the North Sea, the Sea Beggar crippled the enemy's sea communication and at the same time kept the spirit c revolt alive.

Plate 334. Jeton. (1586). *Obverse:* Queen Elizabeth attended by the Earl of Leicester presenting a sword to two envoys from the United Provinces. *Reverse:* sword pointing to a cloud with name of Jehovah in Hebrew.

Plate 335. Jeton (1588). *Obverse:* mai woman, and children praying. *Reverse:* Span ish ship smashed in half. Issued to commemo rate the defeat of the Spanish Armada.

Plate 336 (left). Piacenza (Italy), silver scudo. *Obverse:* Alessandro Farnese, commander of the Spanish army in the Netherlands.

Plate 337 (right). Amsterdam, silver necessity klippe (1578). *Obverse:* two lions supporting city shield. Struck during a siege by the Spaniards.

Famous Sieges

Though William the Silent was a great leader, he had no military talents at all. It is not on record that he ever won a battle, and he lost many. Soon the Dutch were reduced to taking refuge behind the fortified walls of their cities.

Alva thought that the only way to end the revolt was to crush one city after another with frightful massacres. Typical was the siege of Haarlem. After holding out for seven months, the city surrendered in 1573. First Alva collected a ransom of 240,000 florins in return for his solemn promise to spare the inhabitants. Then he put the whole garrison and half the population to the sword, killing others by tying them back to back and throwing them into the river.

Then the Spaniards laid siege to Alkmaar ("all-marsh"), a peaceful town famous to this day for its cheese market. With Spain's well-trained force of 16,000 professional soldiers, they expected to have an easy time of it against the 800 inhabitants. But their training did not help them against the tubs of scalding water and molten lead that the brave women of Alkmaar rained down on them. And when the Dutch resorted to their supreme weapon and opened the dikes to flood the countryside, the Spaniards ran away just as swiftly as any poorly trained soldiers.

Alkmaar was the turning point of the struggle, and it put new heart into the resistance. But it is the epic defense of Leyden that is best remembered. The siege of this city, a cultural center, went on for a year. Plague carried off 7,000 of the city's 16,000 inhabitants. The brave Burgomaster kept up his people's spirits as best he could, striking medals to commemorate their resistance and having musicians parade through the streets playing lively tunes.

At last there came a day when not even a rat or a mouse was left to eat, and the people of Leyden, half-crazed with hunger, begged the Burgomaster to surrender the city so that they could die a quick death. But the Burgomaster, who was in communication with William the Silent by carrier pigeon, refused to give up. He knew that the Dutch leader was waiting for the autumn high tides, when he would open the dikes, flood the land around Leyden, and give the Sea Beggars enough draught to bring their ships in for a devastating raid.

But the Burgomaster could not reveal the plan. He handed his sword to the crowd, and, extending his right arm, he bared it to the shoulder. "Cut this off and eat it, if you will!" he cried to the citizens. "I shall never surrender the city!" Nor did he.

A few days later the Dutch opened the dikes, but the water did not rise high enough to really endanger the besiegers or to carry the Dutch boats inland. Then came the miracle! On October 3 a furious gale swept the waters up and the Sea Beggars sailed in exultantly, wearing their captured armor and wielding their wicked-looking knives and battle-axes.

Plate 338. Leyden, silver show taler (1574). *Obverse:* Sennacherib's mighty Assyrian host melting away before Jerusalem. Note the Biblical reference to 2 Kings: 19. *Reverse:* Spaniards fleeing from Leyden.

Leyden's "Show" Taler

It is to these thrilling events that we owe one of the most interesting of all commemorative coins. To the famished people of Leyden, the deliverance of their city seemed like an Old Testament miracle. And so they issued the famous "Show" Taler—perhaps the heroic Burgomaster Van der Werff was the man who had it struck.

In 1578 Alva, sickened by his tortures and butcheries, or perhaps only by their failure, asked to be relieved of his command. The Spanish King replaced him with Alessandro Farnese, Duke of Parma, considered the finest general of the century.

Although his record has some black marks for cruelty and treachery, he was also a shrewd statesman and a clever peacemaker. Hampered by stupid directives from Madrid, he nevertheless managed to save the Belgian provinces for Spain. His great ambition was to crush England, and he assembled a huge invasion army for that purpose. But when the British destroyed the "Invincible Armada," they dashed his hopes of invasion as well.

Holland's Golden Age

The seventeenth century was the golden age of Dutch sea power, commerce, and exploration.

The herring fleets required many vessels, and soon the Dutch saw quite a few other uses for the ships. They took over the shipping of grain from the Baltic ports to the rest of Europe; they obtained a monopoly of the Russian fur trade; they established extensive trading posts in Brazil.

Despite the efforts of the Barbary pirates, the Dutch captured the trade of the Levant, and even disputed the control of Mediterranean trade with Venice. They edged the Portuguese out of their own overseas markets; from Spain they snatched away the cotton and spice trade with India.

These Dutch sailors and traders were hard-bitten fighters when they had to be. They carried a broom on their masthead—a warning that they meant to sweep the ocean clear of all competition

Cape Horn got its name from a Dutch navigator who honored his native town of Hoorn. Tasmania, the island in the South

Plate 339. Amsterdam, silver trade dollar (1601). *Obverse:* crowned shield with lion rampant. *Reverse:* two lions supporting city shield. This equivalent of the piece of eight was issued by the Distant Company of Amsterdam.

Pacific, is named for Abel Tasman, the Dutch captain who discovered it and New Zealand (which he named for the Dutch province of Zeeland). Dutch whalers reached Spitsbergen and Novaya Zembla, well within the Arctic Circle. Dutch traders founded Kaapstad (now Capetown) at the southern tip of Africa. Dutchmen settled in New Amsterdam (New York), Surinam (Dutch Guiana) in South America, Curacao and Aruba in the West Indies.

All this far-flung trading produced enormous prosperity at home. The Dutch East India Company, founded in 1602, averaged an annual dividend of 18 per cent for the next 200 years. The Dutch West India Company was not started until 1623, but it made such inroads on the commerce with the New World that England passed laws to make it impossible for the American Colonies to ship their produce in Dutch vessels.

As early as 1601 Amsterdam coined its own Trade Dollar to compete with the Spanish piece of eight. Holland's trading boom was too good to last, and in the second half of the seventeenth century three bitterly fought naval wars with England forced the Dutch to admit that Britannia ruled the waves.

Tulips—the National Passion

The Dutch have always been very fond of flowers, and of all flowers, it is the lovely tulip that has fascinated the Dutch.

The tulip had its start in Turkey, where its name was *tulbend* ("turban"). The Austrian ambassador to Turkey brought the beautiful flower back to Vienna in 1554. There Clusius, the court gardener of the Hapsburgs, fell in love with the tulip and introduced it into his native Holland.

By the end of the sixteenth century, the Dutch had already achieved preeminence in tulip growing. Today they have over 2,000 varieties of this colorful and adaptable flower. In fact, they export about $25,000,000 worth of flower bulbs, mostly tulips, every year.

At one time, from 1634 to 1638, speculators traded in tulips. As in modern stock market deals, the speculators never even saw the flowers they traded in. A figure of 10,000,000 gulden was the turnover for one year's tulip-bulb sales in one single city. Eventually the Dutch government had to take energetic steps to put an end to this speculation mania.

During World War II, the Germans featured the tulip on their occupation currency. In the terrible famine winter of 1944-1945 under German occupation, the Dutch kept thousands of children alive by feeding them tulip bulbs.

Plate 340. German Occupation Government, zinc 10-cent piece. *Obverse:* tulip.

Netherlands or Holland?

The correct name for the land of the Dutch is "the Netherlands." Foreigners are so accustomed to calling the country "Holland" that even the natives now accept the name.

The Netherlands is divided into 11 provinces, or districts. One of these is North Holland—the most important of the lot and the one with which foreigners are most likely to be familiar, as it contains the country's three largest cities: Amsterdam, Rotterdam, and The Hague. More and more the term "Holland" has tended to replace the technically correct "the Netherlands."

Northern Europe

The Scandinavian countries—Denmark, Norway, Sweden, and Finland, are noted today for their ability to get along peacefully, for their enlightened social laws, and for their avoidance of extreme wealth or poverty.

It was not always so. A thousand years ago the prayer heard often in many churches of Europe was: "From the fury of the Northmen, deliver us, O Lord!" The blond giants of Scandinavia were mighty warriors, eager for adventure and greedy for plunder.

Viking Conquests

The Vikings, or Norsemen, as they were also called, were magnificent sailors. No coastline of Europe was safe from their raids. They established a kingdom in England, settled in Ireland, sailed further west to Iceland, then to Greenland, and even reached the mainland of North America. (See page 156.) The Vikings raided Antwerp and many French cities, then swept over the Mediterranean. Swarming over the Baltic, they made their way to Russia, penetrated south to establish kingdoms at Novgorod and Kiev, and tried several times to take Constantinople.

As we marvel at the Vikings' tireless wanderings, we wonder how they were able to build seaworthy ships. They were rather tardy in starting to use iron, and their tools were most elementary. Yet they were first-class shipbuilders and some of their vessels are still in existence to prove it.

When a Viking leader died, his ship was hauled up on shore. A burial chamber was constructed inside and there the king was laid to rest, together with his favorite belongings. His followers set the vessel in a deep grave, and covered it with a huge mound.

Many centuries later, when some of these ships were dug up, we discovered that they were light enough to be carried overland—an important feature of "commando" raids. Yet they had room for 40 to 64 oars, and carried close to 100 warriors. The Viking vessels were colorful, with their dragon-prows ornamented with gold scales,

Plate 341. Estonia, aluminum bronze 1 kroon (1934). This handsome coin shows a Viking ship.

their brilliant blue, red, or green sails contrasting with equally striking colors above the water line, and gaily striped pennants streaming in the wind. The old Norse sagas tell of ships large enough to carry a thousand men, and of fleets of 600 and 700 vessels.

The Vikings began their repeated inroads on France in the ninth century. Once they sailed down the Seine to Paris, but spared the city in return for a ransom of 7,000 pounds of silver. At the beginning of the tenth century, Norsemen settled in northern France (later called "Normandy"). Here they carved out vast estates for themselves, accepted Christianity, and became French in speech and customs. They also established kingdoms in the British Isles.

Other Normans went on to attack Spanish cities, entered the Mediterranean, harried southern French and Italian cities, and conquered Sicily and southern Italy in the eleventh century.

The Swedish Vikings who set up their kingdom in Russia developed a profitable trade in the ninth century with Asiatic and Byzantine merchants. The goods brought by the Vikings were shipped north to the Baltic, and on to the town of Visby on the Swedish island of Gotland ("Gothland").

Visby became so wealthy that pirates pillaged it three times, yet each time it amassed new riches. In one of these raids, in 1361, King Valdemar of Denmark filled Visby's public square with barrels and ordered the people to cram them to the top with gold, silver, and other valuables. Visby's decline dates from this raid. Today Visby's museum contains many ancient gold and silver coins from Greece, Rome, Arabia, and the Byzantine Empire.

Vikings had wandered all the way south to Constantinople, and served as mercenaries in the Byzantine armies. Norsemen formed the bodyguard of the Byzantine Emperors, and a Scandinavian legion of the Byzantine army participated in campaigns that ranged through the Holy Land, north Africa, and Italy. The mercenaries must have been well paid, for more than 50,000 Byzantine coins have been dug up in Sweden alone.

Sweden Becomes a Nation

When Denmark, Norway, and Sweden formed the Union of Kalmar in 1397, Denmark was definitely the most powerful and populous of the three and consequently became the dominant partner in the Union. Proud of its preeminence, Denmark adopted a coat of arms with three crowns.

We find this device of three crowns, by the way, on many Swedish coins—not to mention the menus in Swedish restaurants and the smokestacks of Swedish vessels.

***Plate 342.* Sweden, silver 5 kronor (1935). *Reverse:* shield with three crowns. Issued to commemorate the 500th anniversary of the Swedish Parliament.**

The majestic main tower of Stockholm's beautiful Town Hall has three gold crowns. According to some scholars, the three crowns are derived from Denmark's old coat of arms; other experts believe that the crowns represent the Swedish saints Balthazar, Gaspard, and Melchior.

The Swedes were not too happy with their position in the Union. They established their own parliament, the Riksdag,

Plate 343. Sweden, silver taler (1542). *Obverse:* Gustavus Vasa. *Reverse:* Christ. It is interesting to compare this sixteenth century coin of Gustavus Vasa with the next plate.

Plate 344. Sweden, silver 2 kronor (1921). *Obverse:* Gustavus Vasa. Issued to commemorate the 400th anniversary of Swedish independence.

as early as 1435 but its power was limited by the Danish court.

Finally, the unrest in Sweden reached such a point that in 1520 Denmark's tyrannical King Christian II decided on a frightful step—the famous "Bloodbath of Stockholm." He invited 80 of Sweden's leading nobles to a state dinner; at the height of the festivities, the Danish king's soldiers entered, arrested the unfortunates, and after a quick "trial" they were all executed!

The bloodbath horrified the Swedes, but no one wanted to take the risk of organizing a rebellion. However, there was one exception—Gustavus Vasa, the 24-year-old son of one of the victims. After King Christian set a price on his head, he was forced to wander from one end of Sweden to another hiding from would-be informers and Danish soldiers.

At last, tired of hairbreadth escapes and deeply dejected over his failure to gain Swedish support, Vasa mournfully strapped on his skis and fled to the northern wastes, hoping to find a safe refuge. Soon after he left, two men turned up in search of Vasa. Following his trail, they went on doggedly until they caught up with him.

But they were not enemies—they were messengers from his secret supporters, who invited him to raise the standard of revolt. Vasa returned, organized a patriot army and drove out the Danes. In gratitude, the Swedes made him their King, and to this day they revere him as their national liberator and founder of their freedoms. Every year a ski race is held over the route followed by Gustavus Vasa and his pursuers.

As a King, Gustavus Vasa was a "strong man." He introduced many needed reforms, joined the other Scandinavian countries in adopting the Lutheran form of Protestantism, and laid down a policy that Sweden was to follow unsuccessfully for 200 years: striving for control of the Baltic and a foothold on the European mainland.

Sweden's Warrior Kings

Gustavus Adolphus, the first of a series of warrior kings, came to the throne in 1611 at the age of 17. He had a flair for

Plate 345. Sweden, silver 2 kronor (1932). *Obverse:* Gustavus Adolphus. *Reverse:* tablet commemorating the 300th anniversary of his death in the Battle of Luetzen.

Plate 346. Sweden, silver taler (1660). *Obverse:* arm with sword between six arms with smaller swords. Issued to commemorate the death of Charles X Gustav.

Plate 347. Bremen and Verden, silver taler (1674). *Reverse:* coat of arms. An unusually elegant coin.

Plate 348. Riga, silver taler (1660). *Reverse:* hand above placing crown on city coat of arms.

learning quickly; speaking eight languages was only one of his many accomplishments. He was a born general, this "Lion of the North," personally courageous, and an ambitious and far-sighted statesman. Sweden was too poor to afford a large army, so Gustavus Adolphus wisely concentrated on swift mobility, the best available weapons, and intelligent training methods.

In 1631, when it seemed that Protestantism was about to be wiped out in Europe, Gustavus Adolphus became its savior by winning a brilliant victory in Germany at the Battle of Breitenfeld. It was in honor of this battle that the nearby city of Erfurt issued its notable Purimtaler (see Plate 228). A year later he won another famous battle, at Luetzen, but he was killed by an enemy straggler. He died at the age of 38.

In 1638 the Swedes made their only attempt at colonization in the New World by settling in Delaware. Preoccupied with European struggles, they could not give proper support to their colonists, who were driven off by the Dutch in 1654.* In the same year, Charles X Gustav came to the throne. He was a firebrand, living only for war. After winning sensational victories, he died young, and the effects of his victories faded all too soon.

His son Charles XI (1660-1697) was a prudent penny pincher. He built up the royal treasury by confiscating the estates of the nobles and tried to stifle discontent by dismissing the Riksdag. The funds he assembled so laboriously were quickly spent

* See *Coinometry,* p. 31

Plate 349. Breslau, silver taler (1709). *Obverse:* Charles XII in armor. *Reverse:* lion in front of column with candle between palm branches.

Plate 350. Sweden, silver 2 kronor (1938). *Reverse:* ship. Commemorates the 300th anniversary of the Swedish settlement of Delaware.

by his son, Charles XII, who became King in 1697 at the age of 16.

Two years later, when a coalition of Russia (under Peter the Great), Poland, and Denmark declared war on Sweden, it made an astonishing discovery: the youthful Swedish King was the most brilliant military genius of his day. He quickly defeated the Danes. Within three months after marching his army into Russia, and although outnumbered four to one, he smashed part of the Russian army in a blinding snowstorm. Finally—at the age of 24!—he disposed of the Poles.

Unfortunately Charles XII was too ambitious and too daring to know when to stop. Unwisely allowing his forces to be enticed deeper and deeper into Russia, he was decisively defeated by Peter in a battle at Poltava in 1709. Still Charles XII kept up the struggle. His army gone, he fled to Turkey, stirred up the Turks against Russia, made his way back to Sweden, started new wars in the Baltic area, and was fatally wounded at the age of 36.

The colorful, turbulent, and essentially meaningless career of Charles XII left Sweden impoverished, inflation-ridden, and anything but a first-class military power. It took her many years to recover from the effects of her disastrous age of glory.

Calling in all silver coins in 1709, the almost-bankrupt Swedish government issued copper coins from the original dies. Naturally this substitution proved unpopular. Soon a new copper issue appeared with the images of Jupiter, Saturn, and other gods. Popular discontent reached a savage pitch so the government found a convenient scapegoat in Baron de Goertz, the originator of the scheme. He was arrested, tried, and *beheaded!*

The aftermath of the glorious wars was all the more trying in that the Swedes were burdened next by a series of sadly

Plate 352. **Sweden, silver 5 kronor (1935).** ***Obverse:*** **Gustav V, familiar to millions of Americans from films of his tennis-playing at a very advanced age. (This is the obverse of *Plate 342.*)**

incompetent governments. During the involved diplomatic maneuvers of the Napoleonic era, Sweden lost Finland.

Bernadotte became King in 1818 under the name of Charles XIV John. His dynasty continues to this day. The very popular Swedish Kings, like all the modern Scandinavian monarchs, are loved for their friendly ways and simple tastes.

Sweden became prosperous in the nineteenth century after turning away from foreign adventures. In her shipping trade, her farms, forests, and metals she found the wealth that had always been available. Lapland, the northern third of Sweden's area, contains mountains 100 miles north of the Arctic Circle that have the world's purest iron ore. Experts believe there may be as much as 2,000,000,000 tons of this ore which is 60 to 70 per cent pure. There are only 6,000 Lapp residents, nomads who live on reindeer meat, and the region is dark all day except for a brief summer period when the Midnight Sun keeps the night aglow.

Sweden lacks coal, but water power supplies electricity for every need. Like the other Scandinavian countries, Sweden has no slums; industrialization came late enough to enable the Swedes to profit by the mistakes of other countries.

Plate 353. Glueckstadt, silver taler (1624). *Obverse:* Christian IV of Denmark. *Reverse:* Fortuna on globe (Glueckstadt means "town of good fortune.")

Plate 354. Denmark, silver crown (1659). *Obverse:* arm from heaven cutting off the (Swedish) hand which tries to seize crown.

The Danish Empire

The Danes contributed their share of the raids that terrorized the coasts of Europe during the Middle Ages. Medieval Denmark reached its greatest power under King Canute (see Plate 157), who ruled over Norway and England as well as Denmark. The Danes also fought many a battle in Eastern Europe.

At about the time of the Union of Kalmar (1397) with Norway and Sweden, Denmark acquired Schleswig and Holstein, two provinces on the Danish border. The loss of Sweden in 1521 was a great blow. Denmark's story from then on was one of continually being involved in wars with bigger neighbors.

During the Napoleonic wars, Denmark supported the French side and was punished by having to part with Norway in 1814. Fifty years later, Prussia seized Schleswig and Holstein after a lightning war against the Danes. Denmark was now "tiny" Denmark.

In its present form Denmark is made up of some 500 islands of varying size, really submerged mountains sticking up out of the sea.

Some countries have been known to turn ugly after defeat and brood on their revenge. Not so Denmark, which has given

Plate 355. Denmark, silver 2 kroner (1945). *Obverse:* Christian X. *Reverse:* commemorative wreath for the King's 75th birthday and the rebirth of Danish independence.

the world a lesson in how to get along peacefully and make the best of what is available.

After the loss of Schleswig and Holstein, the Danes concentrated on cattle-raising and dairy farming. They produce half the world's bacon, and one-fourth of its butter and eggs, all famous for their quality. Still the Danes devote a great deal of research to make these products even better. Their dairy animals even have stalls equipped with automatic drinking fountains!

Copenhagen is a busy harbor, for these descendents of the Vikings have a great merchant marine. The first Diesel-powered ship (1912) was built in a Danish shipyard. The elegance of Danish work in such fields as silverware, glassware, porcelain, and furniture has always been much admired.

Plate 356. Greenland, silver piaster (1771). *Obverse:* crowned shield. *Reverse:* crowned hemispheres between pillars—an imitation of the pillar design on the Spanish piece of eight (see Plate 462).

Plate 357. Faroe Islands, bronze 1 ore (1941). *Obverse:* inscription with holed center.

Plate 358. Norway, gold 20 kroner (1910). *Reverse:* St. Olaf, patron saint of Norway.

The occupation period during World War II was a period of intense suffering for the Danes. Their underground organization sank the Danish fleet and scuttled the shipping in Copenhagen harbor so that the Germans would not have their use. It blew up supply trains and sabotaged Nazi production. To the Danes, their aged King Christian X was the symbol of resistance to the enemy. Shortly before his death in 1947, he asked to be buried with the emblem of the Danish resistance movement.

Danish Colonies

Greenland, which belongs to Denmark, has one-fourth the area of the United States, but no more than 20,000 inhabitants. And no wonder!—85 per cent of Greenland is ice, some of it 6,000 feet deep. Part of the ice melts from time to time and forms treacherous icebergs that are a menace to shipping. If all this ice were to melt, the surface of the oceans would rise all over the earth.

It is believed that Greenland is rich in minerals, but only the coast is habitable and much of the island is obscured by fog.

Because seals have become scarce, today the natives earn their living by fishing.

Norway

Few of us realize that modern Norway did not achieve full independence until 1905. For centuries it was under Danish domination until it was handed over to Sweden in 1814. Though ill will on both sides brought about the separation of Norway from Sweden in 1905, there was no bloodshed.

Norway is a rugged land, so mountainous that only four per cent of the soil is suitable for farming. Half of the country lies within the Arctic Circle, but the Gulf Stream moderates the rigors of the climate.

The coastline of this long, narrow land extends for about 1,000 miles, curling around to form a common border with Russia at its northern tip. The coast of Norway is broken by hundreds of fjords—bays that are long, slender, twisting indentations of the sea going far inland. The term "Viking" comes from the old Norse word for "bay." Often the fjords flow between lofty mountains that are reflected in the mirror-like surface of the water with an effect that thrills every beholder. It is said that if all the fjords were measured ngthwise, they would reach a combined length of 12,000 miles!

Norway's unpromising soil has forced the Norwegians to make a living from the sea, fishing (sardines, especially) and trading. They have the fourth largest merchant marine—half the size of the United States', although our population is fifty times as large as Norway's. During World War II, the Norwegian merchant marine played a valuable role in bringing about an Allied victory.

Plate 359. **Norway, silver specie daler (1864). *Reverse:* crowned coat of arms in wreath.**

Plate 360. **Finland, copper 10 pennia (1918-1940). *Obverse:* lion on sword.**

Finland

Finland has the misfortune of a highly strategic location on the shores of the Baltic. For centuries it was ruled by the Swedes. Gustavus Vasa founded Helsinki in 1550; the city is famous for its distinguished architecture and spotless streets. It also has a stadium for the Olympic Games, which have been held there several times—most recently in 1952.

Though highly industrialized today, Finland is two-thirds forest land, and has some 60,000 lakes. Much of the land in swampy—*Suomi,* the Finnish name for the country, means "swamp."

The Finns, a hardy people, are descended from wandering tribes that left Asia many centuries ago. The Finnish language, related to Estonian and Hungarian, does not belong to the great family of Indo-European languages.

Finland passed into Russian control in 1809. When the Russian Revolution broke out in 1917, the Finns revolted and broke away from Russia, setting up their own government. Their heroic resistance to Soviet invasion in World War II could not prevent the loss of valuable territory. Today the Finns still maintain their precarious freedom.

Plate 361. **Finland (under Russian administration), copper 10 pennia (1905-1917). *Obverse:* crowned N (for Czar Nicholas).**

Iceland

Though situated on the edge of the Arctic Circle, some 800 miles west of the British Isles, Iceland has a very pleasant climate. It is a volcanic island, and its most famous volcano, Mt. Hekla, once thought to be the rim of Hell, is still active.

Some scholars claim that Iceland was known to mainland Europeans as early as 300 B.C. Irish monks began visiting the island about 500 A.D.

About 870 Iceland was settled by Norwegian Vikings, some of whom had lived in Ireland. In 930 they formed the Althing, their legislature and supreme court. Iceland therefore has the distinction of having established the first parliament organized on

Plate 365 (left). Iceland, silver 10 kroner (1930). *Obverse:* King of Thule with kneeling children.

Plate 366 (right). Iceland, 5 kroner (1930). *Obverse:* Ulfliot the Lawmaker. Both coins commemorate the thousandth anniversary of Iceland's parliament.

democratic lines. Later on, however, Iceland lived through turbulent times, coming first under the domination of Norway and then of Denmark. The island achieved full independence in 1944.

Like all the Norsemen, the men of Iceland were magnificent sailors Under Erik the Red they discovered Greenland about the year 980. Some years later Leif Eriksson, one of Erik's sons, reached the mainland of North America. He called the region Vinland. Today we do not know whether "Vinland" was Newfoundland, Nova Scotia, or New England. At any rate it is now universally accepted that the Norse mariners discovered the New World almost 500 years before Columbus sailed west in the hope of reaching India.

THE BALTIC COUNTRIES

Most of the Baltic lands were under Russian domination until the time of World War I. The Treaty of Versailles which ended that war recognized them as independent nations and they enjoyed a brief taste of uneasy freedom between the two World Wars. During this period (1919-1939) they issued some delightful coins; these were generally of a commemorative nature and revived the glories of bygone days. However, in the period 900-1800, it is hard to discover ten consecutive years of peace!

Poland

The story of the old Polish kingdom was a tragic one. Although they were often heroic in fighting a foreign enemy, the Poles were jealous rivals when it came to domestic affairs. In the end, they fell easy prey to ruthless outsiders.

One of Poland's most warlike Kings, Sigismund III (1587-1632) deserves our attention, though not for his endless wars which contributed to Poland's ruin. Whether out of vanity or sincere love of the arts, Sigismund was responsible for a coin which is one of the world's outstanding numismatic gems.*

A much greater King was Jan III Sobieski (1674-1696), who was greatly admired all over Europe for defeating first the Tatars and then the Turks, each time with a vastly outnumbered army. Jan Sobieski is best remembered for coming to the aid of Vienna in 1683, decisively trouncing the Turks and lifting the siege of that city. This was the last great thrust of the Turks in their attempt to conquer all of Europe.

Good Kings were a rarity in Poland, because they had to be elected by the Diet (legislature) of nobles and were rulers in name only. It took considerable intrigue,

* *See frontispiece for Plate 367.*

late 368. Poland, silver 10 zlotych (1933). *)bverse:* Jan Sobieski. (Commemorates the 50th anniversary of the siege of Vienna.)

'late 369. Poland, silver 5 zlotych (1936). *)bverse:* ship. One of the most beautiful of ll ship coins.

Plate 370. Poland, silver 5 zlotych (1934). *Reverse:* banner of 1830 Revolution.

Plate 371. Poland, silver 10 zlotych (1934). *Obverse:* Joseph Pilsudski, Poland's "strong man." (Twentieth anniversary of entry of Pilsudski's Rifle Corps into World War I.)

ınd often corruption, to find a suitably veak candidate. The Diet worked in a pe-:uliar way. Its measures had to pass unani-nously. If one member objected on any)oint—this was the famous "Polish veto" —the session was over.

Poland, enfeebled by war and misgov-:rnment, attracted the greedy attention of Russia, Prussia, and Austria. Three par-:itions—in 1772, 1793, and 1796—sliced up the country, with the biggest share go-ing to Russia. Three times Polish revolts flared up against hopeless odds, the last revolt (1863) bringing on an exceptionally harsh Russification policy.

Joseph Pilsudski (1867-1935), outstanding leader of the Polish revolutionary movement at the turn of the twentieth century, had served a five-year sentence in Siberia. When he was arrested a second time, he feigned insanity and was sent to a heavily guarded asylum in St. Petersburg from which he managed to escape!

At the outbreak of World War I, Pilsudski organized and led a Polish corps in the German army. After the war, he emerged as Poland's "strong man"; but once in power, he applied many of the tyrannical methods he had fought in earlier times. Poland was Germany's first victim at the outbreak of World War II and has since come into the Russian orbit.

Lithuania, Latvia, Estonia

Lithuania had its glorious age in the fifteenth century when it was about three times the size of Poland, sweeping south to the Black Sea and east almost as far as Moscow. For several centuries Poland and Lithuania were closely associated. One of the fondest memories of the people of both these countries is the stinging defeat inflicted by their combined armies on the Teutonic Knights in the swamps of Tannenberg in East Prussia (1410). Vytatas was the Grand Duke of Lithuania (1392-1430) during its days of greatest glory and cultural flowering.

Both the Latvians (or Letts) and the Estonians have a similar history of constant invasions ending with subjection to Russia. The Estonians are related to the Finns, and their languages are very similar.

Plate 372. Lithuania, silver 10 litu (1936). *Obverse:* Grand Duke Vytatas. *Reverse:* Horseman.

Plate 373. Latvia, silver 5 lati (1929-1932). *Obverse:* young girl in peasant costume. An unusually attractive coin.

Plate 374. Danzig, silver 5 gulden (1923, 1927). *Obverse:* view of Danzig. This coin faithfully reproduces the medieval atmosphere of the old city.

Plate 375. Danzig, silve necessity taler (1577). *Ob verse:* bust of Christ. Struc during a siege, this coin fea tures one of the finest numis matic portraits of Christ.

An Estonian coin of 1933 alludes to the national passion for singing and choral festivals.

Danzig

The former free city of Danzig is located on the Baltic at the mouth of the Vistula River, one of eastern Europe's great waterways. For centuries this picturesque port shipped Polish and Prussian grain which had been brought north by raft along the Vistula.

In time, Danzig became rich and was one of the most important cities of the Hanseatic League of the thirteenth century. Aside from grain and an extensive fishing industry, Danzig was famous for its amber, found in its nearby fossil deposits.

Bristling with fortifications, Danzig endured many a siege in olden times as its neighbors fought over so rich a prize. Its charming twentieth-century coinage admirably conveys the quaint but bustling atmosphere of this historic port.

Plate 376. Estonia, silver kroon (1933). *Ob verse:* lyre. Issued for the tenth Estonian Sing ing Festival.

Plate 377. Estonia, silver 2 krooni (1932) *Obverse:* University of Tartu (commemoratin its 300th anniversary).

Plate 378. Danzig, aluminum bronze 10 pfennig (1932). *Obverse:* codfish.

Plate 379. Danzig, nickel 5 gulden (1935). *Obverse:* sailing ship. Both these coins pay tribute to the old-time glories of Danzig's bustling harbor.

Russia

More than three-quarters of Russia lies in Asia. When you look at the map, the European part of Russia seems no more than an outpost.

The traces of ancient civilization that seeped into Russia from faraway Rome were faint. But Constantinople, the Byzantine capital, was a next-door neighbor. It was from the Byzantine Empire, deeply influenced by Asiatic sources, that Russia took its religion, its Greek-type alphabet, its notions of autocratic government, its imperial symbol of the double eagle, and even its early coinage.

When the Byzantine Empire was destroyed by the Turks in 1453, the rulers of the strongest dynasty in Russia, the Grand Dukes of Muscovy, thought of themselves as the logical successors to the Empire. They developed the theory of "the three Romes," with Russia figuring as the third Roman Empire. It is here that we find the origin of the title "Czar" (Caesar). The first of the Grand Dukes to give himself this title officially was Ivan the Terrible (1533-1584). When the Czarist regime ended in 1917, the theory of a worldwide empire did not die with it; it was merely rephrased by the Communists in more up-to-date language.

Michael Romanov, chosen Czar in 1613 by the boyars, or great barons, founded a dynasty that lasted for slightly more than 300 years. The monarchs of this dynasty varied greatly—some were near-imbeciles and some, like Catherine the Great, were extremely able. But they had one thing in common: they were all absolute rulers. This tradition, too, outlived the Czarist regime and allowed the Communists to establish a dictatorship.

Plate 380. Silver ruble (1913). *Obverse:* the last of the Romanov Czars, Nicholas II (left), and the first, Michael Romanov (right). Issued for the 300th anniversary of the dynasty.

Peter the Great

The greatest of the Czars, Peter the Great (1682-1725), inherited a realm in which brutality, superstition, corruption, and ignorance were widespread. Schools were scarce, representative government was unheard of, the simplest practical techniques unknown.

It was Peter who gave Imperial Russia its army, its navy, and its government bureaucracy. But it was his lifelong at-

Plate 381. Silver ruble (1914). *Obverse:* Peter the Great. *Reverse:* imperial arms with crowned double eagle. Issued for the 200th anniversary of the naval victory at Gangut.

tempt to teach the Russians Western ways and techniques that earned him the title of "the Great." As part of this program, Peter visited Holland and England to study Western skills and to hire technicians.

On his return to Russia, in 1698, Peter gave his subjects a taste of the new ways. A terrific shakeup of the army put all promotion on the basis of ability instead of social position. Every man, boyar or peasant, was to don Western dress and shave his beard. The calendar was drastically revised. He went ahead like a bull, whether people were ready for his changes or not.

It was probably the "ukase" (proclamation) on beards that aroused the most opposition. To the pious Russians, the order was blasphemous—for (so they argued) if God had intended man not to have a beard, He would have created him differently. Even a Czar had to backtrack when met by such powerful reasoning. So Peter issued a new ukase providing that those who wanted the privilege of keeping their beards must pay a tax and would receive a coin—a "beard token"—as a receipt.

Plate 382. Copper beard token. Note the uncanny-looking *reverse* which features nose, lips, mustache, and beard.

Though historians have made much of this "reform," coin scholars believe that the ukases were never enforced. The beard tokens were struck as patterns (or perhaps in quantity) but never used and eventually melted down.

When Peter was 23, in 1695, he conducted his first military campaign—against the Tatars in south Russia. Although he was in charge of the expedition of 120,000 men, he served as a sergeant in the ranks. His army proved no match for the Tatars, but the young Czar had the last word. Commandeering 30,000 men, he built shipyards on the Sea of Azov and turned out 29 vessels. With the aid of his new fleet, he trounced the Tatars.

For the rest of his life, Peter was interested above all in maintaining a southern outlet through the Black Sea and a northern outlet through the Baltic Sea. To this day these aims remain basic Russian policy.

Shortly after his return to Russia in 1698, Peter became involved in war with Sweden. At the same time, he decided to found a new capital on the bleak, unhealthy marshes along the Baltic, hundreds of miles from the nearest Russian habitation. On this grim wasteland, thousands of unfortunate workmen succumbed to exposure and disease in building the new city of St. Petersburg. Neither peasant revolts nor strong Swedish invasions kept Peter from this work. At last, in 1709, he broke Sweden's military power by his victory at Poltava and in 1712 the royal family moved to the new capital.

Peter's last years were clouded by misfortune and disappointment. When Azov was recaptured by the Turks his plans for a southern sea route were destroyed. He imprisoned his son, who was indifferent to reforms and other problems of government. The young man died in prison in 1718—some say he was tortured to death. Worn

Plate 383. **Silver ruble (1763-1796).** ***Obverse:*** **Catherine II (the Great), the German-born wife of Czar Peter III, seized the throne and proved herself the ablest Russian ruler after Peter the Great. Catherine was just as ruthless as any of the Czars, but far more intelligent than most of them. She extended Russia's borders considerably at the expense of Turkey and Poland.**

out by his strenuous life, Peter died in 1725 at the age of 53.

Napoleon's Invasion

In one respect, Peter the Great had been thoroughly successful. He established Russia as a European power—so much so that by 1812, when Napoleon reached his peak, Czar Alexander I was considered his only serious rival for mastery of the Continent.

To invade Russia, Napoleon assembled his Grand Army, the greatest force ever seen up to that time—estimates vary from 300,000 to 600,000 men.

When Napoleon entered Russia, he found that his army had to march through a wasteland of flaming or charred houses and barns. People and animals were gone, the crops destroyed. First the weather was blazing hot, then came chilling rains, leaving mud everywhere. The miserable soldiers became ill from exposure.

When the French entered Moscow they found the city utterly deserted and on fire!

Napoleon gave the order to turn back, choosing a southerly route in the hope of better weather and a richer source of supplies. But, without offering battle, the crafty Russians forced the enemy back to the original, completely ravaged route.

And so, loaded with what loot they could carry from Moscow, Napoleon's wretched soldiers made their way back through the wasteland of burned hamlets. The plodding men kept alive by killing and eating their horses. The Russians, on sleds, easily defeated the remnants of the Grand Army in a battle when the temperature was 40 below zero!

Revolution

The magnificent resistance to Napoleon's invasion gave the Romanov Czars a prestige which they dissipated in the following years. They ruled by stern repression, alternating with reforms that came either too late or too soon. Russia's entry into World War I on the side of the Allies led to a series of battles with fearful losses; on the home front, the railroad system broke down, there were serious food shortages, and discontent was rife. Nicholas II abdicated in March, 1917, in favor of a Provisional Government. In November the Bolsheviks seized power, executed the Czar and his family the following July, and consolidated their regime in a turbulent civil war that lasted well into 1920. After many upheavals, the Russians are still waiting for the brilliant dawn promised on this 1924 coin of the Soviet government.

Plate 384. **U.S.S.R., silver ruble (1924).** ***Obverse:*** **two workers stand before a brilliant dawn.**

The Balkans and Tiny European Countries

Well named the "tinderbox of Europe," the grim, mountainous Balkan Peninsula is bordered on the south by a precious strategic prize—the narrow Straits of the Bosporus and the Dardanelles which separate Russia and the Black Sea on the east from the Aegean and Mediterranean Seas on the west.

The ancient Romans as well as the Byzantines regarded the Balkans as an important objective for their expansion. Time and again this region was also overrun by nomadic tribes pressing ahead fiercely from central Asia. One of these invading peoples, the Ottoman Turks, had the necessary military power and governing skill to conquer virtually all of the Balkans and to rule the area for centuries.

This Empire, the greatest of the Moslem states, was named for Osman, the first outstanding ruler of the Ottoman Turks. Originally Tatar tribesmen of the Asiatic steppes, the Turks intermarried extensively with Europeans in the course of their westward wanderings. Finally they settled in Asia Minor, where they were converted to Mohammedanism about 900 A.D.

Rise of the Ottoman Empire

Soon these ferocious fighters were making conquests to the east, in the Arab countries, and in the Balkan Peninsula, too.

After the Turks captured Constantinople and destroyed the Byzantine Empire in 1453, they remained a constant menace to Europe beyond the borders of the Balkan Peninsula for 250 years.

At its height, during the sixteenth century, the Ottoman Empire excited the wondering admiration of all observers. "No distinction is attached to [noble] birth among the Turks," the Venetian Ambassador reported. "The deference to be paid to a man is measured by the position he holds in the public service."

Yet the Ottoman Empire was despotic, afflicted with all the weaknesses of such regimes. The only way the dynasty could assure its stability was through the custom of having every new Sultan kill all his brothers.

Plate 387. Turkey, silver yuzlik (1789). ***Reverse:*** **four-line inscription. Since the Koran forbids image-making, the coins of Moslem countries are limited to inscriptions and abstract patterns.**

By 1800 Turkey still had a vast Empire, but its government, finances, and army were all in a sad state. Many conflicts arose as the Turkish Empire decayed and the great powers jockeyed for a share of the spoils. In addition, the Balkan Peninsula was in a ferment as the subject peoples struggled for their independence.

Russia was following its age-old policy of seeking control of the Bosporus and the Dardanelles. England and France were both concerned to prevent Russian expansion. They were thus committed to supporting Turkey—a dangerous state of affairs in view of the fourteen major wars between the Russians and the Turks during the preceding 400 years.

One of these conflicts broke out in 1853. When it seemed that Turkey was on the point of being crushed, France and England entered the struggle against Russia. The resulting Crimean War kept the Straits out of Russian hands.

From then on, the Russians pursued an effective policy of stirring up unrest in the Balkans by encouraging their fellow Slavs to revolt against Turkey. Another Russo-Turkish War, in 1877, was disastrous for Turkey, the "sick man of Europe." The Turks had to grant independence to Montenegro, Serbia, Bulgaria, and Rumania. Greece had already won its freedom, with

Plate 390. **Turkey, silver 100 kurus (1934). *Obverse:* Mustafa Kemal Ataturk. *Reverse:* value in wreath. Note the use of the Latin alphabet, Arabic numbers, and Christian Era dating.**

British aid, in 1829; Albania did not achieve complete independence until 1912.

World War I left Turkey a badly defeated country. All that remained of its once huge Empire was a little bit of land in Europe and the bare, rocky Anatolian area in Asia Minor.

Modern Turkey

At this desperate stage the Turks surprised the world with a display of the vigor and resolution which had won them an Empire centuries before. After deposing the Sultan in 1922, they established a republic. Their first President, Mustafa Kemal Ataturk, realized that only the most ruthless reforms could save his tottering country.

Plate 388. **Rumania, gold medal (1939). *Reverse:* peasant mowing. *Obverse:* King Carol on horseback. (Plate 389 uses the same *obverse*. Both these handsome medals appeared in limited quantities as part of an issue of coins.)**

Plate 389. **Rumania, gold medal (1939). *Reverse:* the Wolf of Rome feeding Romulus and Remus, which reminds us that Rumania (ancient Dacia) was once a Roman province.**

Plate 391. Cyprus, silver 45 piastres (1928). *Reverse:* two lions. This Mediterranean island has been occupied by Great Britain since 1878.

Plate 392. Albania, silver 5 franki ari (1925-1927). *Reverse:* plowing scene. Albania has issued some remarkably beautiful coins.

Plate 393. Greece, copper 20 lepta (1831). *Obverse:* phoenix representing Greek freedom from Turkish rule.

Kemal's ambition was to tear out the old Turkey by the roots. He "talked back" boldly to the European nations and drastically curbed the power of the Moslem religious organizations. After establishing free and compulsory public education, he brought in the Latin alphabet and Western numbers. The significant change in the style of Turkish coinage amply illustrates the daring sweep of Kemal's reforms.

In line with his contempt for the old Turkey, Kemal moved the capital from Istanbul in Europe to Ankara in Asia Minor. From 1923, when the change took place, to 1953, Ankara's population grew from 35,000 to 300,000. Kemal Ataturk wanted a modern capital: Ankara's new construction was along Western lines; city dwellers had to wear Western dress; city women enjoyed freedom and could go without veils for the first time in Turkish history.

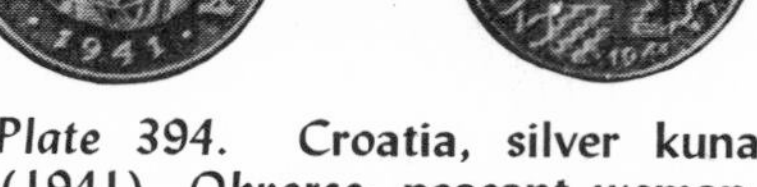

Plate 394. Croatia, silver kuna (1941). *Obverse:* peasant woman.

Plate 395. Croatia, silver 50 banica (1941). *Obverse:* medieval towergate.

Intermingling Cultures

Yugoslavia ("land of the South Slavs") is a good example of the extraordinary intermingling of Balkan cultures and peoples. The South Slavs arrived in this region about 650, and in the course of time were split up among several different rulers. Yugoslavia, uniting Serbia, Croatia and Slovenia into a single nation, did not come into existence until 1918.

Some parts of the country use the Latin alphabet, and the people who live there are Roman Catholic and wear Western dress. In other sections there are many Orthodox Catholics, who use the Cyrillic alphabet (based on Greek letters). Besides this, 500 years or more of Turkish rule have left a considerable number of Moslems, whose culture, alphabet, and dress set them apart from the other Yugoslavs.

Plate 396. Serbia, silver 5 dinar (1904). *Obverse:* Peter I and Kara George.

Plate 397
Bulgaria, silver 5 leva (1930). *Reverse:* knight on horseback.

Plate 398. San Marino, silver 20 lira (1931-1937). *Obverse:* three feathers crowned. *Reverse:* Saint Marinus. Tradition tells us that this 38-square-mile republic was founded in Italy toward the end of the third century by Christian refugees escaping from Emperor Diocletian's persecutions.

Plate 399. Liechtenstein, silver 5 kronen (1900). *Obverse:* Johann II. Because they enjoy low taxes there, some of the world's largest corporations have been chartered in this beautiful Alpine principality, which has an area of 65 square miles.

Plate 400. Luxembourg, silver 50 francs (1946). *Reverse:* Prince John. *Obverse:* King John the Blind on horseback. In the fourteenth and fifteenth centuries several Counts of Luxembourg achieved royal rank. One of them—John, King of Bohemia—sought death in battle after going blind.

Plate 401. Monaco, aluminum bronze 2 francs (1924). *Obverse:* bowman. The principality of Monaco, with its area of half a square mile, is the tiniest country in the world. Yet, as the site of the gambling casino at Monte Carlo, it receives over 1,000,000 visitors a year.

During World War II, Turkey miraculously preserved its neutrality, but all the other Balkan countries were battlegrounds. This was particularly true of Yugoslavia and Greece. After the end of the war the Balkan countries were caught up in the "cold war" between East and West. Yugoslavia, Greece, and Turkey lined up with the West, while Albania, Bulgaria, and Rumania became Soviet satellites.

Luxembourg, Liechtenstein, Monaco, and San Marino are among the tiniest countries in Europe issuing coins.

United States of America

The Indians lived in the Americas long before the ancient civilization of Egypt began to flourish, long before Alexander the Great embarked on his conquests. Scientists believe that the ancestors of the American Indians came to the Americas thousands of years ago by way of the land bridge that once connected Siberia with Alaska. A coin collector totally unfamiliar with American history would get an idea of the important role the Indians have played from the frequency with which Indian likenesses appear on American coins.

Plate 402. Indian Head nickel (1913-1938), *obverse*, or "Buffalo" nickel, so-called because of the bison on the *reverse*.

Plate 403. Indian Head penny (1859-1909), *obverse*. Assembling a set of each year of issue is a favorite collecting specialty.

The Viking discovery of the North American mainland about the year 1000 was no menace to the Indians, for the Norsemen soon left. But when Christopher Columbus landed on an island of the Bahamas on October 12, 1492, he started a process that was destined to turn the Indians out of their homes.

Columbus himself had little profit and little happiness from his discovery. Between 1492 and 1504 he made four voyages, each time in search of proof that Cathay (China) and Cipangu (Japan) could be reached by sailing west from Europe. He scoured the West Indies and the coasts of South and Central America in the futile hope of finding the gold, the gems, the spices of the East.

In 1504 he undertook his last voyage in the bitter knowledge that Vasco da Gama had reached India, and that the Portuguese were already amassing huge profits from their voyages to the Malabar coast of India. But Columbus returned empty-handed; two years later he died, disgraced, ridiculed, broken in health.

Despite the Spaniards' shabby treatment of Columbus, it did not take them many

Plate 404. Columbian Exposition half dollar, silver (1892-1893), *obverse*. The first U.S. commemorative coin ever issued.

Plate 405. Old Spanish Trail half dollar, silver (1935), *obverse*. Issued for the 400th anniversary of the Conquistadores' 12,000-mile travels.

years to realize that his New World offered treasures even surpassing those of the Indies. To exploit the new-found riches, the Spanish Crown sent out the Conquistadores—brave, vigorous men who were born leaders, and cruel, greedy, and treacherous as well.

The Spaniards and the Portuguese had a long lead in colonizing the New World. Then other nations began to stake out their claims—the English at Roanoke and Jamestown, the Dutch at New Amsterdam (later New York), the Swedes in Delaware.

Plate 406. Roanoke Island, N. C., half dollar, silver (1937). *Obverse:* Sir Walter Raleigh, organizer of the English settlers.

Plate 407. New Rochelle, N. Y., half dollar, silver (1938). *Reverse:* fleur-de-lis. Issued in honor of the Huguenots' settling on Long Island Sound.

A new note was sounded in 1620 when the Pilgrims landed at Plymouth, Massachusetts. They made their famous voyage in the *Mayflower* to find religious freedom—a quest that in the course of time would bring millions of people to America.

Some were drawn by promises of a glittering future, others by prospects of a freedom they had never known before. The Thirteen Colonies grew and flourished; by

Plate 408. Connecticut half dollar, silver (1935). *Obverse:* Charter Oak. It was in this tree that the colonists hid their charter from a tyrannical English governor.

Plate 409. Lexington-Concord half dollar, silver (1925). *Obverse:* Minute Man. Issued for the 150th anniversary of the start of the Revolution.

1775 they were no longer satisfied to be colonies. Their conflict with England brought on the American Revolution, which finally established the colonies as an independent country—the United States of America.

Famous Americans on Coins

Of the men who made an independent America possible, the most important was undoubtedly George Washington. Without his military skill, his leadership, his integrity, the American army could hardly have held together until victory was achieved.

Even in England Washington was deeply admired and respected during the Revolution, especially by those Englishmen who sympathized with the American cause. Chief among these was the brilliant Whig statesman, Charles James Fox, who openly proclaimed that he favored the Americans. When Washington lost the Battle of Long Island in 1776, Fox wrote mournfully to a friend about "our defeat."

Just as Washington was indispensable as a military leader, so Benjamin Franklin was invaluable as a diplomat. Washing-

Plate 410. Pilgrim Tercentenary half dollar, silver (1920-1921). *Obverse:* Governor Bradford. *Reverse:* the *Mayflower*.

Plate 411. Washington cent (1791). Issued while Washington was president.

Plate 412. Washington quarter, silver (1932—). Issued on the 200th anniversary of Washington's birth.

Plate 413. Franklin half dollar, silver (1948—). *Obverse:* Benjamin Franklin. *Reverse:* Liberty Bell, famous symbol of American freedom, in Independence Hall, Philadelphia.

ton's military genius would not have been enough without the help that Franklin obtained from France.

Franklin was over 70 when he sailed to France late in 1776. From the start the French were greatly taken with this wise and mellow philosopher, with his serenity, his simplicity, his genial sense of humor.

During the winter of 1777-1778 the American cause reached its lowest ebb. Washington was heroically striving to keep his pitiable army intact at Valley Forge while some of his officers intrigued to have him dismissed. Franklin, surrounded by a net of British spies, was patiently conducting the wearisome negotiations for a French alliance.

At last Franklin succeeded, and the treaty was signed in February, 1778. As soon as the British Government learned from its agents of the signing of the treaty, it made an extraordinary offer of conciliation to the Americans. The desperate proposal even included a complete renunciation of the right to tax the colonies. It was too late; after proclaiming their independence in 1776, the Americans had no intention of returning to colonial status, especially since the French alliance gave them every prospect of success.

When the Continental Congress had proclaimed the Declaration of Independence on July 4, 1776, it had given the army a goal to fight for and created the necessary basis for Franklin's negotiations with France. Thomas Jefferson, the author of the Declaration, later became the third President of the United States.

Jefferson's most important action as President was the purchase of the Louisiana Territory from France in 1803. Originally Jefferson had sent his representatives to purchase New Orleans and some surrounding territory from France. But Napoleon was badly in need of money to fight England. He knew, furthermore, that it was hopeless for him to try to defend the Territory against a possible English invasion. In addition, he had a crafty hope that purchase of the Territory might involve the United States in war with England.

And so Napoleon's reply to the offer to buy New Orleans was, "All or nothing." After a good deal of haggling, the American commissioners bought 800,000 square miles of territory for $15,000,000—four cents an acre. The deal has been called "the greatest bargain in history," but at the time there was considerable American opposition to it. Despite the criticisms, Jefferson courageously seized the opportunity to double the area of the United States. History has amply justified the purchase of the Territory which contained all of Arkansas, Missouri, Iowa, North Dakota, South Dakota, Nebraska, and most of Louisiana, Minnesota, Kansas, Oklahoma, Colorado, Wyoming, and Montana.

Plate 414. **Jefferson nickel (1938—).** ***Obverse:*** **Thomas Jefferson.** ***Reverse:*** **Jefferson's home at Monticello.**

The Louisiana Purchase turned the United States into a big, sprawling country with conflicting sectional interests. The struggle between North and South over the issue of slavery threatened to smash the Union.

When Abraham Lincoln ran for President on the Republican ticket in 1860, he was unknown in many parts of the country. Only a split in the Democratic vote assured his victory in the Electoral College. (In the popular vote, he received 1,800,000 votes to 2,000,000 for his two Democratic opponents.)

Six weeks after Lincoln's election, the Southern states began to secede from the Union. They formed the Confederacy a month before his inauguration. Two days after he was inaugurated, Jefferson Davis, President of the Confederacy, began organizing a Confederate army.

No American President had ever been confronted with such a situation. Lincoln was an inexperienced, virtually untried man, with little formal education. His acquaintance with military matters had been trifling. Even in the North there was a sizable amount of pro-slavery sentiment, and many people looked upon Lincoln as an uncouth ignoramus. The British and French Governments were gleeful over the breakup of the Union, and only waited for an opportunity to extend official recognition to the Confederacy.

Yet Lincoln kept the Union together. Neither inflation, nor war weariness in the North, nor an appalling succession of incompetent generals could undo Lincoln's efforts. The repulse of the Southern forces at Gettysburg, the telling propaganda effect of the Emancipation Proclamation, and the noble statement of Lincoln's war aims in the Gettysburg Address, were all important factors in assuring victory for the North.

Plate 415. **Lincoln Head cent (1909—),** ***obverse.*** **First issued 100 years after Lincoln's birth.**

Plate 416. **Confederate cent, nickel-copper (1861),** ***obverse.*** **Struck, but never issued.**

Plate 417. **Battle of Gettysburg half dollar, silver (1936).** ***Obverse:*** **Union and Confederate soldiers.**

Plate 418. **Confederate half dollar, silver (1861).** ***Reverse:*** **Confederate shield with stars and bars. Only four specimens struck.**

Plate 419. **Grant Memorial half dollar, silver (1922).** ***Obverse:*** **Ulysses S. Grant.**

Plate 420. **Stone Mountain Memorial half dollar, silver (1925).** ***Obverse:*** **Robert E. Lee and "Stonewall" Jackson, the greatest Confederate generals.**

Plate 421. **San Francisco-Oakland Bay Bridge half dollar, silver (1936).** ***Obverse:*** **California bear.** ***Reverse:*** **the bridge.**

The Civil War was fought on the biggest scale of any hostilities before the World Wars. Over 2,000,000 men fought in the war, and more than one-fourth of them were killed. The North outnumbered the South by two to one, but the South had the advantage of better generals, better fighting spirit, and the opportunity of maneuvering on interior lines.

The rehabilitation of the South's ruined economy after the Civil War owes much to a Negro named George Washington Carver. Born in Missouri in the early 1860's, he taught himself to read in early childhood and became in time a great research chemist.

From the potato, Carver developed 118 products, including paste, shoe polish, and ink. But this was nothing compared to his magical transformation of the peanut into over 300 products—shaving lotions, butter, linoleum, axle grease, and many, many others.

Plate 422. **Carver-Washington half dollar, silver (1951—).** ***Obverse:*** **George Washington Carver and Booker T. Washington, famous Negroes.** ***Reverse:*** **map of United States.**

Today the peanut is second only to cotton in the cash-value listing of the South's crops. As for the sweet potato, 70,000,000 bushels are harvested every year. Carver performed other miracles too—making fertilizer from leaves, and plastics from cotton stalks and wood shavings.

Carver gave away all of his discoveries and refused to take a penny or have them patented.

The United States issues many commemorative stamps, but the recent trend is to issue few commemorative coins.

Plate 423. **Woodrow Wilson medal, silver (1920). Issued by the Philippines in honor of the U.S. President during World War I.**

Plate 424. **Roosevelt dime (1946—).** ***Obverse:*** **Franklin Delano Roosevelt.** ***Reverse:*** **torch of liberty between sprays of laurel and oak.**

Plate 425. **Eisenhower commemorative half dollar or 2½ Europinos, silver, 1952. Not an American coin, but struck by the Hamburg mint. This was a tribute to the Allied forces' commander in Europe during World War II.**

Famous Coins and Currency

Plate 426. Nails were so hard to come by in early New England that they were quite acceptable as currency.

Plate 427. Massachusetts Colony, Pine Tree shilling, silver (1652-1684). John Hull, who minted this American colonial coin in Boston, received a fee of one shilling for every 40 struck.

Plate 428. Bar Cent, bronze (about 1785). *Obverse:* USA intertwined. *Reverse:* 13 bars representing the 13 states. Said to have been modeled on a Revolutionary uniform button.

Plate 429. Flying Eagle cent, 1858. Issued from 1856 to 1858 and then replaced by the Indian Head cent.

Plate 430. Citizens' Bank, New Orleans, $10 bank note. This "Dixie" note (from *dix,* French for "10") is believed to have originated the term "Dixie."

Plate 431 (left). Texas token, aluminum (about 1890). *Reverse:* the Alamo. In 1836 a small force of heroic Texans, outnumbered more than 20 to 1, held out against Mexico during a 13-day siege in the Alamo. Not a survivor was left.

Plate 432 (right). Texas Centennial half dollar, silver (1934-1938). *Reverse:* Winged Victory flanked by General Sam Houston and Stephen Austin. Less than six weeks after the Alamo disaster, the Texans won their independence by crushing the Mexican army at San Jacinto.

Plate 433. Confederate $20 bank note (1862). Unable to coin money because of a severe metal shortage, the Confederacy had to rely on paper money.

Plate 434. Two-cent piece, bronze (1864). *Obverse:* shield with motto: "In God We Trust." *Reverse:* value. Issued during the Civil War, this was the first coin to carry the now-familiar motto.

Plate 435. "Mercury" dime (1916-1945). The popular name of this coin is incorrect; it is not Mercury but a Winged Head Liberty.

Plate 436. $50 octagonal gold piece (1915). Issued for the Panama-Pacific Exposition. Note the similarity to Greek coins; Athene is on the *obverse* and the owl on the *reverse.*

Famous American Coin Rarities

Plate 437. Ephraim Brasher, gold doubloon (1787). *Obverse:* sun rising over a mountain, with sea below. *Reverse:* eagle with 13 stars, and the motto *E pluribus unum.* An outstanding rarity of American coinage, this coin is estimated as worth anywhere between $6,500 and $12.000.

Plate 438. Liberty Seated half dollar, silver (1853). This half dollar, without arrows at date, struck at the New Orleans mint ("O" mint mark) is believed to exist in only three copies and is valued at $2,250. A "descendant" of earlier Greek, Roman, and British coins.

Plate 439. Liberty Head dime (1894). Only 24 of these coins were struck with the "S" mint mark. The resulting scarcity has yielded an auction price of $2,350.

Plate 440. $5 gold piece (1822). This "half eagle" has the distinction of bringing the greatest auction price known for a single coin—$11,575 in 1941. Only three specimens are known—one of them in the collection of the United States mint.

Plate 441. Liberty Head nickel (1913). Here is one of the most intriguing mysteries of United States coinage. First issued in 1883, the Liberty Head nickel was discontinued in 1912. Yet five Liberty Head nickels dated 1913 eventually made their appearance!

Plate 442 (left). 1804 dollar, silver. Although mint records show that thousands were issued, only 13 are known of these coins today—six originals and seven restrikes. One original, known as the "Stickney 1804 dollar," sold for $10,500.

Canada

Canada is the third largest country in the world. It is bigger than the United States plus Alaska—bigger, in fact, than all of Europe. With its area of 3,845,000 square miles, Canada is the biggest country in the Western Hemisphere. So vast is this land that its easternmost tip is nearer to the Belgian city of Antwerp than to the western Canadian city of Vancouver!

Canada's border with the United States is almost 4,000 miles long; its north-south length comes close to 3,000 miles at the maximum distance. True, much of Canada's area lies in the Arctic region or near it; but this "wasteland" is now known to be immensely rich in valuable minerals.

Federated Canada is made up of ten provinces and two territories. The Maritime Provinces (Nova Scotia, New Brunswick and Prince Edward Island) and Newfoundland rely on their fisheries, forests and factories as the chief source of income. In terms of money value, Canada is the world's leading fish-exporting country.

Plate 443. Canada, silver 10 cents (1937-1947). ***Reverse:*** **fishing schooner.**

Most of Canada's industry is concentrated in the Central Provinces, Quebec and Ontario. Two-thirds of Canada's people live in this area. Further west are the Prairie Provinces (Manitoba, Saskatchewan, and Alberta) which raise enough wheat to feed seven times Canada's population. British Columbia, Canada's picturesque Far West, is crossed by the Canadian Rockies and has a long Pacific coastline.

Plate 444. British Columbia (province), gold $20 (1862). ***Obverse:*** **royal crown.**

The Yukon and Northwest Territories are mostly wilderness and ice, and a substantial portion of them lies inside the Arctic Circle. They have a population of only about 25,000. The almost deserted Yukon experienced a gold rush in 1897, and both territories are rich in mineral resources.

Both the French and British originally laid claim to parts of Canada. In 1497, only 5 years after Columbus' first voyage, his fellow Genoese John Cabot discovered Newfoundland ("new-found-land"). Cabot, who was a merchant as well as an explorer, sailed in British service, and thus

Plate 445. **Canada, silver dollar (1949),** ***reverse.*** **One of the most beautiful of all ship coins, this commemorates the entry of Newfoundland into the Dominion.**

Newfoundland became the first colony ever acquired by the British Empire. Cabot, like Columbus, thought he had reached the domains of the Great Khan of China.

But though the English were first on the scene, they did not follow up Cabot's voyage with any attempts at settlement. The French took a different course. In 1534 Jacques Cartier, a French explorer, discovered the St. Lawrence River and founded New France. It was he who started barter with the Indians and thus unknowingly brought the fabulously profitable fur trade into existence.

From the first, the French treated the Indians better than any other Europeans did. Far from looking down on the Indian, the French admired his prowess as a hunter and fighter, his skill in the woods, his masterly handling of the fragile-looking canoe.

Samuel de Champlain (1567-1635), the first governor of New France, has often been called "the Father of the New France." The title was well deserved, for the work of this remarkable man had a lasting effect on Canada's development.

Champlain was a dynamic empire builder and forceful leader of men. He loved the New World. The crisp freshness of the "forest primeval" never failed to thrill him, and he was most at home in the grandeur and solitude of an untouched wilderness.

Champlain liked the Hurons and Algonquins, and they returned his affection. He saw the importance of having Frenchmen live in their villages, learn their ways and language, intermarry with them. He was enchanted with the birchbark canoe, and grasped its usefulness in making possible thousands of miles of travel through otherwise trackless forests.

Above all, Champlain immediately recognized the value of the majestic St. Lawrence as an inland waterway. The river is almost 2,000 miles long and affords deep-water navigation for 800 miles. When the Atlantic waterway to connect with the Great Lakes is finally completed some day, it will fulfill the vision Champlain had more than three centuries ago.

In 1608 Champlain succeeded in founding a permanent colony at Quebec where previous efforts had failed. Montreal, the headquarters of the fur trade, was not founded until 1642. Today it is Canada's largest city, with a population of over one million.

Plate 446. La Banque Jacques Cartier, $5 (or 5 piastre) banknote (1886).

Plate 447. Canada, silver dollar (1936). *Obverse:* King George V. *Reverse:* tribute to the *voyageurs* of the fur trade.

Plate 448. Banque du Peuple (Bank of Montreal), copper penny token. *Obverse:* bank building. *Reverse:* Canadian coat of arms.

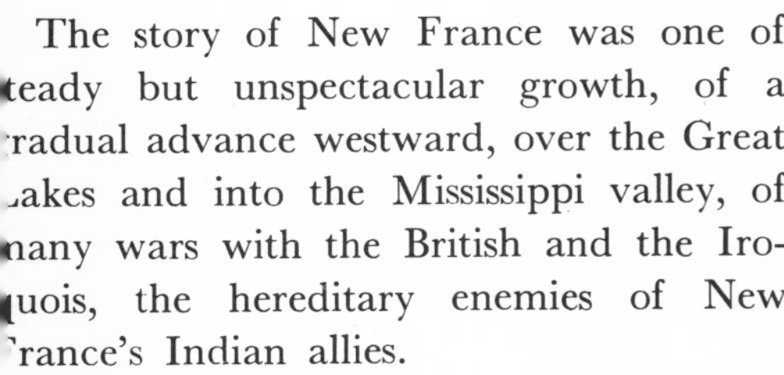

The story of New France was one of steady but unspectacular growth, of a gradual advance westward, over the Great Lakes and into the Mississippi valley, of many wars with the British and the Iroquois, the hereditary enemies of New France's Indian allies.

The eighteenth-century wars between England and France gave the British the two rich prizes of Canada and India. In 1759 a British expedition under General Wolfe upset the calculations of the French. James Cook, the finest navigator in the history of the British Navy, charted the St. Lawrence with such accuracy that he made it possible for the fleet to approach Quebec. Then, under cover of darkness, the British scaled the rock of Quebec and defeated the French on the Plains of Abraham above. Both Wolfe and Montcalm, the French general, were killed in action. A year later all Canada came under British control.

Business Empire

Pierre Radisson, one of the ablest and most daring of the French fur traders, was the pioneer who discovered that the wilderness around Hudson Bay harbored fortunes almost beyond counting. About 1660 he made two fur-trading trips to this region and came back with several hundred thousand dollars' worth of pelts. The Governor of New France was a greedy rascal who deprived Radisson of four-fifths of the proceeds.

Seething with rage over the loss, Radisson sailed for England and revealed his precious secret to the British. On the basis of his information, a number of wealthy men founded an organization known as "the Governor and Company of Adventurers of England trading into Hudson's Bay." Charles II's royal charter, issued in 1670, gave the Hudson's Bay Company title to all rivers emptying into the Bay and to all land drained by the rivers. No man living then could know that this gave the Hudson's Bay Company title to a vast area amounting to 1,480,000 square miles.

Though the Crown did not ask for any share of the profits, it provided for a quaint symbol of its authority over the Company. The charter stipulated that when the British King or his successors entered the Company's domains, they were to receive "two Black Beavers." Such a presentation was made to the Prince of Wales (the present Duke of Windsor) during his Canadian tour in 1927, and to King George VI during his 1939 visit.

From the start, the Hudson's Bay Company realized huge profits. The first venture was the most spectacular. An investment of £650 in trading goods brought returns of £19,000—a profit of 3,000 per cent.

Plate 449. **Canada, 12-sided tombak brass 5 cents (1936). *Reverse:* beaver.**

Plate 450. **Canada, silver 25 cents (1937). *Reverse:* caribou head. Canada is still a paradise for big-game hunters.**

What made the fur trade so profitable was its low overhead. The animals grew their pelts in the wilderness—the Company did not have to raise them on farms at its own expense. Labor costs were trifling, as the Company did not have to employ anyone to trap the animals. The Indians did the trapping, and the Company paid them only a small fraction of the true value of the furs. For a gun costing $5.00, for example, the Indian had to turn in 20 beaver skins that would bring $150.00.

Transportation was also a minor item of cost. Either the Indians brought the pelts to a Company trading post, or the Company sent out *voyageurs* (canoemen) or *coureurs de bois* ("woods-runners") to obtain the skins from the Indians. Canoe transportation was cheap, and the Company's employees received meager pay.

The Company's London stockholders were naturally interested in nothing but dividends; economy meant more to them than plowing back profits into expansion. On the other hand, the Company was lucky with most of its Governors—daring men who widened its operations and generally received shabby rewards in return for their efforts. In general, the Company followed the business practices of the day, and in some ways was well ahead of the average in enlightened policies.

The boldest attempt to break the Hudson's Bay Company's monopoly of the fur trade came from groups of French Canadians, American trappers, and Scottish Highlanders from the English invasion army of 1759. Energetic, resourceful, and well organized to compete with the Hudson's Bay Company, these men formed the North West Company in 1775.

Relentlessly the new firm went after the fur trade of the Northwest wilderness, establishing almost 100 trading posts there. The North West Company had its headquarters at Montreal, and its fleet of 32-foot-long canoes covered thousands of miles of rivers to bring trade goods west and return with pelts. Though these canoes were made to take a cargo of four tons they were light enough to be carried by the *voyageurs* on a portage (an overland trip around rapids or falls that were too dangerous for even the most skillful canoeman).

In some cases, it was necessary to unload and reload cargoes for a portage of as much as 9 miles. But such difficulties meant nothing to the ambitious, ruthless "Fur Barons" who ran the North West Company. Their unscrupulous trading methods dazzled the Indians, and they waged a state of private war for almost 50 years with the Hudson's Bay Company. This brutal competition came to an end in 1821 when the two companies merged.

Plate 451. North West Company, brass beaver token (1820). In dealings with the Indians, the beaver skin was the medium of exchange and the unit of trade.

Plate 452. **Hudson's Bay Company, aluminum 50 cents token (1946). Used in the Arctic region of Labrador.**

The Hudson's Bay Company had a vested interest in keeping as much of Canada as possible in its original wilderness state. The Company was equally interested in the welfare of the Indians who supplied its precious furs. It did not want the forests chopped down to make way for farmers who would drive off the Indians. But here the Company's interest clearly clashed with public policy.

When the Company's license came up for renewal in 1859, the Canadian Government insisted on an investigation of its far-flung land holdings. The upshot was that 10 years later the Company had to return its lands to the British Government for a nominal price of about $1,500,000. However, it was allowed to keep 5 per cent of the land in any new township. With 7,000,000 acres left in its control, it still had a bright future.

The Company played a public-spirited role in advocating the construction of the Canadian Pacific Railroad (1877-1885). The linking of the eastern and western seaboards brought on a tremendous land boom and attracted large numbers of immigrants. In many ways the building of the giant road was a triumph over natural obstacles. For instance, the track over the soggy areas north of Lake Superior had to be laid 7 times before it was no longer in danger of sinking into treacherous underground lakes. In a spectacularly mountainous area, one mile cost $700,000.

Today the Company is more prosperous than ever, with well over 200 trading posts. Motorboats have replaced the old-time canoe. Traders travel by plane and communicate by short-wave radio. Silver fox and mink rather than beaver are now the profitable items. In addition to its trading posts, the Company operates many other enterprises—a string of department stores, for example, spread all over Canada.

The Company is the only business organization in the British Commonwealth that is allowed to fly its own ensign. This consists of the letters "HBC" in white on a red field, and is seen on the Company's ocean liners, freighters, and Arctic icebreakers.

From Colony to Dominion

The British conquest of Canada had brought immigrants from the United Kingdom to the new colony. After the American Revolution, 40,000 refugees—"Tories" to the Americans, "Loyalists" to the British—arrived in Canada from the United States. During the first half of the nineteenth century, close to a million Irish immigrants came to Canada.

Soon there were signs of discontent in Canada because of the lack of self-government. Alerted by several small-scale revolts, British officials were determined not to repeat the unwise policies that had brought

Plate 453 (left). **Canada, bronze 1 cent (1937),** ***reverse.*** **The maple leaf, Canada's favorite symbol, often appears on its coins and stamps.**

Plate 454 (right). **Newfoundland, bronze 1 cent (1942),** ***reverse.*** **The pitcher plant, which attracts insects and traps them to their doom.**

Plate 457 (left). **Canada, 12-sided tombak brass 5 cents (1943),** ***reverse.*** **The "V for Victory" also gives the value of the coin. Dots and dashes in Morse Code around the rim spell out "We win when we work willingly."**

Plate 458 (right). **Canada, 12-sided nickel 5 cents (1951),** ***reverse.*** **Commemorates the 200th anniversary of the isolation of pure nickel.**

on the American Revolution. A statesmanlike policy of reforms gradually widened the scope of Canadian self-government, leading to the formation of a federated Canada in 1867.

The federation, which at the beginning included only Quebec, Ontario, New Brunswick, and Nova Scotia, was patterned on the parliamentary government of Great Britain. The handling of foreign affairs still remained in British hands. One by one the other sections of Canada were incorporated into the federation.

The opening of the transcontinental railroad was a big step forward in the unification of Canada. In 1901 the country had a population of 5,000,000; during the following decade 2,000,000 immigrants arrived to swell the population. Today Canada has three transcontinental railroads, and its first transcontinental highway is being constructed at a cost of $153,000,000. Its total of 43,000 miles of railway track is exceeded only by that of the United States and the U.S.S.R.

Canada came of age as a nation during World War I. Its troops established an imperishable reputation for gallant fighting in such battles as those at Ypres and Vimy Ridge, where they suffered frightful losses. After the war, Canada joined the League of Nations as an independent member, and in 1926 it became a self-governing Dominion, completely free of control by Great Britain, although its nominal head is the British Crown.

In World War II, Canada made an even greater contribution to victory, through its vastly increased industrial production, its enormous enlistment of manpower, its large-scale air-force training program for Allied aviators, and its extensive shipments to beleaguered England.

Canada's Incalculable Riches

In relation to its wealth of natural resources, Canada, with 14,000,000 people, is underpopulated.

Canada leads the world in the production of nickel, radium, platinum, asbestos. One-third of the country is still forest land, enabling Canada to supply 80 per cent of the world's newsprint.

Radium and uranium deposits in the Northwest Territory were accidentally discovered in 1929 by a prospector who was looking for silver in this icy wasteland. He found the silver, but also pitchblende ores which meant that radium and uranium were present.

The underground riches of Canada still await accurate appraisal. Oil has been found in several parts of the country, and Alberta is known to have a reserve of at least one billion barrels of oil. The use of the airplane has enormously eased the search for such resources.

In Labrador, one of the bleakest regions on the face of the earth, U. S. technicians have discovered amazingly rich deposits of high-grade iron ore. One such deposit is believed good for 20,000,000 tons. Thus, although the romantic days of the fur trade and the search for the Northwest Passage are gone forever, they have been followed by an exciting quest along Canada's still untapped industrial frontier.

Mexico

Few countries have had a history as colorful, as turbulent, and as tragic as Mexico's. In the process of enslaving the Indians, the Spanish Conquistadores destroyed two civilizations that were in some ways the equal if not the superior of any of the Old World civilizations.

The Aztecs came to the valley of Mexico from the north about 1300 A.D. They established their capital of Tenochtitlán (the present site of Mexico City) on a shallow lake. Building their houses on rafts, they even laid out gardens in the mud. Gradually the warlike Aztecs conquered the neighboring tribes and intermarried with them.

As the center of a flourishing empire, Tenochtitlán grew into an imposing metropolis, with handsome temples, palaces, and public buildings, busy marketplaces, and skillfully constructed canals.

The Aztecs depended on corn as their important crop. However, they also raised squash, tomatoes, and other vegetables. It was from the Aztecs that the Spaniards learned about the *tomatl,* as the tomato was called. For centuries Europeans refused to eat tomatoes, which they thought were poisonous like other plants of the nightshade family to which it is related.

On the other hand, *xocolatl* (chocolate), a frothy, almost solid beverage made from the cacao bean, became extremely popular in France when the Spaniards introduced this New World product into Europe.

The Aztecs were apparently the first to domesticate the turkey, which was unknown in Europe until the Spaniards brought it back from the New World.

The Aztecs were unacquainted with iron, but they had many materials for their tools and ornaments—gold, silver, jewels, copper, and a darkish, sharp-edged volcanic glass known as obsidian. They had no coinage but they conducted their business dealings with a variety of "currencies" —gold dust, precious stones, jaguar skins, copper shields, axes, live eagles, corn, paper made from the maguey plant, blankets, gourds, salt, hoes, cacao beans, and cochineal dyes. These last were prepared from the dried bodies of the females of an insect which lives on cactus plants.

Plate 459. Bronze 20 centavos (1943-1945). *Obverse:* eagle on serpent (a favorite Aztec motif on Mexican coins). *Reverse:* Aztec Temple of the Sun.

The Aztecs had a great many gods, the chief one being Quetzalcoatl, a gentle, fair-skinned divinity who was the legendary teacher of many useful arts and was said to have given the Aztecs their excellent calendar.

Plate 460. Gold 20 pesos (1916-1921), *obverse.* The Aztec calendar stone, frequently pictured on Mexican coins.

To this day Mexico's coat of arms shows an eagle perched on a cactus, holding a snake in its beak. The Aztecs devised the emblem in 1325, but from 1521 to 1810—the period of Spanish domination—the Aztec eagle never appeared on coins minted in Mexico. The patriots who started the Revolution of 1810 used the Aztec eagle on their coins; and since 1867, when the last foreign invader was driven out, the Aztec eagle motif has been a prominent feature of Mexican coins and stamps.

The Spanish Conquest

Hernando Cortés (1485-1547), greatest of the Spanish Conquistadores, was a man of dynamic energy—a born leader who could demand and get the impossible from his followers. He came to Mexico in a fleet of 11 vessels with 600 men, 17 horses, and 10 cannon. With this tiny force Cortés conquered the Aztec nation—one of history's most remarkable military feats.

The Aztecs had an army of 200,000 warriors, outnumbering the Spaniards by about 350 to 1. Cortés had generalship, determination, and a flair for dealing with the Indians. After landing in Mexico he burned his ships to convince his men they had to do or die.

Cortés naturally had no hope of conquering the Aztecs in the field with his tiny army; but by destroying Tenochtitlán's water supply and setting up a food blockade, he achieved his purpose. Hunger and thirst were enemies that the Aztecs could not resist.

The Aztecs outside the metropolis continued to fight on under the leadership of a heroic chieftain named Cuauhtemoc. Eventually, however, Cuauhtemoc was defeated and captured. After seizing the capital, the Spaniards found gold hoards worth about $15,000,000. But this was only a small part of the Aztec treasures, which had been transferred to various hiding places. Even under torture, Cuauhtemoc refused to reveal the whereabouts of the hidden treasure, lost to this day.

Only the insatiable Conquistadores could have had any reason to be dissatisfied. New Spain, as Mexico was called, was huge; in addition to the present area of Mexico, it included most of what is now California, Arizona, New Mexico, Texas, Colorado and Kansas. Yet Cortés received only ingratitude for his monumental achievement. When he returned to Spain in 1528, he found that Charles V had been turned

Plate 461. Silver 5 pesos (1947). *Obverse:* Cuauhtemoc, the chieftain who refused to tell the Spanish invaders where the Aztec treasures were hidden.

Plate 462 (left). Silver piece of eight or Spanish milled dollar (1793). This is the *reverse* of Plate 310.

Plate 463 (right). The piece of eight was often broken up for small change. Each one-eighth was a "bit." A half-segment was "four bits." A fourth was "two bits"—the ancestor of the American quarter (25¢).

slightly reduced

against him by malicious reports. Cortés spent his last years a disappointed and neglected man.

The Mexico City Mint

For 300 years after the Spanish Conquest, Mexico poured fabulous amounts of silver into the Old World. The expansion of European industry and commerce owed a great deal to the vast bullion shipments carried by the Spanish treasure fleets.

As early as 1504, Ferdinand and Isabella of Spain issued a decree setting up the *quinta* or "royal fifth"—a 20 per cent fee to the Crown on all metal mined in the New World. There was a death penalty for violating the decree.

A royal edict of 1535 established the Mint, which experimented with copper for a while. The metal was of poor quality, and legend has it that the Indians contemptuously threw 200,000 of the coins into Lake Texcoco. The Mint soon discontinued copper coinage, which was not resumed until 1814. According to the Mexico City Mint records, 68,778,411 gold coins and 2,082,260,637 silver coins were struck there from 1537 to 1821. Even after this extensive exploitation of Mexican silver, that country is still the world's leading silver producer, turning out about one-half of the total annual supply.

The Mexico City Mint produced the first coinage in the New World. The early coins were made by rough and ready methods. A sheet of metal was trimmed to the proper thickness, and the individual coins were cut out with a scissors.

About 1580, during the reign of Philip II, the Mint began the coining of "cob" money (from *cabo de barra*—"cut from a bar"). These coins were made by slicing off parts of crude silver bars, which resulted in highly irregular borders. The pieces of metal were then hammered from rough dies. The design was ugly, the coins undated. Specialists enjoy collecting "cobs" because they are the only ones adept at determining the date at which an individual coin was issued, or at least assigning it to a particular period.

The Spanish milled dollar ("taler") of 8 reales, better known as the piece of eight, was the most widely circulated coin of its time. First minted at Mexico City in 1732, it continued to appear until 1821. Some 441,000,000 pieces were produced until 1772; all these featured two globes between the Pillars of Hercules (Straits of Gibraltar). From 1772 on, a Spanish shield replaced the two globes. About 880,000,000 of these were minted to 1814.

Widely circulated as it was, the piece of eight played a role in the coinage of other countries as well. When the United States devised its coinage system, its silver dollar

Plate 464 (left). Silver 5 pesos (1951). *Obverse:* Miguel Hidalgo.

Plate 465 (right). Silver 1 peso (1950). *Obverse: Jose María Morelos.* Hidalgo and Morelos are the national heroes of Mexico's struggle for independence.

was modeled on the Spanish milled dollar. Interestingly enough, Mexican coinage remained legal tender in the United States until 1857—a tribute to the honest silver content of these attractive coins. At the time the coins lost their legal-tender status, well over $2,000,000 worth of Mexican money was in circulation in the United States.

Mexican Struggle for Independence

Two humble parish priests, Miguel Hidalgo (1753-1811) and José Maria Morelos (1765-1815) are revered by Mexicans for their role in the war for independence. In 1810, Hidalgo set up a provisional government which was weakened, however, by rivalries among the rebel leaders. Morelos, like Hidalgo, was a man of singular nobility of character. After these two outstanding leaders were captured by the Spaniards, degraded and executed, the Mexican Revolution suffered serious setbacks.

In 1820 a revolt broke out in Spain as well, and in Mexico a revolutionary leader named Augustín de Iturbide came to the fore. Backed by influential elements, he proclaimed the independence of Mexico in 1821. The following year he became Emperor of Mexico, but his reign was a brief one, and in 1823 Mexico became a republic.

It was the sad fate of the Mexican Republic to be at the mercy of dictators for many years. One of the earliest and most notorious was Antonio López de Santa Anna, who seized power four times and was thrown out four times. Santa Anna, who thought of himself as another Napoleon, was treacherous, greedy, conceited, and incompetent. It was during his dictatorships that Texas broke away from Mexico (1836) and the disastrous war with the United States (1846-1847) inflicted on Mexico the painful loss of most of New Mexico, Arizona, and California.

Juarez and Maximilian

After a civil war which finally drove Santa Anna out for good, power passed to a totally different kind of man: Benito Juárez (1806-1872). Though Juárez was a full-blooded Indian, he managed to receive an excellent education and became a lawyer. A man of scholarly tastes, he was an austere patriot, scrupulously honest, and

Plate 466 (left). Oaxaca, copper 4 reales (1814). *Obverse:* bow. Coinage of Morelos' revolutionary government.

Plate 467 (right). Mexico, silver 2 reales (1823-1869). *Reverse:* liberty cap with rays.

Plate 468 (*left*). Mexican Empire, silver 1 peso (1864-1867). *Obverse:* Archduke Maximilian, who made a futile attempt to establish an empire in Mexico.

Plate 469 (*right*). Oaxaca, silver 2 pesos (1915). *Obverse:* Benito Juarez, revered by Mexicans for his efforts to help the Indians.

passionately determined to improve the lot of the Indians. His reforms came at an inopportune time—just when the Civil War broke out in the United States and when Napoleon III sent a French army of occupation to Mexico. And without bothering to consult the Mexicans, Napoleon selected the Austrian Archduke Maximilian as Emperor of Mexico.

Despite his Hapsburg background, Maximilian was mild and tolerant by nature, eager to found a democratic state, and too naïve to see through the plans of his crafty backers. Disillusionment began the day of his arrival, but pride or perhaps fatalism kept him from fleeing to safety.

Once the Civil War was over, the United States government invoked the Monroe Doctrine and insisted on the departure of the French troops. Deserted by Napoleon, Maximilian was captured by Juárez' troops and executed.

Modern Mexico Emerges

Four years after the death of Juárez, Porfirio Díaz (1830-1915), one of his generals, became dictator of Mexico. This cynical and subtle man was also extraordinarily energetic and capable. Managing to remain in power until 1911, he promoted Mexico's industrial development and built thousands of miles of railways and telephone and telegraph lines.

But there were many painful items on the other side of the Díaz ledger. During his long stay in power he stifled democratic institutions, increased the misery of the Indians by taking away their tribal lands, and made all too sweeping concessions to foreign corporations. In later years this was to cause serious trouble.

The long-delayed explosion came in 1911. Díaz was forced to abdicate and he fled to Paris. The revolution that drove Díaz out led to the most turbulent period in Mexican history. Among the picturesque leaders who assembled private armies in those troubled times between 1911 and 1940 were Pancho Villa, the bandit chieftain, and Emiliano Zapata, who hoped to restore to the Indians their ancient heritage.

During this garish era of glittering promises and monstrous betrayals, three Mexican Presidents were assassinated by treachery—as was Zapata. One "incident" after another strained the relations between Mexico and the United States, and more than once the two countries were on the brink of war. Later, the "Good Neighbor" policy of the Roosevelt administrations did much to ease the tension.

In 1937 President Lázaro Cárdenas' expropriation of foreign oil companies led to a new period of squabbles, but the furor has since died down. In recent years, wild speeches have been replaced by less flashy but more solid achievements: land distribution to the Indians, irrigation projects, large-scale school and sanitation programs, automobile highways.

Central America and the West Indies

Visitors from the United States in increasing thousands are now "discovering" Central America as a tourist paradise. This beautiful area, however, was found and settled thousands of years ago by the Mayas, who established there one of the world's notable civilizations.

Two admirable men stand out by contrast in the sordid story of the Spanish Conquest. One of them was Vasco Núñez de Balboa (1475-1517), a highly intelligent, restless man whose kindness was as remarkable as his physical strength. After becoming bored with the life of a planter on the island of Hispaniola, he stowed away to Panama. Balboa's gentle treatment of the natives gained their confidence, and his marriage to an Indian chieftain's daughter enhanced their friendly feelings. Hearing stories of gold beyond a hitherto unknown sea, Balboa went off in search of treasure.

Plate 472. Guatemala, silver 10 centavos (1949-1950). *Obverse:* Guatemalan coat of arms. *Reverse:* the Quiriguá column, dating from 535 A.D. and the finest of many massive Mayan columns. Made of stone and weighing over 20 tons, they are covered with beautiful carvings and elaborate inscriptions.

On September 29, 1513, Balboa at last beheld the Pacific—the first white man to do so in the New World.

The other friend of the Indians was a Spanish priest, Bartolomé de las Casas (1474-1566), who sailed with Columbus on his last voyage in 1504. Las Casas was so horrified by the Spaniards' treatment of the Indians that he protested vehemently to the King.

As a result, Ferdinand appointed him Protector-General of the Indians of New Spain, and Las Casas spent the rest of his long life interceding for the Indians. He even followed the cruel Pizarro to Peru to do what he could for the Incas. In 1536 he came to Guatemala and spent many years there converting the Indians and trying to improve their living conditions.

The "Impossible" Canal

Only a few years after Balboa's discovery, the idea of building a canal to connect the Atlantic and Pacific through the narrow Isthmus of Panama suggested itself. But 345 years later it was still a dream; when gold was discovered in California, many "forty-niners" still had to use riverboat and stagecoach to cross Panama or Nicaragua.

The need for the canal finally became so great that, despite the difficulties of terrain and climate, a French company undertook the project. After spending millions, they had to give up. When the United States purchased their equipment to finish the job, Colombia, of which Panama was then part, refused permission. Panama revolted, however, in 1903, and the new republic leased the Canal Zone to the United States.

The building of the Panama Canal is one of the most remarkable engineering projects of all time. It required the efforts of 35,000 workmen, at a cost of another $500,000,000, and was not completed until 1914. Colonel George Goethals was the army engineer in charge of construction; it is to him and to William C. Gorgas, Surgeon General of the United States Army, that chief credit for the canal belongs. Gorgas supervised the heroic work of draining the swamps and safeguarding the canal workers against tropical disease.

Goethals dynamited mountains, drained swamps and deflected the course of rivers. The Panama Canal does not follow a direct course; it turns and winds depending on the nature of the terrain. A force of thousands is needed to keep the "Big Ditch" operating. The famous Culebra Cut has to be dredged constantly to remove dangerous accumulations of silt. In other parts of the canal, men work constantly to destroy water plants which if left unchecked would make the route impassable!

Plate 473. Guatemala, 8 reales (1825), ***obverse.*** **This striking view of the sun's rays against lofty mountaintops is a favorite on Central American coins and stamps. Guatemala—its Indian name meant "full of trees"—has the largest population of any Central America country.**

Plate 474 (left). **Panama, silver centésimo (1930).** ***Obverse:*** **Urracá, an Indian chieftain remembered for his courageous struggle against the Spaniards.**

Plate 475 (right). **Guatemala, bronze centavo (1949-1950).** ***Obverse:*** **Fray Bartolomé de las Casas, who befriended the Indians.**

"Banana Republics"

After they achieved independence from Spain in the 1820's, the Central American countries (Guatemala, Honduras, Nicaragua, El Salvador, and Costa Rica) tried to unite for a while. But the experiment proved a failure, and the confederation broke up. Even unity within a single small country has been hard to achieve, because of bad communications, among other things. Education and sanitation are still inadequate and the standard of living is low. Revolutions and dictatorships are still characteristic of Central America.

Coffee is the most valuable export of the Central American countries; the United States buys over 35,000,000 bags of coffee a year from Central America. In the popular mind, however, these lands are "banana republics," and it is true that banana-raising plays an important role in Central America.

Plate 476. Guatemala, silver 25 centavos (1950). *Reverse:* Mayan woman.

Guatemala

Guatemala boasts the largest Caribbean banana-shipping port—Puerto Barrios. Guatemala has a world monopoly of chicle, the basic ingredient of chewing gum, which is also used for surgical tapes, plastics for radio insulation and other industrial products. Bananas are of course much too bulky to be shipped by plane, but most of the chicle produced in Guatemala is now flown right out of the jungle where it is gathered.

Plate 477. Nicaragua, silver córdoba (1912). *Obverse:* Francisco Hernández de Córdoba, a Conquistador who tried to form an empire in Central America.

Nicaragua

In Nicaragua, the largest of the Central American republics, the coffee crop represents well over half the value of all exports. Nicaragua has a remarkably large number of holidays. These include July 4, July 14 (Bastille Day), July 24 (Simón Bolívar's birthday), September 15 (the anniversary of Central American independence), and Columbus Day. September 14 is dedicated

Plate 478 (left). Panama, silver ½ balbo (1930), *obverse.* Panama named a coinag denomination for Balboa.

Plate 479 (right). Honduras, silver lempir (1931-1937), *obverse.* Honduras named a coi for Chief Lempira in honor of his heroic re sistance against the Spaniards.

to the memory of William Walker, a fantastic adventurer from Tennessee who became dictator of Nicaragua in 1856 and president in 1857—a curious reversal of the usual sequence! The country is named for the Indian chieftain Nicarao.

El Salvador

El Salvador is the smallest and most densely populated country of Central America. It has no Caribbean coastline and does not produce bananas. Yet, small as it is, El Salvador accounts for one-fourth of the world's coffee production. In addition to mineral resources, it has sizable crops of tobacco, indigo, balsam, sugar and henequen (a rope fiber). The population is mostly Indian.

Plate 480. El Salvador, gold 20 colones (1925). *Obverse:* Pedro de Alvarado and President Quiñónez, Alvarado was one of the most colorful of all the Conquistadores.

late 481. **Costa Rica, silver 2 reales (1848). rude overstrike on an English shilling of 1844.**

londuras

In Honduras, corn is the leading crop, hough bananas, coffee, cocoanuts, and ugar are raised in quantity. Gold and silier mines have been worked there since he days of the Spanish Conquest. Tegucialpa, the country's capital, is one of the ldest cities in North America—it was the hief city even in Indian times. The most amous product of Honduras is the highly rized wood of the mahogany tree. Some f these trees are 200 years old and measure 6 feet in circumference. The population s mostly mestizo.

osta Rica

In Costa Rica ("rich coast") the Conuistadores came close to exterminating the ndians. A large proportion of the Costa Ricans are of Spanish descent, and the ountry has less than 10,000 Indians. Costa Rica is quite prosperous from its crops of coffee, bananas, cocoa, quinine, pineapples, cocoanuts, and tobacco. Costa Rican coffee is famous for its quality, though coffee-raising did not begin there until 1830, when the first coffee bushes were brought from Cuba.

late 482. **Honduras, 50 centavos (1871). The *obverse* shows the coat of arms, a pyramid elow a crown of feathers, and the tree on the *everse* is the highly prized mahogany.**

The West Indies

The sun-drenched isles of the Caribbean and southern Atlantic have played a colorful role in history. It was here that Christopher Columbus discovered the New World without knowing it. To him the islands were the "Indies" and the people he found there, "Indians."

Europeans made their first New World settlements in the West Indies. Here they introduced Negro slavery on a large scale in order to work the lush canefields. Many a pirate set up his "head office" in the West Indies. The Caribbean was the great highway for the treasure galleons from the rich cities of the Spanish Main to the Atlantic. It did not take long for English, French, and Dutch buccaneers and privateers to make themselves at home in the Caribbean, where they could prey on the ships and also raid the treasure vaults of the Spanish Main. It was here that such "sea hawks" as Drake and Morgan made their rich hauls. Later on, the British and French fought exciting battles over these rich islands. Still later, the struggles of several islands for their freedom produced some of the most stirring dramas of New World history.

In recent years, the West Indies have become one of the great attractions for American tourists. The beautiful tropical scenery and the easygoing tempo of life in the West Indies can be deceptive; there are serious problems of poverty and overpopulation.

Bahamas

The Bahamas are made up of some 700 small islands that are admired for their underwater gardens, tropical vegetation, and brightly-colored birds. It was at one of these islands that Columbus made his momentous landing on October 12, 1492.

It took the Spaniards only 20 years to exterminate the Indians of the Bahamas. Today Negroes number 85 per cent of the population of the Bahamas. The English, who acquired the islands in 1783, freed the Negro slaves in 1838.

Early in the eighteenth century the famous "Pirates' Republic" was established at New Providence (now Nassau) in the Bahamas. The harbor was ideal, for it was large enough to hold 500 pirate craft and yet not deep enough for ships of the Royal Navy. Here the buccaneers auctioned off cargoes to smugglers and other traders. The most notorious of the New Providence pirates was Edward Teach ("Blackbeard").

Plate 483. Bahamas, copper halfpenny (1806). _Obverse:_ George III. _Reverse:_ three-masted man-o'-war. The Latin motto means: "By expulsion of pirates, commerce is restored."

Plate 484. Barbados, copper penny (1788). _Obverse:_ Negro with crown and plume of three ostrich feathers. _Reverse:_ pineapple. Note the inscription "I serve"—motto of the Prince of Wales.

Plate 485. Bermuda, copper penny (1793). _Reverse:_ three-masted fighting ship of the line.

Plate 486. Jamaica token, copper halfpenny (1844). _Obverse:_ coach.

Bermuda

The Bermuda Islands are of course much further north than the West Indies, but are usually considered with them. What we call "Bermuda" is actually a group of 300 coral islands, of which 20 are inhabited. Though Bermuda was discovered about 1510 by the Spaniard Juan de Bermudez, it was settled by accident about a century later, when an English ship was wrecked off the Bermuda coast.

For years, privateering, wrecking, and piracy were Bermuda's chief "industries"; subsequently it became a popular resort. With the coming of the air age, Bermuda is only three hours from New York.

Barbados

In the Windward group, this beautiful island is formed from coral reefs. When the Portuguese first saw the bearded fig trees, they called them *barbudos* ("bearded"); this is the origin of the island's name. The British found Barbados uninhabited when they reached it in 1605. In the early days, Barbados was a favorite pirate lair; cotton and tobacco were often used as currency.

Jamaica

The Arawak Indians called this island *Xaymaca* ("island of springs"). During the seventeenth century, the harbor of Port Royal was a favorite rendezvous of the buccaneers. In 1739 the War of Jenkins' Ear broke out between England and Spain after a Spanish guard cut off an ear from Captain Robert Jenkins, a Jamaican smuggler. It was in this war that the British seized the bullion for their "Lima" coins.

The population of Jamaica is predominantly Negro. The British government abolished slavery there in 1833. As no effective economy has been devised since that time, the picturesque island suffers from a chronic overpopulation and unemployment problem. Among the chief products of Jamaica are cocoanuts, bananas, pimento, ginger, and sugar.

Trinidad

Columbus named this island after the "trinity" of three mountain peaks. Trinidad became an English possession in 1803. Most of the population is Negro, but one-third of Trinidad's people hail from India. Their Hindu temples and Moslem mosques take on added charm in their New World setting.

The chief products of Trinidad include cocoa, sugar, grapefruit, cocoanuts, and petroleum. One of the island's most curious features is its large lake of pitch, which has been known and used since early colonial times. Trinidad is also noted for its Calypso songs, with their clever texts and ingenious accompaniment on such "instruments" as tin cans and discarded machine parts.

Plate 487. Cuban revolutionary regime, silver souvenir (1897).

Plate 488. Cuba, silver 25 centavos (1953). *Obverse:* José Martí, Cuban patriot. *Reverse:* liberty cap and fasces.

Cuba

The largest of the West Indies is Cuba, which we know as the great sugar-producing country.

The Cubans fought a gallant struggle from 1817 to 1898 to throw off the Spanish yoke. The Spaniards crushed one Cuban insurrection after another with the utmost brutality. Among the martyrs of their long battle for freedom the Cubans especially honor José Martí (1853-1895), a scholar and poet who was also a gripping orator and a tireless organizer. When Martí started the revolt of 1895, Americans looked on with intensely sympathetic interest. The explosion of the *Maine* in Havana harbor brought the United States into war with Spain. With their army and navy crushed in short order, the Spaniards surrendered Cuba and Puerto Rico, their last remaining possessions in the New World.

In the treaty ending the Spanish-American War Cuba became an independent republic though under U. S. protection. In 1934 the United States voluntarily withdrew its control, as part of the Good Neighbor policy.

Puerto Rico

With its inviting beaches, lovely tropical scenery, exotic fruits and flowers, and many places of historical interest, Puerto Rico is considered by some the most beautiful of all the West Indies. Juan Ponce de Leon, who naively sought the Fountain of Youth in Florida, gave the island its name, which means "rich port."

Puerto Rico is about 100 miles long and 35 miles wide. During the centuries of Spanish rule much of the island's hilly soil became eroded. With its population approaching 3,000,000, Puerto Rico must import large quantities of food.

Plate 489. Antigua, copper farthing (1836). ***Obverse:*** **palm tree. One of the major Leeward Islands, Antigua was settled by the British in 1632.**

Haiti's Dramatic Story

Haiti's history is among the most exciting epics of the New World. In 1697, France secured Haiti, the western third of the island of Hispaniola. Soon it became extremely wealthy from its sugar, tobacco, indigo, cocoa, and coffee crops. In fact, Haiti was France's richest colony in the eighteenth century. It is said that in those days two-thirds of France's wealth came from Haiti. So many Negro slaves were imported from Africa that by 1760 Haiti had 200,000 Negroes to 15,000 whites.

Haiti was the second New World country to obtain its independence. After the outbreak of the French Revolution, the natives of Haiti rose in revolt, killed their masters, and Toussaint L'Ouverture, the son of an African chieftain, became their leader.

Plate 490. Haiti, silver 50 centimes (1882) ***Obverse:*** **woman's head, symbol of the republic.** ***Reverse:*** **Haiti's coat of arms.**

"The Black Napoleon," as he called himself, cost the French 50,000 soldiers befor he was treacherously captured.

Toussaint's successor was another brilliant amateur general, Henri Christophe who was a remarkable statesman as well His method of building up Haiti's finance was ingenious. First he requisitioned ever green gourd (a kind of vine fruit) in the country. When the coffee crop was ripe he had the dried berries shipped to the capital. Paying the planters in gourds Christophe sold the coffee in Europe, and with the gold he received he was able to start a sound currency.

In 1811 Christophe became Emperor of Haiti. He built himself a magnificent residence, said to be the largest and most elegant palace in the New World. Driving his subjects mercilessly, Christophe enormousl increased the productivity of the island. He used the huge surpluses of sugar, coffee cotton, and other products to increase his monetary supply. Though Christophe was amazingly foresighted and efficient, his subjects wearied of his despotic measures Shortly before he became partly paralyzed in 1820, he shipped out $6,000,000 in gold to be deposited in his wife's name in th Bank of England. Deserted by his soldiers he killed himself—with a gold or silver bullet (the stories vary).

Throughout the nineteenth century

Haiti's history was a turbulent series of dictatorships and uprisings.

Thousands of tourists visit Haiti every year, drawn by its picturesque appearance and its storied past. The countryside is full of small farms and thatched-roof huts. French, or a French dialect, remains the national language of Haiti. Traces of African voodoo practices are still encountered.

Haiti's coffee crop is its chief source of income. Among other products, sisal, a fiber used for binding grain, is of great importance to American farmers.

Dominican Republic

The island later known as Santo (or San) Domingo was named Hispaniola ("little Spain") by Columbus when he visited it. It was on this island that the Spaniards introduced Negro slavery after they found that the Arawaks (the original Indian inhabitants) did not take to forced labor. Ordinarily gentle, peaceful, and affectionate, many of these Indians killed their children and then committed suicide rather than submit to slavery.

Here the Spaniards established the first lasting European settlements in the New World. The eastern two-thirds of the island (today known as the Dominican Republic) boasts the oldest church (1512) and the oldest university (1538) in the Western Hemisphere.

Martinique and Guadeloupe

Martinique, a volcanic island, and Guadeloupe have belonged to France since the seventeenth century. Martinique became very wealthy from its sugar production; the chief crops on Guadeloupe are coffee and bananas. In both colonies, which have a predominantly Negro population, Creole French is the national tongue.

Plate 491. **Haiti, copper centime (1807).** ***Obverse:*** **Henri Christophe.**

Plate 492. **Dominican Republic, bronze centavo (1937).** ***Obverse:*** **palm tree.**

Virgin Islands

The Dutch were the original white settlers, though the islands were also held for a time by Spain and England. St. Croix belonged for a time to the Knights of Malta.

The Danes seized the islands in the early part of the seventeenth century and held them until 1917, when the United States purchased them for $25,000,000. The pleasant, relaxing atmosphere of the islands attracts great numbers of American visitors.

Curaçao

Spain lost Curaçao to the Dutch in 1634; Peter Stuyvesant was the first Dutch governor. Curaçao and the nearby Dutch island of Aruba have extensive oil refineries. The islands, which are only a short distance away from Venezuela, process most of that country's large oil production.

Plate 493. **Netherlands Antilles, silver guilder (1952).** ***Obverse:*** **Queen Juliana. The islands include Curaçao.**

Plate 494. **Danish West Indies (Virgin Islands), bronze 10 bits or 2 cents (1905).** ***Reverse:*** **caduceus, trident, and sickle.**

South America

South America is a continent of violent physical contrasts. The snow-capped Andes extend 5,000 miles from Panama to Cape Horn, and the mountain areas are always freezing cold, even on the Equator. When the sun melts the ice and snow, water rushes down in torrents that form swift rivers as well as large lakes and extensive swamps.

East of the Andes we find the pampas of Argentina and Uruguay. About 1,000 miles long and stretching between the Andes and the Atlantic, these flatlands have no trees and only a few lakes. Grass grows everywhere, sometimes to a height of four feet.

In the north there are steaming jungles, in the south the freezing wastes of Patagonia, in the west thousands of miles of desert.

But there are other contrasts in South America: skyscrapers and primitive villages, airplanes and oxcarts, modern boom towns and ancient Indian ruins, trackless forests and magnificent highways, ancient universities and widespread illiteracy, splendid crops and serious undernourishment.

For centuries, South America's main difficulty was lack of rapid communication. The completion of the Panama Canal, the construction of railroad and highway networks, the introduction of air travel—all these have removed many of the difficulties.

More serious are the difficulties inherited from Spanish rule. In many cases the Spaniards exterminated the Indians; in other instances, they plundered, destroyed, enslaved. The Indian was allowed to exist on the outer fringes of the economy or altogether outside it. But Spain treated its colonies badly in other ways. The colonies were given the least possible amount of self-government; education was neglected; tyrannical decrees squeezed the last bit of revenue out of them.

The tragic fact is that when the Spanish colonies achieved their freedom, they inherited all the difficulties of free government and few of its blessings. The newly established nations have often resorted to dictatorship as the only way they could find to cope with their problems. It is only

Plate 495. Venezuela, silver 5 bolivares (1901-1939), *obverse*. Venezuela honors her "native son" Simón Bolívar.

in relatively recent times that the South American countries have begun to reap the benefits of modern technology and industry. Sanitation and pest control have curbed disease. In agriculture, mechanization has stepped up production and made possible a greater variety of crops.

Since 1933 the United States has intensified its efforts to strengthen its bond of friendship with the South American countries. These lands to the south are among the best customers of the United States, and they also supply many products prized by the *Norteamericanos*: coffee from Brazil and Colombia; copper and vanadium from Peru; manganese, industrial diamonds, and bauxite from Brazil; tin, tungsten, and antimony from Bolivia; oil from Venezuela; and many others.

The Liberator

Simón Bolívar, the liberator of the Spanish-speaking colonies, was born in Caracas in 1783. Educated in Europe, he was deeply influenced by the ideas of the French Revolution and the American Founding Fathers. When Napoelon deposed the Spanish King in 1808, Bolívar, like many other South American patriots, felt that the time had come to overthrow Spanish rule in the New World. In 1817, his third attempt was successful and he became the first President of Greater Colombia (Colombia, Venezuela, and Ecuador). Bolívar planned rebellions for the other Spanish colonies, formed alliances, issued decrees, raised money, collected arms, set up judicial systems, introduced improved mining and farming techniques.

Bolívar knew that constructive effort in the new countries was as important as successful revolt against Spain. He hoped to unite South America into one country, yet he lived to see the liberated countries break

Plate 496. Venezuela, silver 2 reales (1820). *Obverse:* Spanish coat of arms. Issued by the Royalist forces during the War of Independence.

Plate 497. Colombia, silver 50 centavos (1947), *obverse.* An attractive coin portrait of Simon Bolivar.

away from each other. Ill health, ingratitude, jealousies and dissensions, and the assassination of his trusted lieutenant Antonio José de Sucre wore him out.

Argentina

Argentina is large—more than one-third the size of the United States. The country's wealth stems from the pampas, with their 45,000,000 head of cattle and an even greater number of sheep. Argentina is the leading meat and corn producing country in the world, and one of the leading wheat producers.

The picturesque cowboys of Argentina, known as gauchos, are not only superb horsemen; it was the gauchos who made up the army of José de San Martín, the outstanding general of the revolts against Spanish rule. San Martín is especially re-

Plate 498. (Argentina) Rio de la Plata Provinces, silver 8 reales (1836), *reverse.* The sun-symbol of Argentina on an old coin.

Plate 499. **Argentina, silver 2 reales (1842).** ***Obverse:*** **General Manuel de Rosas, dictator.**

Plate 500. **Bolivia, copper-nickel 50 centavos (1939-1941),** ***obverse.*** **The llama, a valued beast of burden in Bolivia and Peru, appears on the coins of both countries.**

membered for his march across the Andes to free Chile and Peru.

A few years after liberation, the notorious Juan Manuel de Rosas became dictator of Argentina as "protector of the poor and persecutor of the rich." Becoming more and more tyrannical, he was finally deposed in 1852.

The Argentines, a proud and sensitive people, are mostly of Spanish, Italian, or German stock. Serious tensions, internal as well as international, made possible the Perón dictatorship in recent times.

Plate 501. **Brazil, silver 4,000 reis (1900),** ***obverse.*** **Commemorates the 400th anniversary of the discovery of Brazil by Pedro Alvares Cabral, one of Portugal's many superb navigators.**

Bolivia

After Peru threw off Spanish rule in 1825, its southern part split off to form a new state, named for the Liberator, Simón Bolívar.

In colonial times, Bolivia was the source of the immense silver shipments from Peru. For several centuries, much of the world's silver coinage — $2,000,000,000 worth — came from Bolivia. Potosí became rich because it was close to a mountain of silver ore. When the metal gave out, Potosí became poor once more.

In modern times the lowly tin can provided Bolivia with an even more valuable asset. Its tin mines supply about 20 per cent of the world's production. Simón Patiño, "the Tin King," started his career by acquiring an abandoned mine and built up a billion-dollar empire. By stark contrast the working and living conditions of the Bolivian tin workers are wretched almost beyond description.

Bolivia is one of the two South American countries that have no outlet to the sea. More than half of the population is Indian, descended from the Incas. There are magnificent ruins of Inca cities on the Altiplano, the desolate plateau high up in the Andes.

Plate 502. **Brazil, nickel 400 reis (1932).** ***Obverse:*** **map of South America; a special issue commemorating the settlement of Brazil in 1532.**

Plate 503. **Brazil, silver 2 milreis (1932).** ***Obverse:*** **João III, Portugal's King when Brazil was settled.**

Brazil

The only Portuguese-speaking country in the New World is the largest country in South America, with an area a little larger than that of the United States. The Portuguese made their first permanent settlement in Brazil in 1532. Sugar and cotton cultivation so enriched the colony that the French, British, and Dutch made repeated attacks to gain a foothold there. Coffee culture started in Brazil in 1727; the rich province of Minas Gerães had a gold and diamond rush during the eighteenth century.

By 1800 Brazil's population was greater than Portugal's. When Napoleon drove out Portuguese King João VI in 1807, that monarch arrived in Brazil with a comment that has been often quoted: "I have lost a kingdom but found a paradise!" João introduced many valuable reforms, and during his reign Portugal and Brazil became a united kingdom. After he returned to Portugal in 1821, Brazil proclaimed its independence, with the King's son, Dom Pedro I, as constitutional Emperor.

Dom Pedro II, who became Emperor in 1840 at the age of 15, was one of the most enlightened rulers in history. Brought up as an orphan by men of culture and patriotic idealism, he became a monarch of simple, austere tastes with strongly republican views.

In his youth, Dom Pedro supported the rebels who overthrew the bloody Argentine dictator, Manuel de Rosas; in old age, Dom Pedro earned such hatred for freeing Brazil's Negro slaves that he was deposed in 1889. Since that time Brazil has been a republic.

Brazil's Amazon River and its tributaries extend 3,900 miles. In the swampy jungles of the Amazon region there is little sunlight and no change in seasons. In the river there are such strange creatures as the piranha, a fish only 10 inches long, with teeth that can bite through steel. The anaconda, a huge snake which kills by constriction, has been known to overcome a 25-foot-long crocodile and eat it whole. The electric eel sends out shocks as far as 50

Plate 504. Brazil, aluminum-bronze milreis (1932). *Obverse:* Martim Affonso da Sousa, who founded the first permanent settlement in Brazil.

Plate 505. Brazil, aluminum-bronze 500 reis (1932). *Reverse:* warrior's quilted jacket.

Plate 506. Brazil, silver 500 reis (1867-1870). *Obverse:* Dom Pedro II, Emperor of Brazil.

Plate 507. Brazil, aluminum-bronze milreis (1922). *Reverse:* torch with crown and liberty cap. Issued for the centennial of Brazilian independence.

Plate 508. Brazil, copper-nickel 200 reis (1936-1938). *Reverse:* locomotive. This coin honors the men who worked on Brazil's railroads.

Plate 509. Brazil, copper-nickel 400 reis (1936-1938). *Obverse:* Dr. Oswaldo Cruz, who devoted his life to checking tropical disease.

feet, killing its prey outright or numbing it into helplessness.

As you might suspect, the "green hell" of the Amazon region harbors every conceivable kind of tropical disease. Brazil pioneered, quite naturally, in the study of such diseases; it was the first country in the Western Hemisphere to found a medical laboratory (1880). One of the most remarkable sights in the bustling and lively city of São Paulo is the Instituto Butantan, which houses more than 10,000 venomous snakes for making serum to combat snakebite.

In a vast sprawling country like Brazil, railway building is absolutely essential to economic progress. In 1870 Brazil had about 850 miles of railway track; 80 years later, the figure had jumped to 30,000 miles. The men who worked on these railroads are among Brazil's unsung heroes; on a single railroad started in 1903, the first five miles of track cost 10,000 lives from tropical disease.

Coffee and rubber were once valuable crops to Brazil, but nowadays the emphasis is on industrialization.

Chile

Chile is one of the queerest-shaped countries in the world. It is narrow, but has a 3,000-mile-long Pacific coastline. English ships sailing around Cape Horn brought many English, Scots, and Irish immigrants to its ports. This explains why we often come across decidedly un-Spanish names in Chilean history.

Bernardo O'Higgins, for example, was the son of an Irish father and an Indian mother. Incisive, daring, and with a genuine gift for military leadership, he became Chile's first President in 1818.

Like Bolívar and other South American liberators, O'Higgins soon found that his followers were anything but grateful. Rather than impose a dictatorship, O'Higgins voluntarily left Chile. After a ten-year period of anarchy, a new constitution in 1833 gave Chile an orderly government.

***Plate 510.* Chile, copper 20 centavos (1942-1944). *Obverse:* Bernardo O'Higgins, liberator of Chile.**

Almost half of Chile's area is desert—but this desert is by no means barren. It is the source of nitrate, valuable in the production of fertilizers, explosives, and chemicals. Other important exports are copper and petroleum.

Colombia

The only New World country named after Columbus, Colombia is one of the largest South American states. It takes in as much territory as California, Oregon, Washington, and Montana, and is the only South American country with both Atlantic and Pacific coastlines. To travel from the coast to Bogotá, the capital, used to take a week. By air the time is now three hours.

It was gold that attracted the Spaniards to this region. Gonzalo Jiménez de Quesada (1495-1576) journeyed inland through almost impassable jungles, mountains, rivers, and swamps in search of "El Dorado," the legendary "gilded man."

It was to Quesada's conquests that Spain owed the rich province of New Granada, which comprised the region now made up of Panama, Colombia, Ecuador and Venezuela. On the western coast of the Spanish Main the Spaniards founded Cartagena, which became a transshipping point for the treasure galleons. The Spaniards imported half a million Negro slaves to fortify the city, a task that took a century.

Plate 511. Colombia, copper-nickel 10 centavos (1952). *Obverse:* Indian with native headdress. *Reverse:* Colombia's coat of arms.

Though the walls of Cartagena were 40 feet high and 50 feet thick, they were not always secure from attack. Sir Francis Drake captured the city no less than three times—in 1572, 1585, and 1595.

Colombia is extremely wealthy in natural resources—bananas, cocoa, coffee, huge stretches of valuable forestlands, extensive gold, platinum, and petroleum deposits. Colombia also has most of the world's emerald supply. The Spaniards worked the emerald mines as early as 1540, but in time the mines were abandoned. Covered with jungle growths, they were rediscovered in 1910 and with the application of up-to-date mining techniques they are more productive than ever.

Ecuador

Ecuador's population is mainly Indian, living for the most part in rather primitive conditions. The country's name is likely to give us some misleading ideas about its climate. Its capital city, for example, is surrounded by snow all year round though it is only 15 miles away from the Equator. This city, Quito, is one of the most charming examples of Spanish colonial architecture. Its elevation of over 9,000 feet in the Andes explains why its climate is so comfortable.

Ecuador has enormous stores of untapped mineral wealth—iron, copper, gold, silver, lead, sulphur. The chief products, well suited to its simple handicrafts economy, are alligator skins, balsa wood for canoes and airplanes, and Panama hats.

Paraguay

During the sixteenth century the Jesuits came to this region and converted the Guarani ("warrior") Indians to Christianity. The priests taught the Indians trades, arranged festivals, and established an exchange economy with no need of money. Protected by the priests from being dragged off to slavery, the Indians lived peacefully and happily in their villages for 150 years. Finally the Spanish government drove out the Jesuits and broke up the Indian communities.

Independence came in 1811, but was hardly a blessing. At last, after 30 years of oppression, Carlos Lopez established a peaceful dictatorship, opening schools and stimulating trade. He was succeeded in

Plate 512. Ecuador, silver 5 sucres (1943-1944). *Obverse:* General José Antonio de Sucre, Bolívar's most trusted lieutenant.

Plate 513. Paraguay, silver peso (1889). *Reverse:* rayed star inside wreath—a favorite design on Paraguayan coins and stamps.

Plate **514. Peru, gold 50 soles (1930-1931).** ***Obverse:*** **Inca Chieftain Manco Capoc.**

Plate **515. Peru, silver sol (1914-1916).** ***Reverse:*** **Peru's coat of arms. The sol ("sun") is a reminder of Inca sun-worship.**

1862 by his half-Indian son, Francisco Solano Lopez, one of the worst power-mad dictators in South American history.

In the futile hope of gaining control of waterways leading to the sea, Lopez involved Paraguay in a war with Argentina, Brazil, and Uruguay. During this fantastic conflict, which lasted from 1865 to 1870, the population of Paraguay went down from 1,500,000 to 200,000.

Later on, Paraguay fought another long destructive war with Bolivia over the Gran Chaco, a wasteland believed to contain great potential wealth.

Peru, Land of the Incas

Many centuries ago, the vast empire of the Incas extended 2,000 miles down the west coast of South America. Much of the huge domain was thousands of feet high up in the towering, snow-covered Andes Mountains.

The Incas called themselves "Children of the Sun"—they had many nature gods, but the sun was by far the most important.

Like Egypt's Pharaohs, the Inca Kings were enormously rich, and all the land, gold, silver, and jewels belonged to them. When one died, his treasure was buried with him. Also like the Pharaoh, the Inca King was considered a god in human form.

The only beast of burden among the Incas was the llama. This animal, a relative of the camel, is wonderfully surefooted as it threads its way along the most dangerous trails of the high Andes. The llama was not only a means of transportation; it also provided meat, wool for clothes and milk for cheese.

Inca officials kept food and llama wool in royal storehouses and used it to pay for work performed. There was no need for money, although there was a limited amount of barter. The Incas mined huge amounts of gold and silver, but the precious metals had no money value. The Incas prized them for their beauty, their durability, their use for ornament, and their suitability for religious ceremonies.

Steadily the Incas enlarged their empire, in much the same way as the Romans. Wherever they conquered, they built masterly roads and bridges through the mountains. They forced their defeated enemies to adopt the Inca religion, language, and customs, but were more merciful to their captives than we might expect.

Efficient as the Inca Empire was, it was too highly organized for its own good. The people had little say about what went on, and they had no chance to follow their own wishes. In the course of time the Empire became top-heavy; like the Romans, the Incas had to divide their domain into two parts.

Francisco Pizarro (1476?-1541), the greediest and cruelest of the Conquistadores, was a brave and capable Spanish officer who decided to seek gold and fame in the New World.

How Pizarro managed to gain control of the Inca Empire with only a handful of soldiers, is one of the gaudiest epics in the colorful story of the Conquistadores. Mas-

Plate 516. Peru, gold libra (1901-1930). *Obverse:* Inca head.

terful, ambitious, cruel, and endlessly resourceful, Pizarro successfully applied the technique Cortés had used in Mexico: exploiting differences among the natives.

United, the Incas could have wiped out the handful of soldiers commanded by Pizarro. Divided, the Indians were an astonishingly easy prey. By treachery Pizarro kidnapped the Inca King Atahualpa after the Indian monarch visited him unarmed. Then, after Atahualpa filled his room with gold (to the value of some $16,000,000) as a ransom, Pizarro took the spoils and had him executed after all.

Though Pizarro got the gold he wanted, he had little pleasure from it. Squabbles broke out among the Spaniards, and during a mutiny Pizarro was killed. Thus ended his lifetime quest for gold and glory.

After the Inca conquest the Spaniards took huge amounts of gold and silver from the province. Despite centuries of extraction, there are still sizable quantities of these metals left. The country's mineral wealth also includes copper, vanadium, lead, and zinc. Among South American countries Peru is second only to Venezuela in petroleum production. Coffee, lumber, and fruits are among Peru's other valuable products.

Plate 517. Peru, bronze 2 centavos (1917-1942). *Obverse:* rayed sun.

Uruguay

The smallest of the South American countries, Uruguay is slightly larger than all the New England states combined. It is the most democratic country in South America and has the most progressive laws. This prosperous land has a comparatively high standard of living (largely from its great cattle herds) with few extremes of wealth and poverty.

Plate 518. Uruguay, aluminum-bronze 10 centésimos (1930). *Reverse:* jaguar. Issued for the centennial of Uruguay's independence.

Venezuela

Large enough to take in Texas, Louisiana, and Arkansas, this country has lofty mountains and rolling plains, as well as steaming jungles.

Back in 1498 Columbus touched on the Caribbean shores of Venezuela during his third voyage. The following year Amerigo Vespucci and Alonso de Ojeda named the region Venezuela ("little Venice") after finding native huts built on stilts.

Venezuela is exceptionally rich in natural resources. Aside from being one of the leading oil-producing countries, Venezuela has gold and diamond deposits as well as huge quantities of high-grade iron ore. Its chief crop is coffee.

After gaining its freedom from Spain, Venezuela was governed by the "benevolent dictatorship" of José Antonio Paez from 1830 to 1873. After his death, there was a good deal of unrest in Venezuela until Juan Vicente Gomez came into power. Gomez maintained his grip from 1908 to 1935 and was responsible for many improvements. But he was a ruthless tyrant—and made himself a multi-millionaire.

Africa

As our planet gets "smaller" with every improvement in communications, Africa takes on greater strategic importance. This became terrifyingly clear during World War II, when the Axis powers controlled Dakar on the West African coast (only four hours' plane flight from Brazil), and came very close to seizing the Suez Canal at the other end of the continent.

Africa, the second largest of the continents, was the last to assume an active role in world history, and the last to be explored and colonized by white men. In 1850 Europeans knew less about Africa than they had known about North America in 1650. During the last 100 years, however, the great powers of Europe concentrated their attention on Africa, where they carved out huge empires.

Geography has played a role in making exploring difficult. Much of the continent is made up of high plateaus extending outward from the interior almost to the coasts and then leveling off abruptly. The problem for explorers was how to reach the interior. Their way was blocked by lofty mountain ranges or impassable jungles or huge deserts. To follow rivers inland from the coast seemed logical; unfortunately, the descent of the rivers as they reach the coast creates powerful falls that cannot be negotiated by ships traveling against the current. The only dependable highway to the interior was the Nile, but it was surrounded by desert on both sides and after 1,500 miles petered out into swamps before resuming as the White Nile and then the Blue Nile.

Travel from the north was equally forbidding, for it meant crossing the Sahara, the world's largest desert, with an area of some 3,000,000 square miles, most of it in French West Africa.

Plate 520. Belgian Congo, brass hexagonal 2 francs (1943). *Obverse:* elephant. The Congo is one of the richest regions in Africa—and one of the least suited for white men.

Plate 519. German East Africa, silver rupee (1910). *Obverse:* Emperor Wilhelm II. The Germans entered late into the scramble for African colonies.

Plate 521. Somalia (Italian protectorate), bronze centesimo (1950). *Obverse:* elephant head.

Plate 522. French Somalia, aluminum 5 francs (1948). *Reverse:* antelope head with fish and shell at sides and fan of feathers above.

The slow exploitation of Africa has left it the continent most plentifully supplied with big game and other creatures that have disappeared elsewhere. The African elephant, the tallest, largest, and heaviest land mammal alive today, is very similar to the mastodons and mammoths that wandered over the earth 50,000,000 years ago.

Present-day elephants reach a maximum height of 13 feet and may weigh as much as 7 tons. The trunk, which is sometimes over 8 feet long, is really an elongated upper lip. As for the tusks, they are actually overdeveloped teeth; the maximum length and weight are 10 feet and 200 pounds.

Strictly a vegetarian, the elephant needs somewhere between 150 and 500 pounds of food a day to keep him happy. It takes a lot of water—say 50 gallons—to wash down the food.

By the time these animals reach maturity, they are so bulky that they sleep standing—this is more comfortable than going to the trouble of getting up after lying down. When it comes to eating, the trunk is a great convenience, as this massive creature would find it difficult to bend down for its food.

Three Independent Countries

Though most of Africa has been carved up into colonies, three countries have maintained their independence—one for many centuries, the other two for a relatively short time.

Ethiopia, or Abyssinia, is an ancient kingdom in northeast Africa. It is a fertile, mountainous country with an area larger than France and England combined. Exceedingly primitive and lacking an outlet to the sea, Abyssinia is rich in undeveloped mineral resources. The country has a large proportion of slaves out of an estimated population of 9,000,000.

The King of Ethiopia claims descent from Solomon and the Queen of Sheba, and styles himself the "Lion of Judah." The rulers have tried to live up to that imposing title. When Italy, in search of an African empire, invaded Abyssinia in the days of Menelik II, the invaders received the worst trouncing ever inflicted on a European force in Africa. Forty years later, in 1936, the Fascist armies of Mussolini succeeded in overrunning Abyssinia and King Haille Selassie became a fugitive. He was restored to power after the Italians lost Abyssinia during World War II.

Plate 523. Ethiopia (Abyssinia) silver talari (1889-1913). *Obverse:* Menelik II. *Reverse:* lion of Judah.

Plate 524. Suez Canal token, brass 20 centimes (1865). Issued by contractors working on construction of the canal.

Plate 525. Liberia, bronze 2 cents (1937). *Obverse:* elephant.

The story of Egypt has been quite different. After the decay of its ancient civilization, Egypt was conquered in turn by the Greeks, the Romans, the Arabs, and the Ottoman Turks. Early in the nineteenth century Mehemet Ali, a swashbuckling Albanian officer in Turkish service, seized power in Egypt, paying nominal allegiance to Turkey. Under the Khedives, his successors, Egypt became more and more a sphere of British influence.

The completion of the Suez Canal in 1869 reduced the sailing distance from England to India from 10,000 to 6,000 miles. This route became the British Empire's "life-line" and intensified British penetration in Egypt. Great Britain purchased a controlling interest in the company which operated the Suez Canal, kept the French out of Egypt, and established a "condominium" (joint rule) with Egypt in the Sudan desert area.

In 1952 an army revolt headed by General Mohammed Neguib deposed playboy King Farouk. General Neguib then applied himself to the problems of raising the Egyptian standard of living and driving the British out of the Sudan and their formidable base in the Suez Canal zone.

The remaining independent country, Liberia, was established back in 1816 when American abolitionists founded the American Colonization Society to establish a homeland in Africa for freed Negroes. The first settlers arrived on the society's land in 1820. The society surrendered its title to the land in 1847, when Liberia was declared a republic.

Belgian Congo

It is curious that one of the first regions in Africa to be exploited extensively was one with a climate which is particularly disagreeable for white men. The publicity attending Henry Stanley's explorations seized on the imaginations of people living in humdrum circumstances. Stanley brought back such picturesque details as his account of the Pygmies who live in the jungles of the Congo. A good many of them are less than four feet tall, though this does not prevent them from being skilled hunters and fierce warriors.

King Leopold II of Belgium was particularly fascinated by Stanley's descriptions. Leopold, a striking-looking man with an imposing beard, had extravagant tastes and great ability. A King could not engage in trade but Leopold saw possibilities.

Here was a region of close to 1,000,000 square miles, almost 100 times larger than Belgium. Leopold worked out a clever scheme. He organized the International African Society, had it approved by the other European powers in 1881, and then

Plate 526. Egypt, copper-nickel 10 milliemes (1938). King Farouk, one of the world's leading coin collectors. He lost his throne in 1952.

Plate 527. Belgian Congo, silver 5 francs (1887). *Obverse:* Leopold II (1865-1909), who gained great wealth from the exploitation of the Congo.

had himself made President of the Congo Free State—not as the Belgian King, *but as a private individual.* Though he did not engage in business, others did. Whoever wanted a concession in the Belgian Congo, simply applied to Leopold. He graciously granted the concession—in return for a 40 per cent share of all profits.

By 1908 Leopold had assembled a private fortune of $200,000,000 from the export of copper, tin, industrial diamonds, palm oil, and other valuable products. But by that time the brutal treatment of the natives had become an international scandal, and Leopold prudently turned over the "Free State" to the Belgian government. Since then Belgian administrators have worked hard to correct the abuses and improve conditions.

Plate 528. British West Africa, copper-nickel penny (1908). *Reverse:* Solomon's Seal with holed center. The Gold Coast is part of this region.

Plate 529. East Africa, copper 10 cents (1936). *Reverse:* elephant tusks.

British Colonies

The Gold Coast Colony, a British possession on the west coast which is about the size of England, Wales and Scotland combined, is another African colony with a climate unsuitable for white men. With few white settlers, the Gold Coast has no economic rivalries between Africans and Europeans. It is the farthest advanced in self-government of all British colonies in Africa.

The Gold Coast has had a colorful history. It was here that the Portuguese started the slave trade in 1442. For years the Ashanti, one of the most warlike tribes on the continent, preyed on other tribes and sold their captives into slavery. From 1825 to 1873 the Ashanti repulsed every British attempt to subdue them. Yet these people are famous for their remarkable sculpture and carving, which have profoundly influenced European art for the past 100 years.

The cultivation of cocoa, which started on the Gold Coast in the 1890's, gradually revamped the economy of the region. The first export crop amounted to 36 tons, but since that time the Gold Coast has become the world's leading producer. As the plantations are of moderate size and are owned by the natives, their standard of living has gone up considerably; prosperity has brought railroads, new towns, an excellent educational system.

Events in Kenya, located clear across the continent in British East Africa, have taken a different course. Though located in the torrid zone, Kenya is a mountainous country with a temperate climate in the highland regions and some of the finest farming country in all of Africa. About the size of Texas, Kenya should theoretically be able to support its 5,500,000 Africans, 100,000 Indians, and 30,000 Europeans in comfort. Instead, this unfortunate land is racked by intricate land disputes which have led to great bitterness, and some terrorism.

Besides Kenya, British East Africa include Uganda and Tanganyika and (until their recent merger with Southern Rhodesia into "British Central Africa") Nyasaland and Northern Rhodesia. The most important segment of British West Africa is Gold Coast. Other colonies are Nigeria, Sierra Leone, Gambia, British Togoland and British Cameroons.

South Africa

The Portuguese succeeded in rounding the Cape of Good Hope in 1487, and established a settlement at what was to become Capetown, at the foot of Table Mountain with its 3,500 feet of sheer wall. Later the Dutch seized the colony and settled there in 1652. These settlers called themselves Boers (Dutch for "farmers" or "peasants") and devoted themselves to farming and sheep and cattle grazing.

The sturdy Boers lived placidly and uneventfully in South Africa for over 150 years, treating the natives as they pleased. When the Cape Colony passed into British hands in 1814, the Boers accepted the change sullenly. The abolition of slavery throughout the British Empire 20 years later infuriated the Boers, however. In 1836, taking their families, their flocks, and their possessions with them, they made "the Great Trek" north to the plateau veldt

Plate 530. Southern Rhodesia, silver shilling (1932). *Reverse:* bird.

Plate 531. Southern Rhodesia, silver florin (1932). *Reverse:* antelope. These are examples of fine African sculpture.

Plate 532. Southern Rhodesia, silver crown (1953). *Reverse:* Cecil John Rhodes. Issued for the centennial of his birth.

("plains") of the Transvaal. They also set up the Orange Free State.

Bad feeling continued to simmer between the Boers and the British for 30 years until a new conflict arose over the discovery of diamonds in Griqualand. Soon there was a wild scramble for the diamond fields, with the Boers, British, and Portuguese laying claim to the area.

The giant De Beers combine built up a monopoly of the richest diamond mines at Kimberley. The dominant man in the enterprise was a young Englishman named Cecil John Rhodes (1853-1902) who had come to South Africa for his health. By the time he was 30, Rhodes, a true "captain of industry," was a multimillionaire. But business was only a means to an end for Rhodes. An imperialist in the best and worst senses of the word, he was obsessed with the idea of adding a vast domain to the British Empire, and establishing a north-south chain of British colonies to be linked by a Cape-to-Cairo railroad. It was due to the daring initiative of Rhodes that the British established themselves in Northern and Southern Rhodesia. This region, north of the Transvaal, has 500,000 square miles of fertile farming land and is ideally suited for white colonization.

Though both the Boers and the British claimed the Transvaal, its administration

Plate 533. Union of South Africa, silver crown (1948). *Reverse:* springbok gazelle. Note that both English and Afrikaans inscriptions appear on South African coins.

Plate 534. Union of South Africa, silver crown (1952). *Reverse:* Dutch East Indiaman entering Table Bay, Capetown. Commemorates the arrival of the Dutch East India Company in 1652.

was in the hands of the Boers. The Boer President was Oom ("uncle") Paul Kruger (1825-1904), a crusty, obstinate, intensely patriotic Boer who hated the British. A new crisis arose when gold was discovered in the Transvaal in 1885. This led to a wild gold rush. Soon the newcomers outnumbered the Boers, who taxed them heavily but refused to let them vote.

With bad feeling on both sides, war was inevitable. To achieve victory, the British had to pour in 300,000 men, but their peace settlement was very generous. Jan Smuts, a Boer, became Prime Minister of South Africa, and in 1910 the newly established Union of South Africa was granted Dominion status.

Despite all British efforts at conciliation, a strong nationalist sentiment continued among the Boers. During both World Wars the Nationalist faction sympathized with the German cause, and only the strong personal popularity of Smuts kept the Nationalists out of power. After his death in 1948, they captured the government.

French Colonies

France has large holdings in Africa with a colonial population of 50,000,000. The French have made many fine technical improvements in their colonies, and have tried to familiarize the natives with French institutions and French culture. In some cases these efforts have been well repaid, notably in French Equatorial Africa.

In 1941, when many governors of French colonies were proclaiming their allegiance to Vichy, Felix Eboué, brilliant administrator and the governor of French Equatorial Africa, refused to follow their example. By his enthusiasm and organizing ability he raised a Free French force of 50,000 men and increased the colony's war production four-fold. What is interesting is that Eboué, who played an important role in saving France's African empire, is a Negro from French Guiana; his soldiers were all African natives.

This is perhaps one reason why the new French constitution of 1946 extended full French citizenship to all inhabitants of French Africa.

Plate 535. Algiers, copper-nickel 100 francs (1950). Algiers, with Tunisia and Morocco, are France's North African colonies.

Plate 536. French Equatorial Africa, brass 50 centimes (1942). *Obverse:* Gallic cock. *Reverse:* the Cross of Lorraine, Free French symbol.

Asia

Asia is by far the largest of all the continents. It covers one-third of the earth and has well over half the people in the world.

Most scholars believe that the origins of civilization lie in Asia; India, China, Persia, and the Arabian Peninsula, among others, all produced imposing civilizations thousands of years ago. In time these empires decayed, and left their successors a disastrous heritage of eroded soil and pitifully unsatisfactory farming methods. Though four-fifths of the people of Asia till the soil, many parts of the continent regularly suffer from large-scale famines. In many cases the farming tools are those of 2,000 years ago; irrigation is unheard of; a peasant's income may be as low as $25 a year, as high as $85.

The colonial era, in which European powers seized great areas of Asia, brought many changes. Europeans built bridges, roads, dams, railways, established modern schools and hospitals, unearthed Asia's riches of rubber, tin, oil, copra, jute, and many other products. They also quickened the tempo of life in Asia. The twentieth century has been an age of profound unrest in Asia, as its people seek to raise their living standards and to obtain national independence.

The Arabs

The Arabian Peninsula, with its bleak deserts, does not look as if a substantial part of it was once called "the Fertile Crescent." Yet this land was so productive that the Sumerians, the Babylonians, the Hittites, the Jews and many other ancient peoples found the Fertile Crescent a rich prize. Eventually the Roman Empire conquered the region and held it for several centuries.

After the ebb of Roman power, the Arabs set out on a remarkable career of conquest that made them masters of Syria, Egypt, Persia, northern India, northern Africa, Spain, and Sicily. At a time when Europe

Plate 537. Persia, silver 5 krans (1902). *Obverse:* lion. *Reverse:* inscription in wreath, crown above. In ancient times Persia (now Iran) had a mighty empire. It possesses one-fifth of the world's known oil reserves.

was deep in the Dark Ages, the Arab civilization had a brilliant flowering of literature and the arts.

By the thirteenth century Arab civilization had begun to decline. One stronghold after another fell to the enemy. Trade went down to a fraction of what it had once been. Under Turkish domination the Arabs became poverty-stricken peasants or nomads with a precarious livelihood.

The discovery of oil in modern times has transformed the Arab lands in many ways. From 1930 to 1950 they yielded more oil than the whole United States oil industry between 1860 and 1940. The productivity of individual wells is fantastic—anywhere from 400 to 15,000 barrels in 24 hours, as compared with an average of 15 in the United States. Native workers in the oil refineries earn about $1.50 a day—roughly a tenfold increase in their income.

Plate 538. **Lebanon, aluminum bronze 5 piastres (1925-1940). *Obverse:* cedar tree. *Reverse:* Phoenician galley. Lebanon, at the eastern end of the Mediterranean, was ancient Phoenicia.**

Plate 539. **Iraq, silver riyal (1921-1933). *Obverse:* King Faisal I. Iraq's name from ancient times was Mesopotamia.**

(Courtesy of Standard Oil Co. of New Jersey)

Plate 540. **Saudi Arabia. An Arab employee looks over his pay statement while waiting to be paid. Arab employees are paid in silver riyals every other Thursday.**

India

This huge sub-continent, which looks like an enormous upside-down triangle on the map, has always attracted conquerors.

The most colorful of the conquerors were the Moghul Emperors, who reigned over a large part of India from 1525 to 1607. (*Moghul* is the Arab word for *Mongol.*) Babar, the first of the Moghuls, was half-Mongol, half-Turk. During their long rule the Moghuls, who were Mohammedans, spread their religion vigorously.

It was actually the British East India Company that established British power in India. At first the company established itself at coastal posts. In order to hold its ground against other European traders, the company raised a private army of Indian troops and British officers. By 1763 India was definitely in English hands.

Plate 541. British East India Company, silver double rupee (1810-1820).

Plate 542. India, gold stater (380-414 A.D.). *Obverse:* Ancient King Chandragupta II shooting his bow at a lion which falls backwards. *Reverse:* goddess seated on lion, holding a lotus in her outstretched hand.

By the beginning of the twentieth century a strong movement for Indian independence had developed. Its leader was a modern saint, Mahatma Gandhi, a frail little man who modeled his life on the teachings of India's greatest religious sages.

In trying to weld together all Indians in one movement, Gandhi, courageously took up the cause of the 45,000,000 "untouchables"—those who belonged to the lowest of the Hindu castes. These unfortunates lived in the deepest poverty and had the humblest occupations, with no chance of ever improving their lot—or their children's.

After years of struggle, Great Britain finally granted Dominion status to India in 1947, after allowing the Moslem groups to split off the predominantly Mohammedan areas into a new state called Pakistan.

Plate 543 *(left)*. Travancore (native Indian state), copper chuckram (1938). *Obverse:* bust of ruler with plumed hat.

Plate 544 *(right)*. Hyderabad (native Indian state), silver rupee (1911-1943). *Obverse:* gateway with minarets.

Plate 545 *(left)*. India, copper-nickel 2 annas (1950). *Obverse:* Asoka pillar with three lions. For its first coinage, free India selected the pillars built for Asoka, who reigned over a large part of India during 273-232 B.C.

Plate 546 *(two on right)*. Pakistan, copper-nickel 2 annas (1948-1950). The first coinage of this Moslem state. Note the crescent and star on the *reverse*.

Plate 547. Ceylon token, vulcanite (about 1890). *Obverse:* Singhalese sailing craft. A British Dominion about the size of West Virginia, Ceylon is an important producer of rubber and copra, the source of valuable cocoanut oil.

China

Of all existing civilizations, China's is the oldest and the most tenacious. Going back well over 4,000 years, it includes extraordinary achievements in the arts, literature, philosophy, religion, and government.

China has the largest population in the world—some 475,000,000 people. Its area is about one-third larger than that of the United States. The enormous size of the country, the richness of its soil, and the wealth of its cities have attracted many invaders. The Chinese built their Great Wall late in the third century B.C. to hold back the Tatar hordes; 1,500 miles long, the wall required the labors of 300,000 men.

Chinese history is extraordinarily rich in clever inventions that did not turn up in the West until a much later date. Thus, as early as the first century A.D. the Chinese were using excellent paper made from old rags, hemp, bark, and fishing nets. By the fifth century the Chinese were making ink from lampblack, and they were printing with wood blocks in 770—possibly earlier.

The use of printing gave the Chinese paper money and playing cards long before these were known in the West. They had devised gunpowder and the compass, and used coal for fuel.

Plate 548. Burma, silver rupee (1852-1878). _Obverse:_ peacock.

Plate 549. Burma, nickel 8 annas (1949). _Obverse:_ lion. After becoming a Dominion, Burma left the British Commonwealth in 1948.

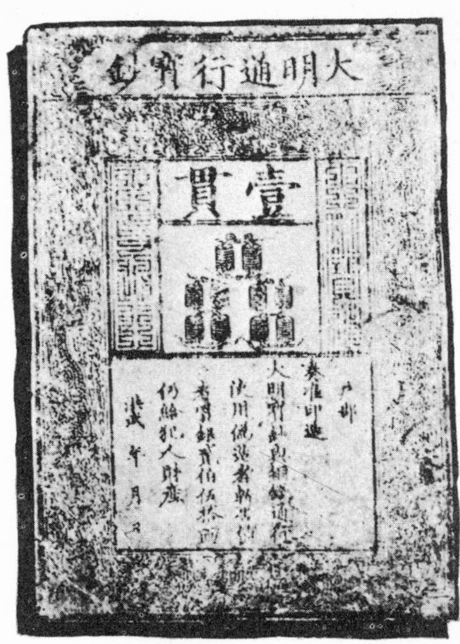

Plate 550. China, Ming Dynasty (1368-1399 A.D.). The oldest known paper money in existence. Part of the text warns counterfeiters that they will be beheaded.

After the Mongols conquered China in the thirteenth century, Kublai Khan, the Mongol Emperor, set up his capital at Peking. Marco Polo the Venetian spent 20 years visiting Kublai Khan's court. When he reached the imperial palace he found that it was built of handsome marble, with a roof brightly painted in red, blue, violet, and green. The grounds were so huge that a horseman needed a whole day to ride around them.

Marco Polo observed many wonders and wrote about them with keen appreciation. But few features impressed him so strongly as Kublai Khan's postal system—the best until the nineteenth century. The Empire had about 10,000 post offices, 25 miles apart and linked by well-kept roads. Messengers carried mail by horseback 300 miles a day in 25-mile relays. Canals and boats rounded out this efficient system.

Plate 551. China, silver dollar (1903). *Obverse:* dragon. Chinese coins often feature dragons. In Chinese mythology they are generally friendly creatures.

Plate 552. China, silver dollar (1933). *Reverse:* Chinese junk. Contrary to Western belief, these vessels are quite seaworthy.

Empires rose and fell, but Chinese civilization retained its extraordinary vitality. Like the ancient Greeks, the Chinese thought of all outsiders as barbarians, but unlike the Greeks they had no use for foreign ideas.

In the nineteenth century, China's contempt for Western ways had disastrous effects. The government of the Manchu dynasty (in power since 1644) became weaker and weaker. Europeans forced their way in ruthlessly, seizing whole regions and extorting trade concessions. Toward the end of the century Japan became a world power and began to take a leading role in the dismemberment of China. Chinese resentment flared out in the Boxer Rebellion, but the Great Powers crushed this outbreak with ease.

By 1912, seething popular discontent forced the abdication of the last Chinese Emperor and the country became a republic. A long period of chaos followed, with war lords trying to gain control of large parts of the country as Japan made ever deeper inroads and Soviet Russia inspired a Communist regime in the north. In 1931 the Japanese marched into Manchuria and set up the huge puppet state of Manchukuo.

World War II freed China from Japanese domination but left the country in the throes of a civil war between the Kuomintang government headed by Chiang Kai-shek and the Communist government headed by Mao Tse-tung.

Plate 553. China (Kwei Chow Province), silver dollar (1928). *Obverse:* automobile. The only coin ever issued to feature a motor car.

Plate 554. China, nickel 20 cents (1935-1942). *Obverse:* Sun Yat-sen, leader of the Chinese Revolution that overthrew the Manchu Dynasty in 1912. *Reverse:* ancient spade once used for money. See Plate 3.

Plate 555. Hong Kong, bronze cent (1925). *Obverse.* George V. *Reverse:* value in Chinese. From 1900-1925, Hong Kong handled more shipping than any other port in the world.

Plate 556. Tibet, silver 10 srang (1948), *obverse.* Located between China and India, Tibet is one of the most mysterious countries in the world.

Plate 557. Annam, silver dollar (1834). Seized by the French in 1856, Annam became part of Viet Nam in French Indo-China.

Japan

Ancient Japan was deeply influenced by Chinese ways. During recent centuries, and until only 100 years ago, the Japanese were determined to keep out foreigners and foreign ideas. Up to 1852 they did not allow the entry of white men. In that year Commodore Matthew Perry led an American squadron to Japan. This visit, followed by another one in 1854, finally resulted in opening up Japan to foreigners.

The great Mikado Meiji, who acquired power in 1868, favored modernization and during his reign the Japanese dropped their attitude of aloofness, adopting Western methods with the same skill with which they had once copied Chinese ways.

Plate 561. Siam, silver tical (1868-1910). *Reverse:* three umbrellas.

Plate 562. Siam, silver tical (1910). *Reverse:* three-headed elephant. Siam, now known as Thailand, managed to retain its independence as a buffer state between British and French colonies.

Plate 558. Korea, nickel 5 chon (1905). From ancient times on, the unhappy Korean peninsula has been a favorite invasion target for the Japanese, Chinese, and Russians.

Plate 563. Straits Settlements (Malaya), copper cent (1919). Malaya is a great rubber and tin producing area.

Plate 559. Hopei (Japanese puppet state), copper-nickel 10 cents (1937). *Obverse:* pagoda.
Plate 560. Manchukuo (Japanese puppet state), bronze (1933-1934). *Obverse:* banner.

Plate 564. Afghanistan, silver afghani (1929-1933). *Obverse:* throne room. Afghans were once aggressive warriors who regularly raided northwest India.

Plate 565. **Japan, copper-nickel 5 sen (1889-1897).** ***Obverse:*** **chrysanthemum. To the Japanese, this flower has both sacred and patriotic meaning.**

Plate 566. **Japan, copper-nickel 10 yen (1953).** ***Reverse:*** **Japanese temple.**

The Japanese modeled their army system on Germany's, their navy on Great Britain's. Their new legal code was borrowed from France, and for business methods they went to the United States. Soon the Japanese were building railways, installing telegraph networks, constructing steamships and battleships.

Japan is made up of 3,000 small islands, though only seven of them are really important. They are mountainous, and the total area of good farming soil amounts to no more than the area of New York State —a meager basis for feeding a rapidly growing population (85,000,000 by 1953). The only answer, as the Japanese saw it, was rapid industrialization and far-flung military expansion.

The policy of military conquest took effect even before the end of the nineteenth century. Japan's amazingly easy defeat of the Chinese in 1895 gave it the rich island prize of Formosa and a chance to operate against Korea. In 1904-5 the Japanese astonished the world by giving the Russians a bad beating, and in 1910 they seized Korea, arrogantly fining the Chinese government $170,000,000 for being "troublesome."

From then on the Japanese followed a lucrative policy of bullying China and detaching rich provinces from their helpless victim. By 1941 the Japanese were ready for undeclared war against the United States and the sneak attack on Pearl Harbor. In a few months Japanese forces seized the Philippines, the Dutch East Indies (Indonesia), Malaya, Indo-China, and huge chunks of China, Siam, and Burma. Here they set up the Japanese "Co-prosperity Sphere," and although they were ultimately forced to surrender, they had shown their fellow-Asians that the white man was vulnerable. Dubious as the ethics of Japanese imperialism were, the Japanese effort to control Southeast Asia was one of the momentous events of world history.

Plate 567. **Tientsin (China) Provisional Government, gold medal (1902). Issued for the defeat of the Boxer Rebellion. The flags of seven nations are represented, including those of the United States, Great Britain, France, Germany, and Japan.**

Australia and Oceania

Though small as continents go, Australia is huge for an island. Despite an area of some 3,000,000 square miles, its population is concentrated in the coastal regions. One-third of Australia's interior is rugged wasteland almost entirely lacking water. Another third, little better as far as water supply is concerned, is capable of supporting only a few people. This explains why Australia's population had reached a figure of only 8,000,000 by 1953.

Dutch, Portuguese, British, and French navigators of the seventeenth and eighteenth centuries often sighted the coast of Australia without exploring further. Captain James Cook, the greatest navigator of them all, charted much of the coast of Australia in 1770 for the British.

Conditions were very hard in this strange land of aborigines who were still living in the Stone Age. What was even stranger was that Australia had many animals found nowhere else in the world, and lacked even the most common ones that are plentiful everywhere else.

Some of these fascinating creatures appear on Australian coins and stamps. Among these is the kangaroo which, like many Australian animals, carries its young in a pouch. Kangaroos can outrun all but the fleetest horses and have been known to jump 40 feet.

Associated with the kangaroo on the Australian coat of arms is the emu, a bird almost six feet tall. Unable to fly, it can hit a speed of 40 miles per hour with its long, muscular legs.

Other animals unique to Australia are the platypus, which is classed as a mammal though it has a flat bill like a duck's and lays eggs which it keeps in a pouch. The platypus has webbed feet and fur—but no outer ear. The spiny anteater, which looks like a porcupine, has a long snout and a long tongue—but no teeth. Among outlandish Australian birds, one of the weirdest is the kookaburra; it is often called "the laughing jackass" because of the way it chuckles and "laughs."

Plate 568. **Australia, silver florin (1910).** ***Reverse:*** **Australia's coat of arms, with kangaroo and emu.**

Plate 569. **Australia, silver florin (1937),** ***reverse.*** **Issued for the centenary of Melbourne and Victoria.**

Plate 570. Australia, silver crown (1937), *reverse*. A strikingly handsome coin.

Plate 571. New Zealand, silver florin (1933-1936). *Reverse*: the kiwi, a bird which cannot fly.

Plate 572. New Zealand, silver crown (1935). *Reverse*: Maori chieftain shaking hands with British naval officer.

Australia became a self-governing Dominion in 1901, and is noted for its many progressive laws.

New Zealand

The two islands that make up New Zealand got their name from a Dutch explorer, Abel Tasman, who discovered them in 1642 and named them after his home province. But the islands were largely ignored until Captain James Cook sailed around them in 1769. On landing, he discovered the native people—Maoris. They were cannibals and brave fighters.

For many decades, missionaries came to New Zealand and proved popular with the natives. At first the British government was indifferent to the idea of colonizing New Zealand; settlement began as late as 1840, and then only to forestall possible European rivals.

About 1890 New Zealand began to acquire a reputation for progressive lawmaking. It is interesting to compare the dates of some of these laws with the years of their passage in other countries:

1893 women received the right to vote.
1894 compulsory industrial arbitration.
1897 the eight-hour work day.
1898 old-age pensions.

The graduated income tax had become law in New Zealand even before these measures were passed. In 1907 New Zealand received Dominion status.

East Indies

When Columbus sailed west, he was seeking the Indies—the East Indies, which became known much later as the Dutch East Indies. Columbus, as we know, failed; but the Portuguese, sailing eastward, discovered the Spice Islands—the home of clove, nutmeg, pepper, and the many other products that made fortunes for the Portuguese back home.

When the first Portuguese mariners arrived in the Indies, they learned that the King of Java had a palace with staircases of alternating gold and silver steps. The floors were likewise of gold and silver squares. For years the Portuguese maintained a monopoly on the riches of the Indies. Eventually the Dutch drove them out and took over the sweltering tropical islands.

Bit by bit the Dutch strengthened their hold on the most important islands—Java,

Plate 573. Dutch East Indies, silver guilder (1802). *Obverse*: sailing ship.

Sumatra, Celebes, Amboina—until they had assembled one of the most profitable empires in history. With a relatively small force they were able to control an empire of 80,000,000 Indonesians in an area 57 times larger than the Netherlands. The valuable products of the islands include rubber, tin, quinine, coffee, rice, pepper, and soybeans.

World War II and Japanese invasion brought fearful destruction throughout the islands. The military weakness of the Dutch was all too clear. On August 17, 1945 the Indonesians declared their independence, and after a sharp struggle they won out.

Plate 574. Indonesia, aluminum 10 sen (1951). *Obverse:* eagle with shield and coat of arms.

Plate 575. Indonesia, copper-nickel 50 sen (1952). *Obverse:* native with turban.

Philippine Islands

There are more than 7,000 islands in this group, many of them tiny and unnamed. Ferdinand Magellan discovered the islands in 1521 and was killed in a fight with the natives. The Spaniards soon took possession and included the Philippines under the rule of the governor of New Spain. After centuries of misrule, the Philippines were ripe for revolt even before Americans appeared on the scene in 1898.

Admiral Dewey's destruction of the Spanish fleet in Manila Bay during the Spanish-American War gave the Philippines a dramatic interest in the eyes of Americans. After the war, the United States bought the islands from Spain for $20,000,000. The Philippines are now an independent country.

Plate 576. United States, Hawaiian Sesquicentennial half dollar, silver (1928). *Obverse:* Captain James Cook, who discovered the Hawaiian Islands. *Reverse:* native chieftain.

Hawaiian Islands

These islands, most of them very tiny, stretch out 1,000 miles in the Pacific. Considered one of the most delightful havens in the world for tourists, they also have a strategic value that was recognized long before the sneak attack on Pearl Harbor.

Captain James Cook discovered the islands in 1778. Although he treated the natives well, he met his death there—perhaps because of some unwitting violation of native religious customs.

For almost a century after Cook's visit, Hawaii was governed by wise native Kings who knew how to steer a judicious course through the growing complications of dealing with foreigners on the island. Later rulers were less skillful, and in 1893 the

Plate 577. Philippine Commonwealth, silver peso (1947). *Obverse:* General Douglas MacArthur.

Plate 578. Philippine Commonwealth, silver peso (1936). *Obverse:* President Roosevelt of the United States and President Quezon of the Philippines.

last King was deposed. Five years later, Hawaii became an American territory.

The Hawaiian Islands make up only one of the many island chains that dot the vast expanse of the Pacific. These groups are set in an area of 55,000,000 square miles; some of the islands in Oceania, as the region is called, are only dots on the map. Most of the islands do not even have that dignity, yet they made the headlines as the scene of some of the most brutal fighting in World War II.

Plate 582. German New Guinea, silver 5 marks (1894). *Obverse:* bird of paradise. Traders amassed fortunes from selling the feathers of this most beautiful of all birds.

Plate 579. British New Guinea, copper penny (1938-1944). The native ornaments pictured on this attractive coin were probably used on the island for money. Native money included shells, porcelain, glass, beads, tortoise shell, cowries, pigs' teeth and tusks.

Plate 583 (left). British North Borneo, copper-nickel (1903-1920). *Obverse:* coat of arms upheld by two Dyaks (aboriginal headhunters of Borneo).

Plate 584 (right). Sarawak, bronze cent (1888). *Obverse:* Sir Charles Brooke, who became the White Rajah of this part of Borneo island after driving off pirates and smugglers. The Brooke family sold out its interest in Sarawak to the British government after World War II.

Plate 580. New South Wales (Australian state), silver 5 shillings (1813). This necessity coin (known as the "Holey Dollar") is a Spanish piece of eight with the center cut out.

Plate 581. New South Wales, silver 15 pence. The center of the previous coin, overstruck with new designs and inscriptions.

Plate 585. Fiji, shilling (1934-1936). *Reverse:* native sailing boat.
Plate 586. Fiji, sixpence (1934-1935). *Reverse:* turtle.

Plate 587. Fiji, aluminum bronze threepence (1947). *Reverse:* native hut.

VALUES OF COINS ILLUSTRATED

NOTE: (a) Six types of condition are given for coins. These are: pr. (proof); unc. (uncirculated); EF (extremely fine); VF (very fine); F (fine); VG (very good).

(b) Coin valuations change from year to year. The general trend is upward, subject to changes of interest in certain countries or certain series. To arrive at the valuations presented here, the compiler has studied standard catalogs, compared the quotations of leading dealers, and consulted authorities in cases of doubt. In several instances of rarities, the range of valuation was so wide that the notation "very rare" seemed most appropriate. In all cases, valuations are dealers' selling prices; a collector disposing of his coins to a dealer would realize lower prices.

Plate No.	Condition	Price
11	VF	$40.00
12	F	15.00
13	EF	300.00
14	VG	7.50
15	EF	very rare
16	EF	1,100.00
17	VF	75.00
18	VF	30.00
19	VF	60.00
20	EF	200.00
21	VF	100.00
22	F	10.00
23	VF	75.00
24	VF	50.00
25	VF	750.00
26	F	30.00
27	VF	60.00
28	VF	9.00
29	EF	very rare
31	F	30.00
32	EF	very rare
33	EF	very rare
34	VF	37.50
35	EF	30.00
37	EF	125.00
38	EF	150.00
39	VF	45.00
40	EF	30.00
41	VF	50.00
42	EF	20.00
43	VF	20.00
44	VF	very rare
45	See Plate 29	
46	VF	1,500.00
47	VF	55.00
48	VF	1,000.00
49	VF	1,000.00
50	VF	very rare
51	F	80.00
52	EF	150.00
53	EF	22.50
54	EF	300.00
55	VF	5.00
56	VF	10.00
57	VF	20.00
58	See Plate 57	
59	VF	6.50
60	VF	6.00
61	See Plate 59	
62	VF	20.00
63	VF	500.00
64	See Plate 69	
65	unc.	150.00
66	VF	50.00
67	See Plate 74	
68	See Plate 66	
69	VF	1,500.00
70	VF	180.00
71	See Plate 70	
72	VF	25.00
73	VF	10.00
74	VF	5.00
75	VF	5.00
76	VF	5.00
77	VF	2.50
78	VF	10.00
79	VF	250.00
80	VF	5.00
81	F	12.50
82	VF	25.00
83	VF	75.00
84	VF	200.00
85	VF	10.00
86	VF	very rare
87	EF	4.00
88	VF	50.00
89	See Plate 85	
90	See Plate 73	
91	VF	10.00
92	VF	15.00
93	VF	15.00
94	VF	75.00
95	VF	10.00
96	VF	10.00
97	See Plate 105	
98	VF	10.00
99	VF	10.00
100	VF	10.00
101	VF	20.00
102	F	20.00
103	VF	4.00
104	VF	2.00
105	VF	20.00
106	VF	7.50
107	See Plate 96	
108	VF	5.00
109	VF	5.00
110	VF	3.00
111	VF	3.00
114	VF	21.00
115	VF	16.00
116	VF	125.00
117	VF	10.00
118	EF	110.00
119	unc.	.15
120	unc.	.15
121	unc.	1.75
122	unc.	2.75
123	VF	7.50
124	VF	10.00
125	VF	10.00
126	F	22.50
127	VF	10.00
128	VF	20.00
129	VF	35.00
130	VF	10.00
131	VF	35.00
132	VF	25.00
133	VF	3.00
134	VF	6.00
135	VF	3.00
136	VF	3.50
138	VF	8.00
139	VF	15.00
140	unc.	250.00
141	VF	6.00
142	F	5.00
144	VF	6.00
145	VF	4.00
146	VF	3.00
147	VF	4.50
148	VF	3.50
149	VF	20.00
150	unc.	5.00
151	VF	1.00
152	VF	.50
153	VF	50.00
154	VF	100.00
155	VF	35.00
156	VF	10.00
157	VF	4.00
158	VF	20.00
159	VF	10.00
160	VF	5.00
161	VF	rare
162	VF	100.00
163	VF	60.00
164	VF	very rare
165	See Plate 164	
166	VF	10.00
167	F	10.00
168	EF	7.50
169	VF	.35
170	EF	5.00
171	See Plate 170	
172	VF	50.00
173	See Plate 172	
174	VF	60.00
175	VF	25.00
176	VF	7.50
177	EF	50.00
178	VF	35.00
179	VF	5.00
180	EF	15.00
181	EF	30.00
182	VF	4.00
183	VF	5.00
184	VF	4.00
185	pr.	200.00
186	VF	5.00
187	EF	10.00
188	VF	1.00
189	VF	1.00
190	VF	1.00
192	See Plate 184	
193	EF	2.50
194	EF	50.00
195	pr.	300.00
196	EF	7.50
197	unc.	15.00
198	VF	4.00
199	unc.	500.00
200	EF	2.50
201	EF	5.00
202	unc.	2.00
203	VF (set)	5.00
204	VF	1.00
205	VF	1.00
206	VF	10.00
207	VF	1.50
208	VF	2.00
209	VF	1.25
210	VF	1.50
211	EF	20.00
212	EF	20.00
213	EF	20.00
214	EF	100.00
215	EF	30.00
216	VF	40.00
217	EF	200.00
218	VF	50.00
221	VF	25.00
222	EF	35.00
223	EF	35.00
224	EF	50.00
225	VF	350.00
226	VF	20.00
227	VF	20.00
228	EF	20.00
229	VF	125.00
230	VF	20.00
231	EF	25.00
232	VF	25.00
233	EF	85.00
235	VF	17.50
236	VF	12.50
237	VF	35.00
238	EF	150.00
239	EF	50.00
240	VF	1.75
241	VF	1.50
242	VF	1.00
243	VF	1.00
245	unc.	3.50
246	unc.	4.00
247	unc.	3.75
248	unc.	3.50
249	unc.	3.00
250	VF	.25
251	VF	.25
252	VF	15.00
253	EF	50.00
254	EF	7,500.00
256	EF	500.00
257	EF	20.00
258	EF	20.00
259	EF	100.00
261	EF	20.00
262	pr.	5.00
263	VF	20.00
264	pr.	150.00
265	VF	15.00
266	EF	125.00
267	VF	75.00
268	VF	.75
269	VF	3.00
270	unc.	2.50
271	unc.	2.50
272	unc.	2.50
273	VF	20.00
274	unc.	4.00
275	EF	1,500.00
277	VF	3.00
278	unc.	3.00
279	VF	375.00
280	VF	450.00
281	VF	175.00
282	VF	5.00

Plate No.	Condition	Price
283	VF	500.00
284	VF	very rare
285	VF	25.00
288	VF	20.00
290	VF	450.00
291	VF	450.00
292	VF	5.00
293	EF	500.00
294	VF	7.50
295	VF	60.00
297	VF	150.00
298	VF	5.00
299	VF	200.00
300	VF	15.00
303	VF	4.00
304	EF	150.00
305	pr.	150.00
306	VF	.35
307	VF	25.00
308	VF	10.00
309	VF	500.00
310	VF	4.00
311	VF	1.00
312	VF	12.50
313	VF	7.50
314	VF	2.50
315	VF	5.00
316	VF	2.50
317	VF	7.50
318	VF	5.00
319	unc.	2.50
320	VF	15.00
321	VF	20.00
322	unc.	5.00
323	F	10.00
324	unc.	5.00
325	VF	.50
326	VF	.35
327	unc.	5.00
329	unc.	2.50
330	unc.	12.50
331	VF	1.00
332	VF	7.50
333	VF	20.00
334	VF	2.00
335	VF	2.00
336	VF	30.00
337	EF	20.00
338	EF	25.00
339	EF	350.00
340	VF	.30
341	VF	2.50
342	VF	7.50
343	VF	50.00
344	unc.	3.00
345	unc.	3.00
346	VF	25.00
347	VF	50.00
348	VF	50.00
349	VF	20.00
350	unc.	5.00
352	See Plate 342	
353	VF	30.00
354	VF	25.00
355	unc.	4.00
356	VF	250.00
357	VF	1.00
358	VF	40.00
359	VF	12.50
360	VF	.35
361	VF	.35
365	unc.	30.00
366	unc.	10.00
367	EF	7,500.00
368	unc.	10.00
369	VF	5.00
370	unc.	10.00
371	unc.	12.50
372	unc.	9.50
373	unc.	7.50
374	unc.	9.50
375	VF	30.00
376	VF	2.50
377	VF	6.00
378	VF	.50
379	VF	3.00
380	unc.	5.00
381	unc.	125.00
382	VF	10.00
383	unc.	12.50
384	unc.	6.00
387	VF	5.00
388	VF	100.00
389	VF	100.00
390	VF	3.00
391	VF	12.50
392	VF	15.00
393	VF	1.50
394	VF	10.00
395	VF	10.00
396	VF	12.50
397	VF	1.00
398	VF	5.00
399	VF	8.00
400	VF	2.50
401	VF	1.50
402	see Coinometry	
403	see Coinometry	
404	unc.	1.50
405	unc.	20.00
406	unc.	8.00
407	unc.	12.50
408	unc.	15.00
409	unc.	5.00
410	unc.	3.00
411	unc.	17.50
412	see Coinometry	
413	see Coinometry	
414	see Coinometry	
415	see Coinometry	
416	pr.	100.00
417	unc.	10.00
418	unc.	5,000.00
419	unc.	5.00
420	unc.	2.50
421	unc.	7.50
422	unc.	2.00
423	VF	20.00
424	see Coinometry	
425	unc.	5.00
427	F	50.00
428	F	15.00
429	unc.	15.00
430	VF	1.00
431	VF	1.00
432	unc.	3.50
433	VF	1.50
434	unc.	1.60
435	see Coinometry	
436	unc.	700.00
437	unc.	very rare
438	unc.	very rare
439	unc.	very rare
440	unc.	very rare
441	unc.	very rare
442	unc.	very rare
443	VF	.50
444	F	very rare
445	unc.	2.50
446	VF	5.00
447	unc.	3.00
448	VF	50.00
449	VF	.50
450	VF	.75
451	VG	40.00
452	VF	2.00
453	VF	.25
454	VF	.50
457	VF	.50
458	unc.	.30
459	VF	.60
460	VF	30.00
461	unc.	2.50
462	see Plate 310	
463	F (2 bits)	5.00
	(4 bits)	7.50
464	unc.	2.25
465	unc.	.75
466	F	75.00
467	VF	.50
468	VF	4.00
469	VF	7.50
472	unc.	1.00
473	VF	4.00
474	VF	.35
475	VF	.15
476	unc.	1.25
477	VF	7.50
478	VF	2.00
479	VF	2.50
480	VF	150.00
481	VF	3.00
482	VF	3.00
483	VF	2.00
484	VF	2.50
485	VF	2.50
486	VF	2.50
487	VF	4.50
488	unc.	.75
489	VF	2.00
490	VF	1.25
491	VF	20.00
492	VF	.25
493	unc.	1.00
494	VF	.35
495	VF	3.50
496	VF	2.50
497	VF	2.00
498	VF	15.00
499	VF	5.00
500	VF	.50
501	VF	60.00
502	VF	1.25
503	VF	3.00
504	VF	2.00
505	VF	2.50
506	VF	1.00
507	VF	.75
508	VF	.50
509	VF	.50
510	VF	.35
511	VF	.25
512	EF	3.00
513	VF	25.00
514	VF	175.00
515	VF	2.00
516	VF	17.50
517	VF	.50
518	VF	.75
519	VF	3.00
520	VF	.50
521	VF	.35
522	unc.	.75
523	VF	7.50
524	VF	1.50
525	VF	.50
526	VF	.50
527	VF	10.00
528	VF	.75
529	VF	.50
530	VF	1.50
531	VF	2.00
532	unc.	2.50
533	VF	2.50
534	unc.	2.50
535	unc.	.75
536	VF	.50
537	VF	7.50
538	VF	.50
539	VF	5.00
541	VF	25.00
542	VF	50.00
543	VF	.50
544	VF	1.50
545	VF	.75
546	VF	.50
547	VF	1.00
548	VF	5.00
549	VF	.50
551	VF	5.00
552	VF	7.50
553	VF	20.00
554	VF	.75
555	VF	.35
556	VF	10.00
557	VF	22.50
558	VF	4.00
559	VF	.35
560	VF	2.50
561	VF	4.00
562	VF	4.00
563	VF	.25
564	VF	5.00
565	VF	.25
566	VF	.25
567	VF	500.00
568	VF	2.00
569	VF	5.00
570	unc.	4.50
571	VF	2.50
572	pr.	60.00
573	VF	5.00
574	VF	.25
575	VF	.75
576	unc.	50.00
577	unc.	2.50
578	VF	6.00
579	VF	.35
580	VF	65.00
581	VF	15.00
582	VF	20.00
583	VF	.50
584	VF	.75
585	VF	1.50
586	VF	1.00
587	VF	.50

CHECKLIST OF AMERICAN COIN CLUBS

(All these clubs are affiliated with The American Numismatic Association. For information about membership, write to Lewis M. Reagan, General Secretary, P.O. Box 577, Wichita, Kansas.)

ALABAMA

ɜirmingham Coin Club

ARIZONA

ᑊhoenix Coin Club

ARKANSAS

ᐱrkansas Numismatic Society (Little Rock)

CALIFORNIA

ȝay Cities Coin Club (Santa Monica)
California State Numismatic Association (Oakland)
Capitol City Coin Club (Sacramento)
East Bay Coin Club (Oakland)
Garden Grove Coin Club
Hanford Coin Club
Hollywood Academy of Numismatics
Long Beach Coin Club
Los Angeles Coin Club (Foresters Hall)
Merced Numismatic Society
Orange County Coin Club (Fullerton)
Orders and Medals Society of America (San Francisco)
Pacific Coast Numismatic Society (Palace Hotel, San Francisco)
Pasadena Coin Club
Redwood Empire Coin Club (Santa Rosa)
San Bernardino Coin Club
San Diego Numismatic Society
San Fernando Valley Coin Club
San Francisco, Junior Coin Collectors (1140 Sutter St.)
San Gabriel Valley Coin Club
San Jose Coin Club

COLORADO

Arkansas Valley Coin Club (Rocky Ford)
Colorado-Wyoming Numismatic Association (Arvada)
Greeley Coin Club
Minnequa Coin Club (Pueblo)
Pikes Peak Coin Club (Colorado Springs)
Rocky Mountain Numismatic Society (Denver)

CONNECTICUT

Fairfield County Numismatic Association (Bridgeport)
Hartford Numismatic Society
Litchfield County Coin Club (Torrington)
Meriden Coin Club
Naugatuck Valley Numismatic Association (Naugatuck)
New Haven Numismatic Society
Uncas Numismatic Association (Norwich)
Waterbury Numismatic Society

DELAWARE

Delaware Numismatic Association (Wilmington)

DISTRICT OF COLUMBIA

Middle Atlantic Numismatic Association (4228 19 St., N.E.)
Washington Numismatic Society

FLORIDA

Clearwater Coin and Stamp Club
Daytona Beach Numismatic Club
Jacksonville Coin Club
Miami Coin Club (2049 Biscayne Blvd.)
Ocala Stamp and Coin Club
St. Petersburg Coin Club

GEORGIA

Atlanta Coin Club (Grady Hotel)

ILLINOIS

Central Illinois Numismatic Society (Springfield)
Central States Numismatic Society (New Holland)
Champaign-Urbana Coin Club
Chicago Coin Club (La Salle Hotel)
Corn Belt Coin Club (Carlock)
Fairmount Coin Club
Hawthorne Coin Club
Illinois Valley Coin Club (Streator)
Kankakee County Coin Club (Kankakee)
Oak Park Coin Club
South Chicago Stamp & Coin Club (3030 E. 92 St.)

INDIANA

Calumet Numismatic Club (East Chicago)
Indianapolis Coin Club

IOWA

Burlington Coin Club
Cedar Rapids Coin Club
Des Moines Coin Club
Fairfield Coin Club
Iowa Numismatic Association (Clinton)
Tri-City Coin Club (Davenport)
Waterloo Coin Club

KANSAS

Coin Collectors' Club (Merriam)
Salina Coin Club
Topeka Coin Club
Wichita Coin Club

LOUISIANA

Baton Rouge Coin Club
Crescent City Coin Club (New Orleans)
Fugio Club (Shreveport)

MARYLAND

Baltimore Coin Club (First Christian Church)
Maryland Numismatic Society (Baltimore)
Martin Coin Club (Baltimore)
Numismatic Society of Frederick, Md.
Telephone Company Stamp and Coin Club (Baltimore)
Western Maryland Coin Club (Cumberland)

MASSACHUSETTS

Boston Numismatic Society (Sheraton-Plaza Hotel)
Cape Cod Coin Club (Hyannis)
New England Numismatic Association (Worcester)
Springfield Coin Club
Worcester County Numismatic Society (Worcester)

MICHIGAN

Ann Arbor Coin Club
Detroit Coin Club (Abington Hotel)
Flint Stamp and Coin Club
Grand Rapids Coin Club
Pontiac Coin Club

MINNESOTA

American Vecturist Association (St. Paul)
Northwest Coin Club (Minneapolis)

MISSISSIPPI

Jackson-Mississippi Coin Club

MISSOURI

Joplin Coin Club
Missouri Numismatic Society (St. Louis)
Heart of America Numismatic Association (Kansas City)

MONTANA

Treasure State Coin Club (Great Falls)

NEBRASKA

David City Coin Club
Lincoln Coin Club
Omaha Coin Club

NEW HAMPSHIRE

Cheshire County Numismatic Society (Keene)
New Hampshire Collectors Club (Concord)

NEW JERSEY

Delaware Valley Coin Club (Westville)
Jersey City Coin Club

CHECK LIST OF AMERICAN COIN CLUBS (Continued)

NEW JERSEY (Cont.)
New Jersey Numismatic Society (Newark)
Pingry School Coin Club (Elizabeth)
South Jersey Numismatic Society (Penns Grove)
Trenton Coin Club

NEW MEXICO
New Mexico Coin Club (Albuquerque)

NEW YORK
Albany Numismatic Society
American Numismatic Society (New York City)
Bronx Coin Club (Concourse Plaza Hotel)
Brooklyn Coin Club (Hotel Granada)
Buffalo Numismatic Association
Cortland Coin Club
Four County Coin Collectors Club (Batavia)
Hudson Valley Coin Club (Kingston)
Long Island Coin Club (Mineola)
Minisink Coin Club (Port Jervis)
New York Numismatic Club (100 Clinton St., Brooklyn)
Rochester Junior Numismatic Association
Rochester Numismatic Association
Syracuse Numismatic Association
Triple Cities Coin Club (Chenango)
Westchester County Coin Club (New Rochelle)

NORTH CAROLINA
Asheville Coin Club
Charlotte Coin Club
Eagle Coin Club (Lexington)
Piedmont Numismatic Coin Club (Winston-Salem)

NORTH DAKOTA
North Dakota Coin Club (Bismarck)

OHIO
Akron Coin Club
Allen County Coin Club (Lima)
Ashland Coin Club
Canton Coin Club
Cedar City Coin Club
Cincinnati Numismatic Association (Hotel Metropole)
Cleveland Coin Club (Hotel Carter)
Columbus Numismatic Society
Dayton Coin Club
East Liverpool Coin Club
Hamilton Coin Club
Marysville Numismatic Society
Norwood Coin Club
Ohio State Numismatic Society (Worthington)
Toledo Coin Club
Western Reserve Numismatic Club of Cleveland (Hotel Carter)
Youngstown Numismatic Club

OKLAHOMA
Oklahoma City Coin Club
Oklahoma-Kansas Numismatic Association (Tulsa)
Ponca City Coin Club
Tulsa Coin Club

OREGON
Oakridge Coin Club
Oregon Numismatic Society (Portland)

PENNSYLVANIA
Armstrong Activities Association (Lancaster)
Brookline Coin Club (Pittsburgh)
Butler Coin Club
Greenville Coin Club
Harrisburg Coin Club
Johnstown Numismatic Club
King Beaver Coin Club (Beaver)
Lehigh Valley Coin Club
Main Line Coin Club (Paoli)
Monroe County Coin Club
New Castle Coin Club
North Penn Stamp and Coin Club (Quakertown)
Numismatic and Antiquarian Society of Philadelphia
Panther Valley Coin Club (Lehighton)
Penn-Ohio Coin Clubs (Mansfield)
Philadelphia Coin Club (Benjamin Franklin Hotel)
Philadelphia Electric Company Coin Club
Philadelphia Transportation Company Coin Club
Pittsburgh Coin Club
Reading Coin Club
Scranton Numismatic Association
Shenango Valley Coin Club (Sharon)
Western Pennsylvania Numismatic Society (Pittsburgh)
Wilkes Barre Coin Club
York Coin Club

RHODE ISLAND
Coin Club of Rhode Island (Providence)

SOUTH DAKOTA
South Dakota Numismatic Society (White Lake)

TENNESSEE
Chattanooga Coin Club
Memphis Coin Club
Nashville Coin Club

TEXAS
Corpus Christi Coin Club
Dallas Coin Club
San Antonio Coin Club

UTAH
Utah Numismatic Society (Salt Lake City)

VERMONT
Chittenden County Coin Club (Burlington)

VIRGINIA
Monticello Coin Club (Charlottesville)
Richmond Coin Club
Stamp and Coin Club of Roanoke

WASHINGTON
Evergreen Coin Club (Centralia)
Inland Empire Coin Club (Spokane)
Pacific Northwest Numismatic Association (Seattle)
Seattle Coin Club (Frye Hotel)

WEST VIRGINIA
Huntington Coin Club
Kanawha Valley Coin Club (Charleston)

WISCONSIN
Madison Coin Club
Milwaukee Numismatic Society
Racine Numismatic Society
Whitefish Bay Coin Club (Milwaukee)

CANADA
Canadian Numismatic Association (Ottawa)
Toronto Coin Club

VALUES OF CURRENTLY-USED FOREIGN COINS*

Country	Currency	*Value in U.S. $ (as of 10/53)*
Afghanistan	Afghani	.0476
Albania	lek	.02
Argentina	peso	.0725
Australia	Australian pound	2.24
Austria	Austrian shilling	.0286
Belgium	franc	.02
Bolivia	boliviano	.002
Brazil	cruzeiro	.0260
	(1000 cruzeiros to 1 conto)	
Bulgaria	lev	.15
Burma	kyat	.21
Canada	Canadian dollar	1.01¼
Ceylon	rupee	.21
Chile	peso	.009
China (Communist)	Jen Min Piao (People's Dollar) *Official rate:*	31,000 for $1 U.S.
Colombia	peso	.40
Costa Rica	colón	.15
Cuba	peso	1.00
Czechoslovakia	crown	.14
Denmark	krone	.145
Dominican Republic	Dominican (gold) peso	1.00
Ecuador	sucre	.058
Egypt	Egyptian pound	2.88
Ethiopia	Ethiopian dollar	.40½
Finland	markka (100 pennis)	.0045
Formosa	Taiwan dollar (hsin Taipi) *Official:*	.0977
	Free:	.065
France	franc	.00286
Germany— (Western Section)	Deutsche mark	.238
(Soviet Section)	No definite exchange value.	
Great Britain and Northern Ireland	pound sterling (£)	2.81½
Greece	drachma	.000033
Guatemala	quetzal	1.00
Haiti	gourde	.20
Hashemite Jordan Kingdom	Jordan dinar	2.81
Honduras	lempira	.50
Hungary	forint	.086
India	rupee	.21
Indonesia	rupia (Indonesian guilder)	.0877

Country	Currency	*Value in U.S. $ (as of 10/53)*
Iran	rial	.03125
Iraq	Iraqi dinar	2.82
Ireland (excluding Northern Ireland)	pound sterling	2.81½
Israel	Israel pound	1.00
	(one of 3 official rates)	
Italy	lira	.0016
Japan	yen	.0028
Korea—So. Korea	whan *Official:*	.0055
	Free:	.00005
Lebanon	Lebanese pound *Official:*	.46
	Free:	.30
Liberia	Liberian dollar	1.00
Libya	Libyan pound	2.86
Luxembourg	Luxembourg franc	.02
	Belgian franc	.02
Malaya	Malay dollar	.327
Mexico	peso	.1163
The Netherlands	guilder	.264
New Zealand	New Zealand pound	2.80½
Nicaragua	córdoba	.20
Norway	krone	.14
Pakistan	rupee	.304
Panama	balboa	1.00
Paraguay	guarani	.0180
Peru	sol	.06
Philippine Islands	peso	.499
Poland	zloty	.25
Portugal	escudo	.035
Rumania	leu (pl. leï)	.0893
El Salvador	colón	.40
Saudi Arabia	riyal	.277
Spain	peseta *Free:*	.026
Sweden	krona	.193
Switzerland	franc	.233
Syria	Syrian pound	.28
Thailand	baht	.057
Turkey	Turkish pound	.357
Union of South Africa	So. African pound	2.82
Union of Soviet Socialist Republics (Russia)	ruble	.25
Uruguay	peso	.34
Venezuela	bolivar	.30
Yugoslavia	dinar	.003

* Figures furnished by the Foreign Department of the Chase National Bank of the City of New York.

INDEX

Aachen 65
Adrian I, Pope 128
Aegina 24
Aenus 17
Aesculapius 129
Aethelred "the unready" 77
Afghanistan 211
Africa 15-16, 31, 36-37, 40, 43, 47, 53, 55-56, 70, 113, 116, 131, 134-135, 147, 149, 190-191, 200-206
Africa Company 87
Agrigentum 27
Akragas 27
Alamo 171
Alaska 166, 173
Albania 163-165, 202
Alberta 173, 178
Alexander I, Czar 161
Alexander VII, Pope 127
Alexander Severus 54, 56
Alexander the Great 6, 13-14, 16, 20-21, 23-24, 26, 28-29, 37, 43, 46, 59, 72, 85, 166
Alfonso I (Portugal) 134
Alfonso XIII (Spain) 133
Alfred III (Scotland) 97
Alfred the Great 76, 77
Algiers 205
Alsace 75
Althing 155
Alvarado, Pedro de 186
Amazon River 195-196
American Numismatic Assn. 9, 219-220
American Revolution 67, 89, 167, 171, 177-178
Amboina 215
Amsterdam 141, 143, 145-147
Andros 25
Anglesea token 91
Annam 211
Anne, Queen (England) 88-89
Anson, Admiral George 89
Antigonus Gonatas 16, 22
Antigua 190
Antioch 35, 62, 126
Antoninus Pius 29, 50, 55, 85
Antony, see Mark Antony
Aphrodite 16, 32, 42, 44
Apollo 15-16, 23, 28, 32, 42
Appenzell 137
Arabia 28, 59, 149, 206
Arabs 58-59, 65, 101, 121-123, 131, 134, 162-163, 202, 206-207
Aragon 101
Arethusa 17, 27
Argentina 192-195, 198
Arizona 180, 182
Arkansas 168, 199
Armenia 35
Arsinoe 13
Artabanus II (Parthia) 43
Artemis 15, 27
Aruba 147, 191
Ashantis 203
Asia 206-212
Asoka 208
Assyrians 59, 146
Astarte 38
Athene (Athena) 15-20, 23, 26, 29, 32, 85, 128, 172
Athens 14-19, 23-29, 97
Augustus 39, 45-50, 52-53, 55, 59, 61-62
Aurelian 53, 56
Austin, Stephen 171
Australia 213-214, 216
Austria 65-66, 68-71, 73-74, 107, 109, 111, 113-120, 129, 132, 136, 139-141, 147, 157
Aztecs 179, 180

Babylonians 13, 52, 59, 206
Bacchiocchi, Felix 129
Bahamas 166, 188
Balboa, Vasco Nunez de 184, 186
Balkans 117, 119, 162-165
Baltic countries 156-158
Bank of England 90, 190, of France 72
Barbados 188
Barbary pirates 146
Bar cent 171
Bar Kochba 60-61
Basta, George 119
Bastille 68, 186
Batavia 142
Bavaria 100, 115-116
Beard tokens 160
Belgian Congo 200, 202-203
Belgium 65, 73, 113, 137, 140-141, 146, 173, 202-203
Bermuda 188
Bermudez, Juan de 188
Bernadotte, Jean see Charles XIV John
Berne 136-138
Bible 59, 61-62, 79-80, 105-106, 146
Boers 204-205
Bohemia 100-102, 107, 113-114, 119-120, 165
Bolivar, Simon 186, 192-194, 196
Bolivia 193-194, 198
Bombay 116
Bonaparte, Elisa 129, Joseph 133
Bonaparte, see Napoleon
Bosnia 118
Boulton, Matthew 92
Bourbons 73-74, 129
Boxer Rebellion 210, 212
Bracteates 101
Bradford, William 167
Bramante, Donato 126
Brandenburg 102, 109
Brasher doubloon 172
Brazil 6, 135, 146, 193-196, 198, 200
Bremen 103, 151
Breslau 151
Britannia 29, 50, 81, 85-86, 90, 93, 147
British Cameroons 204, Central Africa 204, Columbia 173, Commonwealth 99, 177, 209, East Africa 203-204, East India Company 83, 207-208, Empire 6, 8, 70, 83-84, 93-94, 174, 202, 204, Isles, see Great Britain, New Guinea 216, North Borneo 216, Togoland 204, West Africa 203-204
Brooke, Sir Charles 216
Brunswick 100, 106, 108, 110
Brutus 45-46
"Buffalo" nickel 166
Bulgaria 163, 165
Buonarotti, Michelangelo 125, 127-128
Burma 209, 212
Byzantine Empire 58, 63, 78, 101, 121-123, 125, 149, 159, 162

Cabot, John 81, 173-174
Cabral, Pedro Alvares 194
Caesar, see Julius Caesar
California 82, 170, 180, 182, 184, 196
Caligula 48-49, 51-52
Canada 6, 8, 67, 173-178
Canute the Great 76-77, 153
Cape Colony 204
Capetown 147, 204
Caracalla 52, 56
Cardenas, Lazaro 183
Carol II (Rumania) 163
Cartagena 196-197
Carthage 27-28, 36-38, 40-42, 89, 122
Cartier, Jacques 174
Carver, George Washington 170
Carver-Washington half dollar 170
"Cartwheels" 86, 89, 92
Casas, Bartolomé de las 184-185
Castile 132
Castor 42
Catherine the Great, 159, 161
Cattaro 71
Celebes 215
Cellini, Benvenuto 80, 126
Central America 133, 166, 184-187
Ceres 75
Ceylon 135, 208
Chaldeans 7
Chandragupta II (India) 208
Charlemagne 6, 64-65, 72, 100, 122, 128
Charles I (England) 84-85
Charles II (England) 29, 66, 85-89, 175
Charles III (Spain) 90
Charles IV (Holy Roman Empire) 102
Charles IV (Spain) 90, 132
Charles V (Holy Roman Empire) 105, 113-115, 131-133, 180
Charles VI (Holy Roman Empire) 115
Charles X (France) 73
Charles X Gustav (Sweden) 151
Charles XI (Sweden)151
Charles XII (Sweden) 151-152
Charles XIV John (Sweden) 152
Charter Oak 167
Chiang Kai-shek 210
Chile 194, 196
China 8, 22, 122, 166, 174, 206, 209-212
Chrismon 128
Christ 57-58, 61, 96, 103, 123-124, 128, 150, 158
Christian II (Denmark) 150
Christian IV (Denmark) 153
Christian X (Denmark) 153-154
Circus Maximus 6, 51
Civil War (American) 138, 169-171, 183
Claudius 35, 48-49, 52
Clement VII, Pope 126
Clement VIII, Pope 126
Clement IX, Pope 128
Cleopatra 13, 44-47
Coin cleaning and storing 9, condition 7-8, machinery 9-10, valuation 8, 217-218
Cologne 101-104, 107
Colorado 168, 180
Colombia 185, 193, 196-197
Colosseum 51
Columbian Exposition half dollar 166
Columbus, Christopher 6, 81, 131, 134-135, 156, 166, 173-174, 184, 186-188, 191, 196, 199, 214
Confederacy 169, 171
Congo Free State 203
Connecticut Tercentenary half dollar 167
Constantine the Great 41, 50, 53, 56-57, 65, 126-127
Constantius II 57
Cook, James 175, 213-215
Cordoba Francisco Hernando de 186
Corinth 21, 24-26, 29, 41, 76
Corvey 109
Costa Rica 185, 187
Crassus 41, 43, 55, 59
Crete 24
Cricklade penny 77
Croatia 116-117, 164
Cromwell, Oliver 85
Croton 26-27
Crusades 59, 93, 101, 123
Cruz, Dr. Oswaldo 195
Cuauhtemoc 180
Cuba 187, 189
Curacao 147, 191
Cyrillic alphabet 164
Cyprus 164
Cyrus the Great 59
Czechoslovakia 116, 120

Dacia 30, 49-50, 53, 55-56, 163
Dalmatia 71
Danegeld 76
Danish West Indies 191
Danzig 6, 103, 158
Dardanelles 162-163
Declaration of Independen 168
Delaware 151, 167
Demanhur 29
Denmark 53, 76-77, 111, 148-150, 152-155, 191
Dewey, Admiral George 21
Diana, see Artemis
Diaz, Porfirio 183
Dinkelsbuhl 112
Diocletian 53, 56-57, 93, 16
Dionysus 28
Distant Company of Amstedam 146
"Dixie" notes 171
Dominican Republic 191
Domitian 49, 52, 55
Donauwerth 113
Drake, Sir Francis 6, 81-82, 96, 187, 197
Durer, Albrecht 112
Dutch, East India Co. 147, 205, East Indies 212, Guia 147, West India Co. 147
Dyaks 216

East Indies, see Indonesia
Ecuador 193, 196-197
Edward II (England) 96
Edward III (England) 78
Edward IV (England) 79
Edward VI (England) 81, 8
Edward VII (England) 93, 9
Egypt 11-13, 16, 20-21, 23-2 29, 33, 44-46, 48, 59, 70, 72, 136, 166, 198, 202, 206
Eire, see Ireland
Eisenhower, Dwight D. 170
Elagabalus 56
El Dorado 196
Elis 16-17, 25
Elizabeth I (England) 81-8 144
Elizabeth II (England) 96-9
England, see Great Britain
Eretria 25
Erik the Red 156
Eriksson, Lief 156
Esterhazy 116
Estonia 6, 148, 155, 157-158
Ethiopia 116, 201

Faisal I (Iraq) 207
Farnese, Alessandro 145-146
Faroe Islands 154
Farouk I (Egypt) 202
Ferdinand I (Holy Roman Empire) 113-114, 132
Ferdinand III (Holy Roma Empire) 106
Ferdinand V (Spain) 131, 181, 184
Festival of Britain 96
Fiji 216
Finland 148, 152, 155, 157
Florence 63, 102, 107, 124-12
Florenzia 83
Florida 190
Flying Eagle cent 171
Formosa 212
Fortuna 108, 153
France 21, 53, 63-75, 78-79, 85-86, 89, 91, 94, 109, 111-112, 115-116, 119, 121, 124, 132, 135-136, 138-141, 143-144, 148-149, 153, 161, 163, 168-169, 173-176, 179, 183, 185, 187, 190-191, 195, 201-202, 205, 211-213
Frankfurt am Main 101, 107
Franklin, Benjamin 167-168, half dollar 168
Franz Joseph (Austria-Hungary) 117
Frederick Barbarossa 100-101, 122
Frederick II (Holy Roman Empire) 63, 85, 101-102
Frederick II (the Great) 10 111, 116
Free French government 20
French Equatorial Africa 20 Guiana 205, Indo-China 7, 211-212, Somalia 201, West Africa 200

INDEX

Fribourg Shooting Festival 138-139
Fugger 114-115, 122

Gambia 204
Gangut, Battle of 160
Gela 19
Geneva 139
Genoa 122, 139, 173
George I (England) 89
George II (England) 89, 109
George III (England) 87, 89-90, 93, 188
George IV (England) 93
George V (England) 95-96, 175, 210
George VI (England) 96, 175
German East Africa 200, New Guinea 216
Germany 10, 57, 63-66, 73, 75, 89, 91, 100-112, 115, 118-122, 132, 135, 140-141, 144, 147, 149, 151, 154, 157, 161, 200, 205, 212
Gerona 133
Gettysburg half dollar 169
Gibraltar 36, 133, 181
Glossary 10
Glueckstadt 153
"Godless" florin 94-95
Goertz, Baron de 152
Goethe, Johann Wolfgang von 112
Gold Coast 87, 203-204
Golden Hind 10, 82, 96
Gorgon 25
"Gothic" crown 94-95
Gotland 149
Grant Memorial half dollar 169
Great Britain 6-8, 29-31, 53, 66-67, 69-70, 72-74, 76-99, 103, 112, 121, 123-125, 131-132, 135-137, 140, 143, 146-149, 153, 155, 160, 163-164, 167-169, 172-178, 187-191, 194-196, 201-205, 207-208, 211-213
Greece 8, 9, 11, 13-29, 31-33, 35-37, 40-44, 46-47, 51, 58-59, 65, 68, 76, 98, 101-102, 104, 122, 125-126, 128, 149, 159, 163-165, 172, 202, 210
Greenland 148, 154, 156
Gregory XIII, Pope 45
Griqualand 204
Guadeloupe 191
Guatemala 184-186
Guinea 87
"Gun-money" 85, 96-97
Gustav V (Sweden) 152
Gustavus Adolphus 106, 150
Gustavus Vasa 150-151, 154

Hadrian 29, 31, 47, 50, 54-55, 60, 85
Haiti 190-191
Hannibal 18, 37-38, 40-41, 137
Hanseatic League 102-103, 158
Hapsburgs 72, 103, 113-116, 118-120, 136, 183
Harold II (England) 77
Hawaiian Islands 215-216, Sesquicentennial half dollar 215
Haydn, Joseph 116, 118
Helvetia, Switzerland, 136
Henri Christophe 190-191
Henry IV (England) 97
Henry VI (England) 79
Henry VII (England) 79-80
Henry VIII (England) 80-81
Henry the Lion (Saxony) 100
Hera 15-16, 26, 32, 41
Herakles (Hercules) 23, 25, 29, 32, 42, 62, 70
Hermes 15, 17, 32, 141
Hesse 101
Hidalgo, Miguel 182
Hindenburg, Paul von 112
Hispaniola 184, 190-191
Hohenzollerns 109
"Holey Dollar" 216
Holland, see Netherlands
Holstein 111, 153
Holy Land, see Israel and Judea
Holy Roman Empire 63, 65, 100-102, 104-106, 113-116, 120, 127, 129, 131, 136
Honduras 185-187
Hong Kong 210
Hopei 211
Houston, Sam 171
Hudson's Bay Company 175-177
Huguenots 138, 167
Hull, John 171
"Hundred Days" 73-74
Hungary 100-101, 113-114, 116-117, 119-120, 155
Hyderabad 208

Iberian Peninsula 131-135
Iceland 28, 148, 155
Incas 184, 194, 198-199
Incuse 10
India 20-22, 55, 67, 70, 134-135, 146, 156, 166, 175, 189, 202-203, 206-208, 211
Indian Head penny 6, 166, 171
Indonesia 212, 214-215
Iowa 168
Iran, see Persia
Iraq 207
Ireland 84-86, 89, 97-99, 148, 155, 177, 196
Isabella 131, 181
Israel 6, 59-62
Italy 9, 15, 24, 26, 35, 37-38, 40, 43-44, 53, 63-66, 70-71, 73-74, 80-81, 86, 91, 100-102, 112-113, 116-117, 119, 121-132, 134-135, 149, 165, 194, 201
Iturbide, Augustin de 182
Ivan the Terrible, Czar 159

Jackson, "Stonewall" 169
Jamaica 188-189
James I (England) 84, 96
James II (England) 98
James VI (Scotland) 84
Jamestown 167
Janus 32, 42, 47, 49
Japan 112, 166, 210-212, 215
Java 214
Jefferson, Thomas 7, 168-169, nickel 7, 169
Jesus, see Christ
Joachimstal 107, 113-115
Joachimstaler 107, 115
Joao III (Portugal) 194
Joao VI (Portugal) 195
John the Blind 165
Juarez, Benito 182-183
Judas Iscariot 62
Judas Maccabeus 59
Judea 28, 49, 55, 59-62, 123, 149, 206
Juliana (Netherlands) 191
Julius II, Pope 127
Julius Caesar 6, 13, 21, 28, 35, 39, 41-45, 47-48, 72, 142
Juno, see Hera
Jupiter, see Zeus
Justinian 58

Kalmar, Union of 149, 153
Kansas 168, 180
Kara George (Serbia) 164
Kemal Ataturk, Mustafa 163
Kenya 203, 204
Khan Kublai 209
Kimberley 204
Knights of Malta 191
Koran 162
Korea 211-212
Kruger, Paul 205
Kuomintang 210
Kuttenberg mines 117

Labrador 177-178
Lapland 152
Latin (language) 30, 65, 77, 81, 85, 88, 101, 117, 163-164
Latvia 157-158
Laurium 24
Lebanon 207
Lee, Robert E. 169
Leeward Islands 190
Leicester, Earl of 144
Leipzig, Battle of 109, 111
Lempira, Chief 186
Leon (Spain) 132
Leonardo, see Vinci
Leontini 28
Leopold I (Belgium) 141
Leopold II 141, 202-203 202-203
Levant 111, 116, 123, 125, 146
Lexington-Concord half dollar 167
Leyden 145-146
Liberia 202
Liberty Bell 168
Liberty Head nickel 172
Liechtenstein 165
Lima 89-90, 189
Lincoln 50, 169, Head cent 169
Liszt, Franz 120
Lithuania 157
Livia 61-62
Loewenstein 108
Lopez, Carlos 197
Lopez, Francisco Solano 198
Lorenzo the Magnificent 125-126
Lorraine 75, 205
Louis IX (France) 66
Louis XIII (France) 66
Louis XIV (France) 66-67, 143
Louis XV (France) 67
Louis XVI (France) 67-68, 73, 138
Louis XVIII (France) 73-74
Louisiana 168-169, 199, Purchase 168
Louis Philippe 74
Low Countries 125, 131-132, 141, 144
Lübeck 102-103
Lucca 129
Lucerne 138
Luetzen, Battle of 150-151
Luneberg 103
Luther, Martin 81, 104-105
Lycurgus 17
Lydia 18, 22-23
Lysimachus 13, 20, 29, 85

MacArthur, Gen. Douglas 215
Macedon 13, 16, 20-21, 23-25, 28-29, 46
Magdeburg 106
Magellan, Ferdinand 82, 215
Magnentius 57
Maia 33
Maine 118
Mainz 102, 107
Malabar coast 135, 166
Malacca 9, 135
Malaya 9, 211-212
Man, Isle of 97
Manchukuo 210-211
Manchuria 210
Manco Capoc 198
Mantua 122
Maoris 214
Mao Tse-tung 210
Marathon 18-19, 26, 29
Marco Polo, see Polo
Marcus Aurelius 50
Maria Theresa 115-116, talers 116
Mariazell 118
Marie Antoinette 67-68, 72, 138
Marie Louise 72
Marius 34, 43, 47
Marius (Roman Emperor) 54
Mark Antony 13, 42, 45-48, 55
Mars 32, 35, 42, 148
Marseilles 15
Massachusetts 84, 171
Marti, Jose 189
Martinique 191
Masaryk, Thomas G. 120
Massalia 15
Maundy money 96-97
Mauretania 55
Maximilian (Archduke) 74, 182, 183
Maximilian I (Holy Roman Emperor) 113, 115, 132
Maximinus 54
Mayas 184, 186
Mayflower 84, 167
Medicis 125-126
Melbourne 213
Melkarth 62
Mende 28
Menelik 11
Mercury, see Hermes
"Mercury" dime 7-8, 16, 31, 171
Messana 15
Mestrelle, Eloye 83-84
Metapontum 21, 26, 76
Mexico 74, 88, 90, 132-133, 171, 179-183, 199
Mexico City Mint 181
Michelangelo, see Buonarotti
Minerva, see Athene
Ming dynasty 109
"Mining" taler 110
Minnesota 168
Mint mark 7-8
Mint, Royal 83-85, 88-90, 92-93, 95, 97, 116
Mirandola 121
Missouri 168, 170
Mithras 31
Monaco 165
Montana 168, 196
Montcalm, General Louis de 175
Monte Carlo 165
Montenegro 163
Monticello 169
Montreal 174-176
Moravia 120
Morelos, José Maria 182
Morgan, Henry 187
Morocco 205
Morse Code 178
Mosher, Stuart 7
Mozart, Wolfgang A. 118
Murat, Joachim 129
Muscovy, Grand Duchy of 159

Naples 129
Napoleon Bonaparte 12, 21, 31, 55, 69-71, 86, 89-91, 93, 97, 102, 109, 116, 124, 129, 132-133, 135-136, 140, 152-153, 161, 168, 182, 190, 193, 195
Napoleon II 72
Napoleon III 74-75, 183
Nassau 188
Nebraska 168
Nebuchadnezzar 13, 59
Neguib, Mohammed 202
Neptune, see Poseidon
Nero 48-49, 52-55, 126
Nerva 49
Netherlands 65, 69, 73, 83, 86, 88, 113, 123, 132, 135, 140-147, 151-160, 167, 187, 191, 195, 204, 213-215
Netherlands Antilles 191
New England 156, 171, 199
Newfoundland 81, 156, 173-174, 177
New Granada 196
New Mexico 180, 182
New Orleans Mint 172
New Rochelle half dollar 167
New South Wales 216
New Spain 115, 180, 184, 215
Newton, Sir Isaac 88
New Zealand 147, 214
Nicaragua 185-186
Nicholas II, Czar 155, 159, 161
Nicholas V, Pope 127
Nigeria 204
Nike 29
Nordhausen 101, 112
North Dakota 168
North Rhodesia 204
North West Company 176
Northwest Passage 178
Northwest Territory 173, 178

INDEX

Norway 76, 103, 148-149, 153-156
Nova Scotia 156, 173, 178
Numismatist, The 7, 9
Nuremberg 103, 107
Nyasaland 204

Oaxaca 182-183
Obverse 10
Oceania 135, 214-216
Octavian, see Augustus
O'Higgins, Bernardo 196
Ojeda, Alonso de 199
Oklahoma 168
Olbia 24
Old Spanish Trail half dollar 160
Olympia 25
Olympic Games 16-17, 25, 155
Ontario 173, 178
Orange Free State 204
Oregon 196
Otto I (Holy Roman Empire) 100
Ottoman Turks, see Turkey
Ouriques, Battle of 134
Overstrike 10

Patagonia 192
Patino, Simon 194
Pattern 10
Paul III, Pope 126
Peace Dollar 31
Pedro I, Dom (Brazil) 195
Pedro II, Dom (Brazil) 195
Pegasus 25
Pergamum 17, 48
Pericles 19
Peron, Juan 194
Persephone 16, 27
Perseus, King 24
Persia 13, 18-24, 26-28, 31, 59, 206
Perry, Comm. Matthew 211
Peru 82, 88-89, 184, 193-194, 198-199
Peter I (Serbia) 164
Peter III, Czar 161
Peter the Great 152, 159-161
Pakistan 208
Palatinate 102, 107
Panama 82, 184-186, 192, 196, Canal 184-185, 192
Panama-Pacific gold piece 29, 172
Papacy 64-65, 81, 100, 102, 104-105, 122-123, 125-129
Papal States 121, 126-127, 129
Paraguay 197-198
Parma 128, 146
"Parson's Foe" taler 106
Parthia 28, 43, 46, 55
Parys Mines Co. 91
Philadelphia 133
Philip of Macedon 16, 20, 23, 28
Philip II (Spain) 82, 114, 131, 132, 135, 143, 181
Philip the Arab 31, 56
Philippines 170, 212, 215
Philistis, Queen 27
Phoebus, see Apollo
Phoenicia 36, 38, 62, 207
Phrygia 68
Piacenza 129, 145
Piece of eight 181-182
Pidcock token 97
Pilgrim Tercentenary half dollar 167
Pillars of Hercules 181
Pilsudski, Joseph 157
Pine Tree shilling 171
Pistrucci, Benedetto 93-96
Pius IX, Pope 127
Pizarro, Francisco 184, 198-199
Plymouth 167
Poland 6, 74, 100-101, 112, 114, 116, 119, 152, 156-158, 161
Poliziano, Angelo 126
Pollux 42
Polo, Marco 122, 209
Pompey 42-44, 47, 59
Port Royal 189
Portugal 30, 73, 81, 90, 115, 122, 131-134, 146, 166-167, 188, 194-195, 203-204, 213-214
Poseidon 15-16, 22, 86, 108
Potosi 90, 194
Prince Edward Island 173
Probus 56
Proof sets 8
Prussia 68-69, 73-75, 100, 109, 111-112, 116-117, 153, 157-158
Ptolemies 13, 23, 29, 46
Puerto Barrios 186
Puerto Rico 189-190
"Purim" taler 106, 151
Pythagoras 26

Quebec 173-175, 178
Quesada, Gonzalo Jiménez de 196
Quezon, Manuel 215
Quinonez 186
Quirigua column 184

Radisson, Pierre 175
Rainsford, Sir John 81
Reeded edge 10
Renaissance 63, 80, 121-122, 124-126, 128
Reverse 10
Rhegium 15
Rhodes, Cecil John 204-205
Richard III (England) 79
Riga 151
Roanoke Island half dollar 167
Roma 31-33, 40-42
Romanovs 159, 161
Rome 6, 8, 13, 18, 21, 28-65, 68, 76-77, 85, 88-89, 93, 97, 102, 104, 115, 121-124, 126, 129, 131, 136-137, 139, 149, 159, 162, 171, 198, 202, 206
Roosevelt, Franklin Delano 170, 183, 215, dime 170
Rosas, Juan Manuel de 130, 194-195
Rudolf, Crown Prince 117
Rudolf I (Holy Roman Empire) 113
Rumania 30, 50, 55-56, 116, 163, 165
Russia 66, 73, 103, 109, 112, 117, 119-120, 146, 148-149, 152, 154-157, 159-163, 178, 210-212
Ruthenia 116, 120

Sabina 54
St. Andrew 84
St. Balthazar 149
St. Croix 191
St. Francis of Assisi 121
St. Gaspard 149
St. George 84-86, 93-96
St. Helena 73
St. Joachim 115
St. John the Baptist 124
St. Ladislaus 119
St. Marinus 165
St. Mark 123-124, 128, 130
St. Melchior 149
St. Michael 79-80, 141
St. Olaf 154
St. Paul 21, 126
St. Peter 126-128
St. Stephen 119
St. Sylvester 126
St. Vitus 109
Salazar, Antonio de Oliviera 135
Salisbury penny 78
Salvador, El 185-186
Salzburg 114
San Francisco mint 172
San Francisco-Oakland Bay Bridge half dollar 170
San Jacinto, Battle of 171
San Marino 165
San Martin, Jose de 193
Santo Domingo see Dominican Republic
Sarawak 216
Sardinia 121, 129-130
Saskatchewan 173
Saudi Arabia 207
Saxony 64, 100, 102, 104-105, 109-111, 116
Scandinavian countries 97, 101, 148-156
Schleswig 111, 153
Schlick, Counts 115
Schubert, Franz 118
Scotland 83-85, 89, 176, 196
Seaby, Peter 86, 92
Seleucus 21
Seltman, Dr. Charles 22
Sennacherib 146
Septimius Severus 56
Serbia 117, 163-164
Sforzas 122, 125
"Show" taler 146
Siam 211-212
Siberia 157, 166
Sicily 15, 23-24, 26-27, 36-38, 40, 73, 97, 101, 121-122, 129-132, 144, 149, 206
Sierra Leone 204
Sigismund III (Poland) 156
Sihtric III (Ireland) 98
Silenus 15
Silesia 109, 116, 120
Skidmore token 92
Sluys 79
Smuts, Jan 205
Sobieski, Jan III (Poland) 114, 156-157
Somalia 201
Sousa, Martim Affonso da 195
South Africa 204-205
South America 82, 89, 130, 133, 147, 166, 192-199
South Dakota 168
Southern Rhodesia 204
South Sea Company 89
Spain 15, 28, 30-31, 37, 40-41, 52-53, 55, 64, 66, 69, 73, 81-84, 88-90, 107, 113-116, 122-123, 131-133, 135, 140-141, 143-144, 146-147, 149, 166-167, 179-181, 184-194, 196-199, 206, 215
Spanish-American War 189, 215
Spanish Main 187, 196
Spanish milled dollar see Piece of eight
Sparta 17-19, 23
Spice Islands 134-135, 214
Stickney 1804 dollar 172
Stone Mountain Memorial half dollar 169
Story of the English Coinage, The 86, 92
Straits Settlements see Malaya
Stuarts 84
Sucre, José de 193, 197
Sudan 202
Suez Canal 200, 202
Sulla 35, 42-43, 47
Sumatra 215
Sun Yat-sen 210
Surinam 147
Sweden 53, 73, 103, 106, 109, 146, 148-155, 160, 167
Switzerland 65, 101, 113, 136-139
Syracuse 16-17, 26-27
Syria 20, 28, 35, 56, 206

Talers 107-109
Tanganyika 204
Tanit 38
Tannenberg, Battle of 157
Tartu, University of 158
Tasman, Abel 147, 214
Tasmania 146
Tegucigalpa 187
Tell, William 136
Tennessee 186
Teutonic Knights 157
Texas 171, 180, 182, 199, 203, Centennial half dollar 171
Thailand, see Siam
Thalers, see Talers
Thebes 25
Thrace 20, 29
Thuringia 101
Tiberius 48, 61-62
Tibet 211
Tientsin 212
Tigranes the Great 35
Titus 49, 51, 60
Toussaint l'Ouverture 190
Tokens 97
Tours 64
Trajan 6, 49-52, 55-56
Transvaal 204-205
Transylvania 119
Travancore 208
Triquetra 97
Trinidad 189
Tudors 79-80
Tunisia 205
Turkey 58-59, 70, 74, 114, 117, 119, 132, 147, 152, 156, 159-165, 202, 207
Tuscany 122, 124
Tyre 62

Uganda 204
Umbria 52
Una 95
Union of South Africa see South Africa
United States of America 6, 7, 10, 15-16, 23, 29, 30-31, 68, 94, 102, 107, 112, 120, 133, 139, 154-155, 166-173, 176-178, 181-185, 187, 189, 191, 193, 195, 207, 209, 212, 215
United States Mint 7-10
Urraca 185
Uruguay 130, 192, 198-199
Utrecht 143

Valdemar IV (Denmark) 14[illegible]
Vatican 126-128, 138
Venezuela 191-193, 196, 199
Venice 103, 107, 122-124, 126 129-130, 146, 162, 209
Venus, see Aphrodite
Verden 151
Vespasian 49, 51, 54-55, 61
Vespucci, Amerigo 199
Vichy state 75, 205
Victor Emmanuel II (Italy) 130
Victor Emmanuel III (Italy) 130
Victoria, Queen 93
Viet Nam 211
Vigo 88-89
Vinci, Leonardo da 80, 125-12[illegible]
Virgin Islands 191
Visby 103, 149
Vladislav II Jagiello 119
Vogelweide, Walther von der 118
Vytatas, Grand Duke (Lithuania) 157

Wallenstein, Albrecht 106-10[illegible]
Washington, Booker T. 170
Washington, George 144, 167-168
Washington quarter 168
Washington (state) 196
"Wedding" taler 115
Weimar Republic 111-112
West Indies 147, 166, 187-19[illegible]
West Virginia 208
Wilhelm I (Germany) 100
Wilhelm II (Germany) 111, 200
William III (England) 88
William IV (England) 90
William of Orange 144-145
William the Conqueror 77-78
Wilson, Woodrow 170
Wyoming 168
Wyon, William 93

Yugoslavia 164-165
Yukon Territory 173

Zeeland 142, 147
Zeus 15-17, 23, 26, 28-29, 31-33, 42, 152